The Michigan Historical Reprint Series

Reprints from the collection of the University of Michigan University Library

This volume is produced from digital images created through the University of Michigan University Library's preservation reformatting program. The Library seeks to preserve the intellectual content of items in a manner that facilitates and promotes a variety of uses. The digital reformatting process results in an electronic version of the text that can both be accessed online and used to create new print copies. This book and thousands of others can be found in the digital collections of the University of Michigan Library. The University Library also understands and values the utility of print, and makes reprints available through its Scholarly Publishing Office.

For access to the University of Michigan Library's digital collections, please see http://www.lib.umich.edu.

The Scholarly Publishing Office seeks to disseminate high-quality, cost-effective scholarly content through both print and electronic publishing. Information about the Scholarly Publishing Office can be found at http://spo.umdl.umich.edu.

The Scholarly Publishing Office
the University of Michigan
University Library

WHY FOUR GOSPELS?

OR,

THE GOSPEL FOR ALL THE WORLD.

A MANUAL DESIGNED TO AID CHRISTIANS IN THE STUDY OF THE SCRIPTURES, AND TO A BETTER UNDERSTANDING OF THE GOSPELS.

BY

D. S. GREGORY, D. D.,

PROFESSOR OF THE MENTAL SCIENCES AND ENGLISH LITERATURE IN THE UNIVERSITY OF WOOSTER; AUTHOR OF "CHRISTIAN ETHICS."

NEW YORK:
SHELDON AND COMPANY.

RIVERSIDE, CAMBRIDGE:
STEREOTYPED BY H. O. HOUGHTON AND COMPANY.

TO MY WIFE,

H. B. G.,

TO WHOSE CONSTANT ENCOURAGEMENT AND ASSIDUOUS HELPFULNESS
THE CHRISTIAN PUBLIC OWES WHATEVER OF VALUE THIS
VOLUME MAY CONTAIN, IT IS, WITHOUT
HER KNOWLEDGE,

Affectionately Dedicated.

PREFACE.

It is admitted on all hands that the central point of attack upon Christianity in the present age is found in the Gospels. "The life of Jesus," says Tischendorf, "is the most momentous of all questions which the Church has to encounter, — the one which is decisive whether it shall or shall not live." The assailants demand that the Christian apologist shall put his system to the test of exhibiting its philosophic basis and its rational explanation. Whether the demand be reasonable or unreasonable, it is certain that this scientific age will continue to press its questions of *why* and *how*.

While it is absolutely certain that God's Word will stand all legitimate tests and remain intact to the end of time, it is no less certain that some of the old modes of viewing, exhibiting, and defending it must be abandoned for others which are more truly scientific, or, in other words, more in harmony with the divine truth and thought.

It is a growing conviction in many Christian minds, that the most conclusive argument for the divine origin of the four Gospels is not that furnished by the external evidences but by the Gospels themselves; that whoever can be brought to take a truly scientific view of them, that is, to see them as they really are in themselves and their relations, will need no further arguments to convince him that these productions are each and all from God.

The present work is designed to aid the intelligent reader in his efforts to see the Gospels as they really are, that they may present their own claims — based upon their unity, harmony, completeness, and perfect adaptation to human needs — to be from God, divinely inspired, and worthy of God. It is the application of simple, common-sense principles to the study and elucidation of the productions of the Evangelists, with the hope that the result may be helpful to Christians who would go beyond the old conventional methods and seek to gain clearer, fresher, truer, and more reasonable views. It is desired especially that the present essay may commend the study of the Gospels to the minds of that class of thinkers, daily increasing, who are to be satisfied only by a reasonable explanation of the facts, whether of the world or of the Word, with which they come in contact.

The studies which led to this work originated in the efforts of a pastor to awaken a new interest on the part of his flock in the study of the Word of God. The encouragement received led to the embodiment of portions of the subject, in a form different from the present, in a series of articles for one of the leading Quarterlies. In response to the urgent request of many earnest laborers in the Gospel, the thought has been embodied — during the intervals of a life filled with most pressing duties — in the present form, in order to bring it within the reach of a larger number of intelligent readers. Should it be owned of God in helping inquiring minds to a clearer and more comprehensive view of the Gospel of Christ, and to a firmer faith in its Divine origin and aim, the highest and chief end of its preparation will be secured.

WOOSTER, O., October 2, 1876.

CONTENTS.

INTRODUCTION.

PART I.

THE PURPOSE OF GOD AND THE GOSPEL.

CHAPTER I.

CHAPTER II.

PART II.

MATTHEW, THE GOSPEL FOR THE JEW.

CHAPTER I.

CHAPTER II.

PART III.

MARK, THE GOSPEL FOR THE ROMAN.

CHAPTER I.

CHAPTER II.

PART IV.

LUKE, THE GOSPEL FOR THE GREEK.

CHAPTER I.

CHAPTER II.

PART V.

JOHN, THE GOSPEL FOR THE CHURCH.

CHAPTER I.

CHAPTER II.

CONCLUSION.

INTRODUCTION.

THE QUESTION AND THE PROPOSED ANSWERS.

Question stated. The one Gospel of Jesus Christ appears in the Sacred Scriptures in four forms, — a first, according to Matthew; a second, according to Mark; a third, according to Luke; and a fourth, according to John. Why not in three, or five, or twenty forms? Or, why not, in accordance with a prevailing desire of the present age, in only one form?

Since the *fact* of four Gospels cannot be escaped, wherein and why do they differ? Do the order, harmony, and design, which are found everywhere in God's world, appear also in that other work of God, his Word? In particular, did the infinite Reason preside in the production of the Gospels, so that we may confidently look for a divine plan in each of them considered by itself, and a like plan in the whole of them taken together?

Answers proposed. For eighteen hundred years, these brief productions, occupying but a few pages in a single book, have evinced their power to raise such questions as these, and to keep the world employed in the effort to answer them.

In all ages thoughtful men, and especially the great souls of the Church, have shrunk from looking upon the Gospels as aimless and disjointed productions, mere medleys of fact and truth. But in seeking to reach the order and unity which their natures craved, they have tried different and often irrational methods.

The *harmonists* have attempted to construct, from the four Gospels regarded as a poorly arranged mass of material, one complete life of Jesus, or, at least, to remove the obstacles to the construction of such a life.

The *allegorists*, seizing upon certain available scriptural symbols, have done their best, in their arbitrary and fanciful way, to put aim and plan into the Gospels.

From such irrational methods, pursued through centuries with no definite and valuable product of the kind sought after, resulted the method and work of the modern *rationalists*. From the despair of plan and aim, or the assertion of unreasonable plan and aim, there came, as a natural and inevitable reaction against the old unreason, the vehement and unreasoning denial of any plan and aim.

Against all these the method of *right reason* is now vindicating itself. The course of modern progress in this, as in so many other fields of investigation, has been from irrationalism through rationalism to the true reason.

A comprehensive view of this line of work — irrational, rationalistic, and truly rational — of the past centuries, will best open the way for a new attempt to solve the old and ever-recurring problem.

SECTION I.

THE HARMONISTS.

The Christian Fathers seem to have made little effort to find any plan in the Gospels. Very early, however, they began to produce what may, in a loose way, be called *Lives of Christ*. These did not so much aim to explain apparent discrepancies, or even to ascertain the exact chronological order of the events, as to reduce the four Gospels to one continuous narrative. They were unlike the modern so-called Lives; for although in those as in these the writings of the Evangelists were torn member from member, yet the scattered members were not wholly whelmed in a flood of weak and vapid sentiment, nor entirely lost in the mazes of a cheap but ambitious rhetoric. They shared with some of the moderns the error, that uninspired man can give a better form to the material of the Evangelists than the divine form given by inspiration; but they did not share with them the more monstrous modern error, that uninspired man can improve upon the divine material by adding to it either his profound philosophy or his sentimental twaddle.

As early as A. D. 170, Tatian the Syrian compiled his *Diatessaron*, — that is, his Gospel according to the four Evangelists, — a work now lost. It was substantially a life of Christ, compiled in accordance with the view of its author, that the ministry of Jesus lasted only one year.

Ammonius of Alexandria prepared a similar work, about A. D. 220, which he entitled a *Harmony*. He divided the four Gospels into short Sections, which he numbered according to the order in which they were to be placed in his combined Gospel or Harmony.

The *Canons* of Eusebius, A. D. 315, was in fact a harmony upon a somewhat different plan from the Ammonian Sections. There are ten of the Canons or Tables, — one exhibiting the Sections common to all the Gospels; three, those common to any three of the Gospels; five, those common to any two; and one, those peculiar to any one Gospel. Very little advance has been made upon the work of Ammonius and Eusebius in this direction.

The necessity for explaining in a systematic way the apparent discrepancies of the Gospels made itself felt at a later date. The best known, and, perhaps, the most valuable of the Harmonies, constructed under pressure of this necessity, is that of Robinson (A. D. 1845), based upon the earlier works of Newcome (1778) and Le Clerc (1699). In the class of works of which it is the representative, learning the most varied and profound has been brought to bear in the discussion of times, places, and circumstances, with the aim of reconciling apparent discrepancies and contradictions, and of arranging the material of all the Gospels in exact chronological order in one narrative.

The Harmonists have done good and worthy work so far as they have assisted to explain the apparent inconsistencies of the Gospels and to make the true relations of the various portions better understood. So far, however, as they have undertaken to construct one continuous and complete narrative of the career of Jesus of Nazareth, they have attempted an impossible task. There are no sufficient data upon which to base a just conclusion concerning the precise time when many of the events recorded in the Gospels occurred. It will appear subsequently in this discussion, that it was no part of the aim of the Evangelists to give a complete account of the life of Jesus strictly arranged in the order of time. Their chronology is clear and distinct, at the most, only in the opening and concluding chapters. But even if the exact time of each event could be ascertained, it would still be impossible to combine the four Gospels in one consistent whole. The writers were themselves unlike in nature and culture, and so the style of each is different from that of all the others. They wrote, as will be shown, for different classes of readers, each class requiring a different mode of presentation. Each of them looked at Jesus from a different point of view. Some one has compared their four productions to four photographs of the four different sides of a house, — each is distinct, and the four sides could not possibly be taken in one picture.

Results. It is hardly too much to affirm that the efforts to make a complete and harmonious whole out of the Gospels have failed.

Says Dr. Isaac Da Costa: "Unhappily by far the most of these Harmonies, for want of any principle of solution drawn from the very nature and organical construction of these writings, have contributed rather to embarrass than to resolve the problem, owing to the purely mechanical and forced manner in which its solution has been attempted."[1]

Dr. J. Addison Alexander, in an article on Harmonies of the Gospels, ably sums up the whole matter. "What then, it may be asked, is the use of all this harmonistic labor, from the second to the nineteenth century? We answer, much every way — or rather, every way but one — and that the very one on which the heart of the harmonical interpreter is often set — the undesirable, impracticable, and chimerical reduction of these four inestimable gems to one bright but artificial compound. The true use of Harmonies is threefold, Exegetical, Historical, Apologetical. By mere juxtaposition, if judicious, the Gospels may be made to throw light upon each other's obscure places. By combination, not mechanical but rational, not textual but interpretive, harmonies put it in our power, not to grind, or melt, or boil four Gospels into one, but out of the four, kept apart, yet viewed together, to extract one history for ourselves. And lastly, by the endless demonstration of the possible solutions of apparent or alleged discrepancies, even where we may not be prepared to choose among them, they reduce the general charge of falsehood or of contradiction, not only *ad absurdum*, but to a palpable impossibility. How

[1] *The Four Witnesses*, p. 4.

can four independent narratives be false or contradictory, which it is possible to reconcile on so many distinct hypotheses? The art of the most subtle infidelity consists in hiding this convincing argument behind the alleged necessity of either giving a conclusive and exclusive answer to all captious cavils and apparent disagreements, or abandoning our faith in the history as a whole. This most important end of Gospel Harmonies has been accomplished. It has been established, beyond all reasonable doubt, that however the Evangelists may differ, and however hard it may be often to explain the difference, they never, in a single instance, contradict each other. This is a grand result, well worthy of the toil bestowed upon it by the Fathers and Reformers and Divines for eighteen hundred years; while, on the other hand, the minute chronology, which some of these have viewed as the great object to be aimed at, is as far from its complete solution now as in the days of Tatian or Augustine; so that the inquirer may still say to the most able harmonists, with one of Terence's dramatic characters: Fecistis probe, incertior sum multo quam dudum!"[1]

When one has clearly grasped the characteristics of each of the Gospels, the attempt to mass them all in one, while preserving the glory of each, will appear as absurd as would the attempt of an architect to construct, from the materials of Sòlomon's Temple, of the Parthenon, of the Coliseum, and of Westminster Abbey, a new temple which should preserve and harmoniously combine the peculiar features of them all, and be neither Jewish, Greek, Roman, nor Gothic.

[1] *Princeton Review*, vol. xxviii. p. 395.

SECTION II.

THE ALLEGORISTS.

While the Harmonists have been engaged in their impossible task, another class of minds, delighting in allegory and given to imagination, has been engaged upon a work equally impossible. The *Cherubim* of Ezekiel and the *Four Living Creatures* of the Apocalypse have played as important a part in their interpretation of the Gospels as the cycles and epicycles played in the theories of the old astronomers. There are four Gospels and there are four of these figures of prophecy. Is not that a wonderful coincidence? Besides, have not all scriptural symbols an inexhaustible fullness of mystic, prophetic signification and application? Why, then, were not those symbols of Ezekiel and John intended by the Spirit of God to symbolize the four Evangelists, — or, at least, those aspects of the person and office of Christ which they respectively exhibit in their Gospels? Who could say they were not so intended?

Irenæus, Bishop of Lyons in the second century, began with the vision of the four Cherubim, in the first chapter of Ezekiel. That vision, in its symbolical meaning, he applied to the distinctive peculiarities of the Gospels. "As for the likeness of their faces, they four had the face of a man, and the face of a lion, on the right side; and they four had the face of an ox on the left side; they four also had the face of an eagle." The man, according to Irenæus, symbolizes Matthew's Gospel; the lion, Mark's; the ox, Luke's; the eagle, John's. So happy a thought could not fail, in the circumstances, to perpetuate itself. The later Fathers adopted and developed the idea of Irenæus. At the end of two centuries, Jerome completed the development, and proposed that special arrangement and application of the symbols which the Latin Church adopted, and which Art has perpetuated. His order is that of Ezekiel.

The Rhemist fathers interpreted and applied the vision, in accordance with this order of Ezekiel and Jerome. "St. Matthew is likened to a man, because he beginneth with the pedigree of Christ, as he is a man; St. Mark to a lion, because he beginneth with the preaching of St. John the Baptist, as it were the roaring of a lion in the wilderness; St. Luke to a calf, because he beginneth with a priest of the Old Testament (to wit, Zacharias, the father of John Baptist), which priesthood was to sacrifice calves to God; St. John to an eagle, because he beginneth with the divinity of Christ, flying as high, as more is not possible." This is plainly worse than childish, — absurd! It explains nothing. It opens to view no aim or harmony before invisible.

The great Augustine was dissatisfied with the explanation of Irenæus. So were some even before his day, and more after it. He preferred the order in John's vision of the *Four Living Creatures*, as found in Revelation iv. 7: "And the first beast was like a lion, and the second beast was like a calf, and the third beast had a face as a man, and the fourth beast was like a flying eagle." Matthew's Gospel, according to this view, is symbolized by the *lion*, because he sets forth Christ as the Lion of the tribe of Judah; Mark's by the *calf* or *ox*, because he exhibits Christ as the servant in a life of patient, humble service; Luke's by the *man*, because he hold's forth Christ as the perfection of humanity; John's by the *eagle*, because of his heavenward gaze and flight in unfolding the mysteries of Christ's Deity. This was better, — if anything better be attainable by a method so arbitrary, — for it suggests a half-truth in connection with each of the first three Gospels, to which Jerome's inter pretation did not open the way. Still there was room for new efforts in attaching to the Gospels the symbols of these prophets of the two dispensations.

Among the latest adaptations is that of Lange, in his "Life of Jesus," — an adaptation approved by Stier. The ox, the lion, the man, the eagle, is Lange's order. His view is presented in his introduction to the commentary on the Gospel according to Matthew. "The first Gospel is preëminently that of history, and of the fulfillment of the Old Testament by the sacrificial sufferings and death of Christ and the redemption thus achieved. Hence, the sacrificial *bullock* is the appropriate symbol of Matthew. The second Gospel presents to our minds the all-powerful revelation and working of Christ as direct from heaven, irrespectively of anything that preceded, — the completion of all former manifestations of the Deity. Symbol, the *lion*. The third Gospel is preeminently that of humanity, — human mercy presented in the light of divine grace, the transformation of all human kindness into divine love. Symbol, the figure of a *man*. Lastly, the fourth Gospel exhibits the deep spiritual and eternal import of the history of Christ, — the divine element pervading and underlying its every phase, — and with it the transformation of all ideals, in connection with Christ. Symbol, the *eagle*." Very different, truly, is the symbol of Lange for Matthew from that of Augustine, — the *ox*, from the *lion*, — ignoring entirely the order of divine revelation, — yet with his explanation it serves to bring out another half-truth concerning the priestly character of Messiah as taught in prophecy and realized in Jesus of Nazareth.

Results. But accommodating as these symbols of prophecy have been, the various and never-ending changes in the attempts to apply them to the Gospels show most clearly that the thing attempted is purely arbitrary. Admitting that they may have been of some use in the past, in helping to group some of the facts peculiar to the respective Gospels, — of use just as the cycles and epicycles were in the old astronomy, or the nebular hypothesis in the modern, — still they are scarcely worthy to be taken into serious account in any attempt to reach a philosophic and common-sense view of the existence and structure of the four Gospels.

It is not too much to say that the attempts to put a plan into the Gospels, in this arbitrary way, have failed no less utterly than the attempts of the harmonists to put the material of the Gospels into a new form better than the divine.

SECTION III.

THE RATIONALISTS.

Out of these irrational modes of treating the Gospels has come the modern reaction, which has taken form, on its worst side, in Rationalism. The Rationalist accepts the failure of the irrational method as conclusive against all aim and plan in the Gospels. As the Gospels are a medley, they are therefore not from God. Still, the medley — a very extraordinary one certainly — remains to be accounted for. To account for it without the aid of the supernatural is the aim of the rationalist.

Pantheistic form. David Friedrich Strauss, who has but recently passed away, was the man who first gave literary shape — in his "Life of Jesus," published in 1835 — to a view of the Gospels which had been for some time floating in dim and undefined form in the German mind of his age.

The reality of our Lord's life may be attacked in two, and only two, ways; it may be urged that the Gospel history is pure fable, without any better basis of historical fact than the "Arabian Nights," or that it is a mixture of fact and fable, like the Grecian and Roman legends, which can only be separated by the aid of critical intuition. Strauss took the former method of attack.

His work was the inevitable last outcome of German Pantheism. Pantheism denies a Personal God. The Gospel history must therefore be false or at least mythical, because the notion of a Personal God and Creator of men, and of a Son of God, revealing the will of the Heavenly Father, is *unphilosophical*, — a dream of superstition, and not a truth of reason as expounded by its latest and highest prophet, Hegel.[1] It was not by his science, but by his fundamental hypothesis, the assumption of the truth of Pantheism, that Strauss aimed to rid the world of the Gospel facts.

His scientific method led him to apply both philosophy and criticism to the Gospels, and in his hands, with the truth of Pantheism postulated, both were of course equally destructive.

As Strauss adopted the philosophy of Hegel, we accordingly find the Hegelian idea prominent in all his speculations on the Gospels. He maintained that he believed as an *idea* what others believed as *history*. The idea is before the facts and creates the so-called facts. The need of a deliverer created the idea of a Saviour. The old prophecies, misinterpreted, fashioned in the popular mind a character to be attributed to that Saviour. The whole Gospel history is an attempt of the ruling idea of the Jewish race in that age to realize itself in fact. The imagination, or *mythus*, to which the need of a deliverer gave rise, grew in process of time into the great four-fold fable of the Gospels.

The facts in Christianity were temporary, the ideas eternal. Christ was the type of humanity. His life, death, and resurrection were the symbol of the life,

[1] See Tulloch, *Lectures on M. Renan's "Vie de Jésus,"* p. 32.

death, and resurrection of humanity. The former was unimportant and temporary, the latter momentous and eternal. An exoteric religion for the people might exhibit the one; the esoteric for the philosopher might retain the other. In short, the dogmas of the Gospel are true, but the history false.

With his Hegelian philosophy and criticism, Strauss would have done for the Gospels what Niebuhr and Grote have done for the Roman and Grecian legends of the pre-historic age, given in poetry and tradition; and he would have relegated the Jesus of the Evangelists to the same shadowy place in history with Æneas, Hercules, the early kings of Rome, and the Brutus of England. It is already acknowledged by all competent critics that, in spite of all his marvelous learning, the attempt of Strauss was, philosophically, a complete and miserable failure. Jesus of Nazareth lived not in fabulous but in historic times, — in fact, in the most cultivated age of antiquity. The four Gospels are, on the very face of them, not poems, or legends, or myths, but simple, life-like, historical narratives, which could have been produced only by or with the aid of eye-witnesses. It can be proved that they all existed in their present form before the close of the first century, so that no time is anywhere given for the growth of the wonderful myths of Strauss. It were far easier to prove Julius Cæsar a myth, than to prove Jesus Christ a myth. The principles by which Strauss would prove the life of Jesus a fable, would as readily prove the life of Napoleon a fable.

Positivist form. In the acknowledged failure of Strauss is found the secret of the changed plan of attack by M. Ernest Renan, in his "Life of Jesus." It is impossible to show the Gospel history to be all fable; the next thing to that is to show it to be a mixture of fact and fable. There must be a basis of fact. M. Renan will pick it out according to his own taste. He has a monopoly of the intuition of Gospel fact. So he gives the world his "Fifth Gospel," — his "Life of Jesus." It might more appropriately be styled M. Renan's "Romance of Jesus;" since there is no Gospel left in it except what may be found in the author's very French notions of sentiment and morality.

This work was the inevitable outgrowth of French Positivism. Positivism affirms that the universe is governed by necessary law, and its order is therefore unchanging. The notion of a personal Will interposing in human affairs is therefore incompatible with science. The miracles of the Gospels, in short whatever professes to be a manifestation of the supernatural or of a personal Will, must be false.[1]

The chief problem of positivist criticism must therefore require the separation, by some power of critical intuition, of the true in the Gospels from the false, of the fact from the fable. To this work Renan, with his brilliant erudition and his still more brilliant style, sets himself.

Renan finds three periods in the life of Jesus. In the first, the hero has some features of the Jesus of the Evangelists left. M. Renan would make him appear as a moralist and a gentle reformer of the noblest and purest character, according to the attenuated French idea of moralist and reformer and of nobility and purity. In the second, Jesus is brought under the influence of the gloomy Baptist, and his sweet nature is changed by close contact with that sterner character. Somehow the notion of a strange ideal kingdom gets into his head, and he sets about establishing it. In this he fails, and the third period is marked by a radical change of character and conduct. Disappointed and embittered, he raves

[1] See Tulloch, *Lectures on M. Renan's "Vie de Jésus,"* p. 33.

against all classes of men; is tempted to make use of deception and yields; and, in the belief in some coming world-revolution, hurries on his own violent death, and is buried in a grave from which M. Renan does not allow the stone to be rolled away. This is the basis of fact, according to Renan, on which the great romances of the Gospels were constructed.

Naturally not a few readers have inquired how it happens that the brilliant Frenchman has a monopoly of that critical intuition which is absolutely necessary to cull the facts of the Gospels from the fable. Those inclined to receive him as their teacher have gone farther and insisted on claiming a share of that intuition for themselves. The intuition of the equally brilliant author of Ecce Homo differs from that of the Frenchman and from that of everybody else. Even M. Renan's intuition changes from time to time; and there is no one to decide where the rationalistic doctors all disagree.

Men of sense begin to see clearly that this new principle once admitted would destroy all the foundations of History, no less surely than would the older principle of Strauss. As they read the grand story of the Gospels, they feel that the life, character, and mission of Jesus of Nazareth are "one in idea, in purpose, in accomplishment, and result." They turn away from M. Renan's no-gospel as a repulsive thing, and the polished Frenchman's romance, after being a nine-days' wonder, is making haste to the upper shelves or the waste basket. Not even with the aid of French vivacity and genius can such a baseless and sentimental production hold its own against the clear unity, the intense reality, and the divine spirituality of the Gospel narratives.

Results. On the whole, Christianity has little reason to complain of the final results of these German and French ventures. The year in which Strauss published his life of Jesus is as memorable in theology as 1848 in politics. Theologians of all classes saw that it called for a reconstruction of the whole subject of the origin and foundations of Christianity. If it formed the starting point of the new literature of unbelief, it likewise awakened Christian thought and directed it to the central facts of Gospel history, and above all to the Divine Person revealed there. The life of Jesus has thus called forth from Christian scholars the richest results of critical investigation and exposition of the place of the Gospels in literature and history, and has given the historical Christ a firmer hold on the intelligent faith of mankind than he has ever before had. In fine, both pantheism and positivism did their best in Strauss and Renan, and failed.

The conflict that has since been waged is but the necessary disagreement of the inquiring in passing from the blind and worthless agreement of the ignorant to the priceless unanimity of the intelligent and enlightened. But for the efforts of Strauss and his successors, the Church might still have known nothing of the common-sense, historic criticism, to which it already owes so much, and from which it may reasonably hope for so much more.

SECTION IV.

THE COMMON-SENSE CRITICS.

The modern reaction from the irrational and rationalistic methods has given rise to a common-sense criticism, which promises to lead ultimately to a correct and full understanding of the Gospels. It asks men to look at the Gospels as they are, and to study them in the light of the times and forces that shaped them. It aims to do for the Gospels the work that the Baconian philosophy has done for the world of nature.

Says Matthew Arnold: "Of the literature of France and Germany, as of the intellect of Europe in general, the main effort, for now many years, has been a critical effort; the endeavor in all branches of knowledge, — theology, philosophy, history, art, science, — to see the object as in itself it really is." We accept this as certainly the proper aim of all critical study of words from God, if not of the proper study of merely human productions, — to come to see them as they really are. The practical question in connection with the criticism of the Gospels is, How can this end be attained? Through a long period of honest, earnest work the Christian Church has been approximating to the true method, and through it to the true answer.

It is obvious, however, from what has already been presented, that the progress toward the goal has not been made in a right line. Human reason, when employed on these great divine subjects, has a most unreasonable way of taking to by-ways and cross-roads of investigation, and of losing sight of the one main track.

Along the line of Gospel study two things have been prominent: the divine records themselves; and the ever-increasing mass of related facts, geographical, biographical, and historical, drawn partly from those records and partly from independent sources.

There are, therefore, three possible methods of procedure. The true method and the best results obviously require that both these sources of knowledge shall be taken into account. In the actual work of criticism, however, one class of critics has looked only to the records, and another only to the related facts; and both, by adopting wrong methods, have failed of securing the most valuable results. The work of the former class has too often degenerated into a barren consideration of petty details or of the mere letter of the Scriptures, while that of the latter has sunk into equally barren geographical, biographical, or historical speculation on subjects only remotely connected with the truths of the divine revelation. But it is a satisfaction to be assured, that even the departures from the right line of progress must ultimately assist in reaching the truth, by showing that the truth does not lie in the directions in which these departures have been made, but somewhere midway between them.

The history of Gospel study, up to the present time, may be said to have fairly demonstrated that the old commentary of petty detail, which sticks to isolated facts and to words and letters, to the neglect of the more important things of the Scriptures, will not greatly help men to see the productions of the Evangelists as they really are. It ignores the divine system and the infinitely varied relations that must exist wherever God's thought finds expression. It is a fatal mistake to fix the attention upon verses and phrases, upon names and dates, upon words and syllables, and to lose sight of that spirit which is infinitely above the mere letter, and of that truth of the entire Gospels which is infinitely grander than the mere sum of the separate parts. In a whole library of commentaries constructed after this microscopic method, one can scarcely find a trace of the truest, highest glories of the writings of the Evangelists.

In like manner it has been shown very clearly that the commentary which devotes itself to things external and incidental to the Gospels, and which so generally sinks into petty biographical, historical, or geographical criticism, can give even less aid toward understanding the productions of the Evangelists as they really are. It is doubtless important, in the examination of literary works, to consider the personality, the circumstances, the country and the career of the author. But when this degenerates into petty search after curious facts, often more useless than curious, it fails to lay open the secret of an author's life, and does little toward making his productions intelligible. Of what imaginable help is it, in understanding the mighty work of a Newton in the world, to know that he was "small enough, when he was born, to be put into a quart mug, and that if he had any animal taste, it was for apples of the red-streak sort?" Of what possible service in understanding the sublime tragedies of Æschylus, is the much-paraded story, that the old man had his bald head broken by an eagle, which, high in air, mistook it for a stone, and dropped a tortoise on it to crack for a meal? And yet how much of so-called gospel illustration deals with facts and fables as petty and worthless as these! Thoughtful men are beginning to see that valuable lives may be worse than wasted by scholars who give themselves up to such work in connection with the history of the Evangelists. A whole library of such materials may fail to give any one the least insight into the real spirit of Matthew, Mark, Luke, and John, or the slightest glimpse of the true spiritual power of their productions.

Results. The final result of these erroneous methods has been to turn the attention toward the true method, which may be characterized as that of genuine textual and historical criticism. It gives due attention both to the sacred records, in their minute details and in their grand unities, and to the important related facts.

The fundamental law of this criticism requires, on the one hand, that he who wishes to understand the Gospels shall devote the proper study and accord due weight, to the agents and forces, human and divine, individual and national, which wrought in producing them, and to the ideas, customs, circumstances, relations, and aims which gave them final shape. Without proper regard to this canon no right understanding of the Gospels in their completeness and unity is possible. The same law requires, on the other hand, that he who wishes to understand the Gospels as they really are shall devote no less earnest study to the sacred records themselves, — seeking in the light of all the related facts to grasp them in detail and in completeness, in part and in whole; making use of the previously sought out secret of the author's age and life and genius, and of the revelation of the divine purpose, to reach the still higher secret of the glad tidings to all men.

In the "Life, Times, and Travels of St. Paul," Conybeare and Howson have applied this method with notable success in dealing with a portion of the Acts of the Apostles and with the Pauline Epistles. Their work has thrown new and marvelous light upon apostolic times in general, and especially upon the career of the Apostle to the Gentiles.

A proper application of the same method to the Gospels cannot fail to bring out something of the divine system, which most certainly inheres in the mass of Gospel facts of which Jesus of Nazareth is the central figure. The light which it must cast upon the productions of the Evangelists cannot fail to invest them with a new, fresh, yet common-sense and historic, interest. The Gospels themselves will at the same time be permitted to present their own best vindication against both rationalism and irrationalism; and will furnish, in their respective aims and plans, and in their complete unity and harmony, a new and most convincing argument in favor of the Christianity based upon them.

Topics. In the course of such a work the questions: Why are there four Gospels? and, Wherein and why do they differ? will, it is trusted, be satisfactorily answered; or, at least, the direction along which the true answer can alone be found be clearly pointed out.

It will appear incidentally how false is the common notion that the divine work for the redemption of the world might have been accomplished just as well by one Gospel, or any other number than four, — so false, indeed, that history would have to be transformed, the world revolutionized, and the nature of the races radically changed, before the divine purpose could have reached its fulfillment through one or three or five or any other number than the divinely chosen *four*.

The method. The proposed application of this common-sense method will require: —

First, the consideration of such introductory topics as the preparation of the world for the advent of the Messiah; the advent and career of the Messiah; and the actual origin of the four written Gospels.

Secondly, the special consideration of each of the four Gospels, in its origin, design, and authorship, and in its adaptation in structure and matter to those for whom it was originally prepared.

PART I.

THE PURPOSE OF GOD AND THE GOSPEL.

"Careless seems the Great Avenger; history's pages but record
One death-grapple in the darkness 'twixt old systems and the Word;
Truth forever on the scaffold, Wrong forever on the throne, —
Yet that scaffold sways the future, and, behind the dim unknown,
Standeth God within the shadow, keeping watch above his own."
JAMES RUSSELL LOWELL.

"For after that in the wisdom of God the world by wisdom knew not God, it pleased God by the foolishness of preaching to save them that believe."
1 CORINTHIANS i. 21.

CHAPTER I.

THE PREPARATION FOR THE ADVENT OF THE MESSIAH.

THOUGH man often works irrationally and without plan, God never does. In the introduction of Christianity into the world there was a divine plan whose working out reached through all the ages until the complete embodiment of the one Gospel in the four forms in which it appears in the Bible. Into that plan the ancient world, Jewish and Pagan, consciously or unconsciously entered. In general terms, it has been said that "Judaism prepared salvation for mankind, and heathenism prepared mankind for salvation."[1] This statement may perhaps be shown to be only a half-truth, — since it will be found that Judaism did a chief part

[1] Kurtz, *Text Book of Ch. History*, vol. i. p. 44.

of the work of preparing mankind for salvation, — but a most important half-truth nevertheless.

Two parts may be seen in this plan: a first, which includes the preparation made for the Advent, or the coming of Messiah; a second, which includes the coming and career of Messiah and the preaching and written embodiment of his Gospel.

The preparation for the advent of Jesus Christ involved the missions of Jew and Pagan. In the case of the former, the work of preparation was carried on by means of revelation; in the case of the latter by means of free experience. So, in substance, writes Pressensé.[1] It will be seen, however, that revelation had much to do, through the Jewish dispersion, with the preparation of the heathen world for Messiah.

SECTION I.

THE PREPARATORY MISSION OF THE JEWS.

"The salvation is of the Jews."[2] These are the words of Jesus Christ himself to the woman of Samaria by the well of Sychar. Salvation is the one necessity of the race. No religion, therefore, that has not salvation as its essence can meet the wants of the race.

It was the mission of the Jew to receive directly from God, and, in due time, transmit to the whole human race the only religion of salvation, and therefore the only true world-religion. Everything connected with the history of the Jews had reference to the completion of this one religion for mankind. Each revelation and dispensation, all discipline and punishment, every promise and threatening, their constitution, laws, and worship,

[1] *Religions before Christ*, p. 191.

[2] John iv. 22. The definite article used in the original gives the meaning: *The* (promised and only) *salvation comes from the Jews.*

every political, civil, and religious institution (so far as they were legitimate and proper), tended toward this one goal.[1] In the light of providential developments and later revelations, the divine plan as connected with the Jews may readily be traced, in its great outlines, from the calling of Abraham to the advent of Christ.

The history of the chosen people has been providentially divided into two periods, the first of which ended with the captivity and the extinction of national independence, and the second, with the Advent. The first was, in general terms, a period of national unity and integrity, and of complete separation from the outside world. The second was a period of national disintegration, of dispersion throughout the whole world, and of most varied union with mankind.

To the careless glance there seems a contradiction in the parts of this divine plan. Why first the policy of complete isolation, and then an abrupt change to the opposite? As always elsewhere, so here, to a closer inspection, the unity and consistency of the divine purpose clearly appear. The one purpose was twofold. The work of the period of isolation may be characterized as the revelation of the world-religion to the chosen people and the establishment of its sway over them. The work of the period of dispersion may be characterized as missionary in its nature, and as intended to impress the world-religion, in the form in which it had been revealed to the chosen people, upon the pagan races, in order to prepare them for the reception of the Divine Saviour with his salvation.

I. *The Jewish Isolation.*

Two great epochs are to be distinguished in the history of Judaism during the period of isolation. In the

[1] Kurtz, *Text Book of Ch. History,* vol. i. p. 43.

first, the Jewish system was definitely constituted, receiving its institutions from God, in the Covenant, through Abraham, and in the Law, through Moses. In the second, Israel was established in the land of Canaan, and the power of the new religion developed by the growth and perfection of its institutions and by a cycle of sublime revelations throwing vivid light upon the future. The first epoch was characterized by the predominance of the legal element, the second, by that of the prophetic, — though neither element was ever altogether absent. The Covenant, the Law, and the Prophets thus represent the three aspects of the Jewish religion during the age of isolation.

The Covenant. The first stage of the divine work of salvation began when Abraham of Ur of the Chaldees was called to be the head of a privileged family, and the progenitor of a race privileged for the world's sake.

In the covenant which Jehovah made with Abraham are found a command, a promise, and a seal.

"Get thee out of thy country, and from thy kindred."[1] "I am the Almighty God; walk before me and be thou perfect."[2] So ran the command. It called to a separation from paganism with its many gods and to a dedication to the one Almighty God. Its monotheism and its separation foreshadowed the more complete revelation and law which were to come by Moses.

"And I will make of thee a great nation, and I will bless thee, and make thy name great; and thou shalt be a blessing: and I will bless them that bless thee, and curse him that curseth thee: and in thee shall all the families of the earth be blessed."[3] So read the promise. While assuring to Abraham and his descendants special blessing and grace, whereby they should be exalted and the

[1] Genesis xii. 1. [2] Genesis xvii. 1. [3] Genesis xii. 2, 3.

true religion preserved, it reached out to the whole human race and was made in its interests, and so foreshadowed the world-religion to be brought in by Christ. It involved the germ of all the subsequent prophecies of Messiah and all the later developments of God's plan for the salvation of the world.

"This is my covenant, which ye shall keep, between me and thee, and thy seed after thee; every man child among you shall be circumcised."[1] Such was the seal. It was a "fit symbol of that removal of the old man and renewal of nature which qualified Abraham to be the parent of a holy seed."[2]

Thus were furnished the germs of the world-religion.

The Mosaic System. The holy seed which was called and created[3] in Abraham grew into a nation and in due time was called out of Egypt to receive, by the hand of Moses, a fuller revelation of God's law and grace. This was the second stage of the divine work.

The era of the Law began with the experience in the wilderness, on the way from Egypt to the promised land. It was then that the descendants of Abraham received those divine revelations which shaped their whole national life. They were, at the foundation, revelations of law, and expressed what it was God's will that the chosen people should do and become; but they were likewise revelations of grace, unfolding the method by which the people might, in conduct and character, attain to the fulfillment of the divine will.

The legal element of the divine revelation through Moses embraced the Jewish civil code and the moral law. The chosen people, already united by common suffering

[1] Genesis xvii. 10.

[2] Murphy, *Commentary on Genesis*, xvii. 9–14.

[3] Hebrews xi. 12.

and blessing, were thoroughly organized as a nation, and their union confirmed and consolidated at Sinai, by the establishment of a civil code. This code — the similarity of which to our own has been remarked by the eminent French jurist, De Tocqueville — was subordinate to higher than civil ends.[1] The moral law, summed up in the Decalogue, addressed to the understanding, sanctioned by suitable authority, and enforced by adequate penalties, was designed to impress upon the people God's moral attributes. It was "the clearest expression of the holy will of God before the advent of Christ. It set forth the ideal of righteousness, and was thus fitted most effectually to awaken a sense of man's great departure from it, and to give the knowledge of sin and guilt (Rom. iii. 20). It acted as a school-master to lead men to Christ that they might be justified by faith (Gal. iii. 24)."[2]

The gracious element in the Mosaic system, as distinguished from the legal element, was embodied in concrete and sensible form in the ceremonial law. This was necessary, for abstract statement was not enough. God's purpose both of law and grace needed to be put into such a form that it could be impressed upon the mind through the senses, — needed to be put in the form of a perpetual object lesson. This was accomplished by the ritual of the Mosaic religion. That religion was embodied in the four institutions which were at the basis of all the ancient religions: sacrifice; the priesthood; the sanctuary, or sacred place of adoration; and religious festivals, or periods consecrated to adoration. These institutions were purified from all heathen elements and given their full significance.

It was necessary that the grace element should be

[1] See Wines, *Commentaries on the Laws of the Ancient Hebrews.*

[2] Schaff, *History of the Apostolic Church*, p. 39.

added and placed over against the law, for mere law was not enough to save men. There was therefore attached to the Mosaic rites "both a symbolical and typical value, representing important truths having a present application, and being at the same time the shadow of good things to come."[1] They spoke at once of present duty and future blessing. The moral law brought despair and death; the sacrifices brought in the idea of reparation, of atonement, by death for death, and typified the great coming atonement. The moral law made man feel his unfitness to approach Jehovah; the priest, set apart and purified, appeared between the sinner and an offended God, symbolizing the separation while typifying the great High Priest by whom the race should be brought nigh to God. There was needed a permanent centre for this sacrificial system, a sanctuary; this was found at first in the tabernacle (afterward in the temple), which perpetually symbolized the salvation of God, and typified the better things to come. The people must be brought into close and frequent contact with this great centre that they may effectually learn the lessons of their religious system; the sacred festivals, with the daily sacrifices and sabbatic ordinances, were for this end.

The Mosaic ritual and the whole system of Judaism, given in the wilderness, were developed and perfected in the land of promise. Judæa was as admirably situated in that age, for maintaining the isolation of the Israelites from all the world, as it proved to be, in a later age and in altered circumstances, for bringing them into closest connection and union with all the world. It was at the common centre of the three grand divisions of the old world, and surrounded by the great nations of ancient culture; but it was separated from them by deserts on the south and east, by sea on the west, and by mountains

[1] Pressensé, *The Religions before Christ*, p. 207.

on the north.[1] The Mosaic legislation reared a still more impassable barrier than deserts and seas and mountains, between God's people and the pagan world.

What with the land and the legislation and the destruction of the Canaanites, freedom for the full development of Judaism, without disturbing influences from the heathen at home or abroad, was secured. When the monarchy reached the height of its glory, under David and Solomon, the ritual reached its most complete and magnificent embodiment in the temple then erected and made the centre of the Jewish system.

Development of Prophecy. The third stage in the divine work had already been entered upon. While the law was advancing toward its most perfect unfolding, the element of prophecy began to assume increasing prominence.

The Pentateuch opens with the promise that the seed of the woman shall bruise the serpent's head. That promise had always kept its place in the unfolding of Judaism. To Abraham it was made more definite; from his seed was to come the mysterious benefactor who was to restore the whole human race. Thus the promise of the world-religion, the theme and burden of prophecy, was given. Each new phase of Jewish history enriched it.

In the time of Samuel, some eleven centuries before Christ, prophecy received an organized form in a permanent prophetical office and order, and was thus prepared to take its place as a leading element in the Jewish religious development. It was the vocation of the prophet to keep alive the fundamental truth of the covenant, to keep before the minds of the people their high vocation, to call them back from idolatry, and to inspire them with a living faith in their glorious destiny. Borrowing his

[1] Schaff, *History of the Christian Church*, p. 36.

symbols from the times in which he lived, and thus securing an ever-present freshness, the prophet of the Lord pointed, with a clearness increasing to the last, to the Messiah in whom all the promises should be realized to Israel and to the world.

Says Dr. William H. Green, in an essay on "The Matter of Prophecy": "The prophetic exhibition of Christ is accomplished by successive teachings, each suited to its own age and its own special design, but all combining to produce the general effect. The prophets may thus be likened to a grand orchestra. Each musician plays a part adapted to his own particular instrument, which, taken by itself, is designed to give a particular effect to the piece; and yet they are attuned in such precise harmony, and so contrived with reference to the various possibilities of the melody, that, combined upon the oratorio of the Messiah, they bring out, as could in no other way be done, the full power of that magnificent production. The necessities of one period call for the presentation of the coming Saviour and his work under one point of view; those of other periods lead to the contemplation of them from different sides. And the necessities of the people, as they arise in the progress of their history, are themselves accommodated to the grand end to be accomplished, being of such a variety and character, that the instructions which they demand may complete the total of the revelations to be made respecting Messiah before his advent." [1]

When the prophetic era closed, the idea of the coming Messiah, to whom the whole ritual pointed and in whom all prophecy centred, had been made as prominent in the Jewish mind as was the law when it had become enshrined in the temple of Solomon at the close of the legal period. Every eye was turned toward the coming Christ.

[1] Princeton Review, *The Matter of Prophecy*, October, 1862.

But before this great work had been fully accomplished and the voices of the prophets hushed, the chosen people had passed from the period of isolation from all the world to the period of dispersion through all the world.

II. *The Jewish Dispersion.*

Certain events in the progress of the prophetic period, and especially toward its close, prepared for the transition from the early condition of national unity and isolation to the later one of disintegration and dispersion. The extraordinary material prosperity of the Jewish monarchy began the work of breaking down the barriers between the chosen people and the world ; the judgments of God completed it. In the prosperity and the judgments originated the system of means divinely employed for disseminating the truths of the world-religion.

Prosperity and judgments. In pushing the bounds of his kingdom out to the limits of the other great nations of the earth, King David made the Israelites one of the most prominent nations of that age, the rival in power and splendor of Egypt and Assyria, and a fit object for their fear and jealousy.

Still later, the necessity for gold and silver and other building materials, arising from the construction of the temple of Solomon and the various works in which that monarch attempted to rival the other great empires, gave an impulse to a world-wide commerce and intercourse. The sea on the west ceased to be a barrier, and became instead a highway to the nations, even as far west as Tarshish or Spain. The ports of Ezion-geber and Elath, at the head of the Akabah, opened the way for an active trade, both to the south and east, with the nations along the Red Sea and the Indian Ocean. The deserts on the east, north and south, no longer shut them out from the older nations of the world from which the Jewish race originally sprung. By building Tadmor, or Palmyra, on an oasis midway between Damascus and the Euphrates, Solomon gained control of the immense trade of Egypt and Asia Minor with the east by caravan, and thus made the wealth of both the east and the west tributary to the prosperity of his own realm. A highway for trade was opened into Egypt, and Solomon allied himself to Pharaoh by marrying his daughter. The way was thus prepared for the Jews, who were by nature a race of merchants, to become the merchants of the world.

The story of the very general departure of the Jewish race from the true God and of their lapse into idolatry, which resulted from their connection with the heathen nations, is too familiar to need rehearsal. In this defection Solomon himself — who, with all his wisdom, was unable to withstand the seductive influences of prosperity — took the lead, by the introduction and establishment of idolatry in the various forms in which it was practiced by his heathen wives. He had taken these wives in disobedience to God's plain command, thereby showing his own early departure from the true religion.

The story of the divine judgments which followed the apostasy of the chosen people is equally familiar. The divine wrath did not delay, but fell even upon Solomon. At his death the vast empire of David had already shrunk to its original narrow limits, and the Lord declared that even what remained should be rent from his successors. Jeroboam, when he had drawn off the ten tribes in revolt, established the idolatrous worship as the religion of the State, and from that time Israel, or the ten tribes, made haste to destruction, in spite of the many warnings and judgments of God. The final blow fell when Shalmanezer, king of Assyria, took Samaria, razed it, destroyed the kingdom of Israel, and carried the captives away to Halah and Habor (Chebar). Judah followed in the idolatry of Israel, and a little more than a century later its people were carried away captive to Babylon, save a remnant that fled into Egypt.

The prophetic activity reached its height during the decline and captivity. It was then that the sins against the covenant needed most to be rebuked. Early in that period appeared Elijah and Elisha, who wrought more miracles than any prophet since the days of Moses and Joshua. Just before the overthrow of Israel, Isaiah and Micah flourished in Judah, contemporary with Hosea and Amos in Israel. The two former survived that overthrow, and were succeeded by Nahum and Zephaniah, through whom, in the reign of Hezekiah and Josiah, a partial and temporary reformation was wrought in Judah.

It is obvious, moreover, that in the captivity the hopes of the Messiah needed to be kept most clearly before the people. Still more earnestly, therefore, did the prophets then ply their vocation among the captives of Judah, directing them in working God's purposes, — Jeremiah with the remnant in Egypt; Ezekiel among those by the river of Chebar; Daniel at the court of the great eastern monarch; Ezra and Nehemiah in leading back the band that rebuilt Jerusalem and the temple. Haggai, Zechariah, and Malachi, after the restoration, concluded the communications of God, in that age, touching the coming of Messiah and the great events of the future, using the deliverance from captivity as the type of Messiah's work. With them the roll of the prophets ended, and the voice of prophecy ceased till the near approach of the Advent.

Dissemination of the World-religion. The work of transmitting the true religion from the narrow limits of the Jewish race, where it had been prepared, to the widest limits of the human race, for which it had been prepared, had already begun.

Providentially, in connection with the prosperity and the judgments, there was somehow perfected the most complete system of means possible for the dissemination of the truth. It may now be seen that everything wrought together marvelously in God's plan, and for the accomplishment of his ends. It is manifest from history that the captivity and dispersion made the profoundest moral impression upon both Jew and Gentile, and that the restoration of the Jews resulted in the most constant and intimate intercourse of Jerusalem with all the world.

The captivity produced a revolution in the sentiments of both Jews and Gentiles respecting the true Judaism.

It cured the Jews of their idolatry, bound them as never before to their sacred records, and urged them on to make proselytes of all the world. Says Dr. Schaff: "As to religion, the Jews, especially after the Babylonish captivity, adhered most tenaciously to the letter of the law, and to their traditions and ceremonies, but without knowing the spirit and power of the Scriptures."[1] This is the universal testimony on the subject. Neander has shown how the Pharisees, or strict Jews, labored to make proselytes. The wavering authority of the old national religions, the unsatisfied religious necessities of so many, came in to aid them. Hence, the inclination to Judaism, particularly in the large capital cities, became very marked.[2]

The character of the Jew, as elevated by the judgments of the captivity, turned the favorable attention of the heathen world to the true religion. The Jew was the cultured religious man of that age. With Egypt he

[1] Schaff, *History of the Christian Church*, p. 37.

[2] Neander, *Church History*, vol. i. p. 67.

had shared the early knowledge of the arts. In the exodus, before the origin of Greek letters, his written language exhibited the fruits of his sojourn in the land of the Nile. He belonged to that Semitic race which has given the world, besides so many precious words of science and art, the three great and only systems of Theism.

It is obvious, too, that the religion of the Jew, unlike that of the heathen, was bound to a law of moral purity. Men might complain that they could not see the God of the Jew; but they could not help feeling the morality of his law. As a slave in heathen households moulding the young, as a steward overseeing his master's business, as a counselor of kings directing the destinies of nations, the true Israelite was everywhere doing in his measure, by the purity and diligence of his life, the work which Daniel the prophet did, in the highest positions, by his personal influence in winning men to his own pure and lofty faith.

The Jew, moreover, was then as ever the thrifty man of the world. Born with a tendency to acquisition, made by his religion a man to be trusted, he was prepared by his tact and thrift and enterprise to be the banker, merchant, and executive man of business, and so to coöperate in the work for heathendom which God was carrying forward both by natural and supernatural agencies. Xerxes, who attempted the conquest of Greece, had a Jewish cupbearer, a Jewish consort, and a Jewish prime minister.

But the most striking impressions made upon the nations in favor of the true religion were due to the special manifestations of divine power.

These manifestations were very marked during the exile. They were needed both to correct and comfort the people of God, and also to impress the character of Jehovah, as the only true God, upon the greatest of the

Oriental Empires. In all this miraculous work, the prophets were the representatives of God. Foremost among them all was Daniel, the most faultless character of the old dispensation, and one of the grandest of all the prophets. The book which bears his name is one continued record of miracles of power and foresight, wrought at the very centre of oriental magnificence, and exerting an influence on the future destiny of the nations that witnessed them, perhaps greater than those wrought in Egypt and at Sinai. Kings heard his prophecies, and knew that God spoke by him. They witnessed his miraculous works and his striking deliverances, and acknowledged the God of the Jews to be "the God of gods." By royal decrees they did what was in their power to make their own feeling the universal feeling of western Asia. Influenced by the prophet, Cyrus issued the decree for the rebuilding of the temple and provided the requisite means for the work. The reëstablishment at Jerusalem of a grand religious centre, from which light was to go out into all the world while men were waiting for the advent of Messiah, was therefore one of the most impressive proofs of the wonderful revolution wrought by the exile,in Oriental heathendom.

The New Religious Centre. Never was there a more complete and marvelous provision of God than that for making the most of this moral impression, upon Jew and Gentile, in giving the true religion the widest possible influence. The restored city and temple, the completed canon of the Scriptures, and the synagogue system constitute the chief features of that provision.

Jerusalem was restored to be henceforth not a national centre, as under David and Solomon, but simply a religious metropolis to the whole dispersed nation, from which should go forth the spiritual influences which should fashion the future of mankind.

Hence the edict of Cyrus, which originated in the divine counsels, was a permission and not a command. The long period of war and desolation had changed the aspect of Judæa. It had ceased to be in the old sense "a land flowing with milk and honey." It could never again be the great natural centre of wealth it had once been, for the line of trade had been changed, and its history was to be one of dependence. Henceforward it must be sought as a home chiefly for the memories of what it had been, or for the hopes of what it should again become through the Messiah.

No decree of earthly king could have brought back more than a small portion of the descendants of Abraham. The great mass had become engaged in commerce, banking, and retail traffic, and would not make the Holy City their place of residence. "The emigrants doubtless consisted chiefly of the pious and the poor; and as the latter proved docile to their teachers, a totally new spirit reigned in the restored nation."[1] Jerusalem thus became comparatively pure, as a religious centre, and was fitted to elevate the Jews of the dispersion who came up from year to year to the great festivals.

While the Holy City and the temple were thus being restored, the divine religion, which gave them their significance and their sacredness, was receiving its final and unalterable written form.

One step toward securing this result was taken in the gathering up of the sacred writings and the completion of the Old Testament canon, by Ezra, the prophet and scribe. From that time forward nothing was to be added to the word of God until Christ should come, and the Jews guarded it with jealous care against all attempted additions whatsoever.

Another step was taken when the Hebrew ceased to

[1] See Kitto, *Cyclopædia*, article "Captivities."

be a living language. Living languages change; old words die or receive new meanings; new words are constantly produced. With a living language, in constant contact with new phases of Oriental and Greek thought, the Jews might have greatly corrupted the sacred records. But in the violent disruption and the foreign intercourse, the Hebrew became a dead tongue, and Judaism, in its divinely revealed form, thus became fixed and incapable, through the centuries preceding the advent of Messiah, of any extensive corruption. From the day of the restoration the true religion spoke out from that spiritual centre of the world with no uncertain voice.

The establishment and development of the synagogue system furnished the connecting link between the temple with its divine religion, and the Jew of the dispersion, and the heathen world wherever the Jew was to be found.

The synagogue probably originated during the captivity. At all events, its great development took place then. When the temple had been destroyed, the Jews naturally established the synagogue to take its place in keeping up their religion. The rule was, that "a synagogue was to be erected in every place where there were ten *Batelnim*, that is, ten persons of full age and free condition always at leisure to attend the service of it."[1] The services to be performed in these synagogue assemblies were prayers, reading the Scriptures, and expounding them. Morning and evening the Law was read on three days in the week, and then on the Sabbath it was reread. Each year the five books of Moses were read through and repeated. Besides, each day had its reading of the Prophets, and of certain passages of the Law called the *Shema*. The greatest familiarity with the let-

[1] See Prideaux, *Old and New Testament Connected*, vol. i. pp. 298, 299.

ter of the Scriptures was thus secured wherever the wanderings of the Jews carried the synagogue system.

After the restoration of the temple, the cessation of prophecy turned the attention of the religious leaders at that great centre with tenfold eagerness to the study of the Scriptures, especially of the prophecies concerning the Messiah. The Jews of the dispersion, who went up annually in immense numbers to Jerusalem to the great religious festivals, carried back from the temple to the synagogues, in all parts of the pagan world, the latest developments of this study. The extent of this intercourse may be imagined from the statement of Josephus, that, when Jerusalem was besieged by the Romans under Titus, three millions of Jews, who had come up to the Passover, were shut in by the besiegers.

By this vast telegraphic system the latest thought at Jerusalem was speedily made the property of all the Jews, and through them was borne to the doors of the entire pagan world. As the time of the Advent drew nigh, the expectation of a coming Messiah, deepened and directed to the times designated in prophecy, had been awakened in all lands. All men were looking for a great Deliverer to come out of Judæa.

The old religion in its Jewish form had done its part of the preparatory work for the Christ, in accordance with the divine plan.

SECTION II.

THE PREPARATORY MISSION OF THE GENTILES.

A view of the preparation for the Messiah would be incomplete if confined to the Jews alone. Salvation has been seen to have come forth from Judæa, but to be adapted to the necessities of the world. Three great historic races, the Oriental, the Greek, and the Roman, successively entered, along with the Jew, into the work of preparing the world for the advent of Messiah and the spread of his divine salvation.

This was in accordance with the prophecies of Daniel, contained in the second and seventh chapters of his book. These great empires were to precede and prepare the way for the mightier kingdom of Messiah which the God of heaven should set up, and which should be an everlasting kingdom. Each will be found to have accomplished a twofold preparatory work.

I. *The Mission of the Oriental Races.*

The Oriental empires which entered into this work were the Babylonian, represented by the head of gold in the great image of prophecy, and the less magnificent Medo-Persian, represented by the arms and breast of silver. In the later prophecy, of the four beasts, the former is symbolized by the first beast, which was like a lion, and had eagle's wings; since it was a lion in strength and an eagle in swiftness: the latter is symbolized by the second beast, which was like a bear; since, in the desire for conquest, it was all-voracious like the bear.

The Oriental Problem. These great Oriental races represented material riches, power, and grandeur. It was a subordinate part of their mission to prove the insufficiency of the greatest wealth, luxury, and splendor to satisfy and save man. It was the problem on which Solomon wrought, and whose solution he gives in Ecclesiastes when he brings back from his varied experience the conclusion: "Fear God and keep his commandments, for this is the whole of man," — the same problem, only on a vastly grander scale. The nations of the Orient came from its attempted solution wretched and perishing. But the more important part of their mission was to furnish the agencies and theatre for the Jewish dispersion, and for the early dissemination of the germs of the world-religion. For this they were eminently fitted. The Jew was their proper representative, belonging to their own race. He had come forth from the valley of the Euphrates, in Abraham the Chaldee. The captivity was but a return to the primitive home. Who was so entitled as the Jew to be called the representative Oriental?

The Oriental races could most easily come into sympathy with Judaism, and could most readily furnish the conditions requisite for the fuller development of the germs of the true religion. In the Oriental mind, therefore, the Jew was to place the grand truths of his religion first, and thus to open the way to reach, at a later date, the Greek and Roman. By their self-will and brute force the Oriental races were meantime to chastise the Jewish race and cure it of its idolatry.

II. *The Mission of the Greeks.*

The eastern empires fell successively under the sentence which the handwriting on the wall passed upon Belshazzar, and which history repeats against every despotism to the end of time: "Thou art weighed in the balance and found wanting," — wanting in fulfilling the true ends of states and governments, in securing the welfare of mankind and their union in the bonds of social life.[1]

In the later period of its history, when in the height of power under Xerxes, the Medo-Persian empire came into direct and open conflict with the West as represented by Greece, the nation which was divinely appointed to work out another problem, — whether man's free energy in poetry and art, in learning and philosophy, could perfect his social state, and thus accomplish

[1] See Philip Smith, *History of the World*, vol. i. p. 242.

that in which the East with its despotic power and wealth and magnificence had failed.

The Greek empire under Alexander was the third kingdom which was to rule over all the earth. Its strength is represented by the brass of the image of the vision, in Daniel, and the rapidity of its conquests and the insatiableness of its ambition, by the third beast, the leopard, with its four wings and four heads.[1]

The Greek Problem. In its career the Greek race tested the insufficiency of the human reason with the highest human culture to satisfy and save man; while in the conquests of Alexander it gave the world the highest human civilization of the ancient ages, and the most perfect of languages in which to embody the true religion. These are the main points of interest in the mission of the Greek. In fact, Greek wisdom exhausted its free energies upon the same great problem which despotic Oriental power and magnificence had failed to solve.

For a millennium the Greek race directed its varied powers and consummate genius in vain to the work of perfecting humanity. It achieved the greatest results in thought ever permitted to unaided human effort. Its civilization was one of the grandest the world has ever seen, — grand in its recognitions of humanity, in its poetry and philosophy, in its science and art. But its culture was purely intellectual, having no religious and moral ground of support capable of withstanding every shock and indestructible under all changes, and in the natural course of its development it could only degenerate into false civilization and end in social corruption. It had no light and life from God. "There was yet no salt to preserve the life of humanity from decomposing, or to restore it back again when passing to decomposition."

[1] Daniel ii. 32, 39; vii. 6.

It is not too much to say that the Greek did everything toward the perfecting of man that could be done by a purely intellectual civilization. He demonstrated for all time what human reason, when situated most favorably and tasked to the utmost, could accomplish for the salvation of a race with endowments superior to the other races. The later ages showed it to be very little.

It became manifest that the glory of the Greek thought needed to be saved from its own corruption, — saved for the good of mankind. This could only be accomplished by extending its sway over the Oriental empires, and bringing it in contact with the saving influences of the world-religion which was being diffused everywhere by the scattered and exiled seed of Abraham.

The World Hellenized. When the Greek had voiced his wonderful thoughts of beauty and power in a language made for them and by them, and, therefore, the most perfect of the languages of the ancient ages, — the one most worthy to become the world-language, — and before the blight and decay had fallen upon the race, Alexander of Macedon appeared to perform the needed office of Hellenizing the world.

Of the work of Alexander, Howson says: "He took up the meshes of the net of civilization, which were lying in disorder on the edges of the Asiatic shore, and spread them over all the countries which he traversed in his wonderful campaigns. The East and the West were suddenly brought together. Separated tribes were united under a common government. New cities were built, as the centres of political life. New lines of communication were opened, as the channels of commercial activity. The new culture penetrated the mountain ranges of Pisidia and Lycaonia. The Tigris and Euphrates became Greek rivers. The language of Athens was heard among the Jewish colonies of Babylonia; and a Grecian Babylon was built by the conqueror in Egypt and called by his name."[1]

When Alexander passed away leaving his vast plans unfinished, in his dying words, "to the strongest," he left his empire to the only men who could have carried out the work of making the world permanently Greek, — his own great generals whom he had trained to command. When the empire was broken into four, the four were Greek, and Antioch and Alexandria rivaled Athens and Corinth as centres of Greek learning and art.[2]

From Alexander to the Advent Judaism and Hellenism were in world-wide contact. The man of prophecy was elevating the view of the man of reason, while the man of reason was widening the vision of the man of prophecy. Even where the Greek contemptuously held himself aloof from the Jew, the Jewish religion was one of the most powerful influences in breaking down the old paganism. At the bar of reason, polytheism could not stand before the doctrine of one God. It was doomed from the hour when the Greek heard the first whispers concerning Jehovah. But the Greek did not everywhere hold himself aloof; the two modes of thought came into direct contact; the philosopher and the scribe met and became one. This occurred especially in the great centres. At Alexandria, the Septuagint, or Greek version of the Old Testament Scriptures, was made three centuries before the Advent, for the use of those employing the Greek language, and the old revelation of the world-religion was thus scattered abroad for the Greek-speaking communities. At the same centre of culture Platonism and Judaism came together and were consoli-

[1] See Conybeare and Howson, *Life, Times, and Travels of St. Paul*, vol. i. p. 9.

[2] See Döllinger, *The Gentiles and Jews in the Court of the Temple of Christ*, vol. i. p. 341.

dated in the Neo-Platonism which exerted such an influence both before and after the Advent.

In this twofold manner, by despair of reason and hope from prophecy, the Greek was borne onward to the completion of his part in the work of preparation for the coming of the Messiah, until mankind was found in possession of the world-religion with its predictions of the coming Redeemer, written in the perfected world-language, and made capable of greater expansiveness by the Greek forms of thought.

The Greek mission was thus evidently essential in the preparation for Messiah. It forced the thinking men of that age to feel and confess the insufficiency of human reason, even in its most perfect development, for the deliverance and perfection of mankind, and left them waiting and longing for one who could accomplish this work. It brought in a dawning sense of human brotherhood, and so helped to bring mankind together into the true unity. It aided men to cut loose from the hoary but unreasonable traditions of the past, and thus prepared them to receive the reasonable truth of God. It made ready and living the better and broader forms of thought and speech in which the Gospel with its grander truths — too grand and living to be put into the narrow and dead Hebrew — should be proclaimed to all the world.

III. *The Mission of the Romans.*

Rome was already the rising power of the West when Alexander gave the Greek civilization to the East. The Roman Empire was the fourth kingdom of the prophecy of Daniel. Its strength is represented by the iron of the great image, since it was to be "strong as iron;" its terrible character, by the fourth beast, which had more than the power of the lion, more than the greed of the bear, and more than the swiftness and insatiable cruelty of the leopard, and to which no name could be given.[1]

The Roman Problem. The Roman was to try another solution of the problem on which the Oriental and the Greek had failed. He was to try whether human power, taking the form of law, regulated by political principles of which a regard for law and justice was most conspicuous, could perfect humanity by subordinating the individual to the state and making the state universal. "The power which was destined at length to raise a universal empire on the ruins of the Eastern Monarchies, of the free states of Greece, and of the commercial oligarchy of Carthage, combined in itself the strongest points of the systems which it superseded,"[2] — more than the material power of Oriental despotism; much of the freedom and intelligence and more than the social order of Greece; a stronger and better aristocracy than that of Carthage.

In the old Roman race, the will, or that part of man which pushes to action and enables him to control and mould nature and mankind, was the predominant element, associated with conscience or the natural sense of justice. Its herculean tasks and its universal empire furnish the highest expression of the human soul as the repository of the energy for shaping the world to law and order. The Roman, as the man of power, was to attempt the solution of the same problem of perfecting man in which the man of prophecy and the man of reason and taste had already failed, and in his failure was to complete the preparation for the coming of him who could solve the hitherto insoluble problem.

The World Romanized. Before the time of the Advent, Rome had demonstrated the powerlessness of hu-

[1] Daniel, ii. 33, 40; vii. 7, 19, 23.

[2] Smith, *History of the World*, vol. i. p. 131.

man power to save mankind. It had done its best, but its best was little, — practically nothing. It needed the coming Christ that itself might be saved. Imperialism was as helpless as Orientalism and Hellenism.

But the Roman performed a still more important part in preparing the world for the Messiah and the spread of the world-religion. It was Rome that cast up the highways along which the Jews plied their traffic and carried out to the ends of the earth the truth of God and the expectation of a coming Deliverer. It was Rome that made the influence of the divine religion free, rapid, and world wide.

But more than all, Rome did for the whole world that law-work without which man never feels the greatness of his need of the Gospel. In carrying out his mission of power the Roman was, as already hinted, the representative of natural justice in the world. It was doubtless some alleviation that the moulds into which the Roman power so remorselessly crushed men and nations were moulds of justice; yet in proportion as the world was a wicked world was the justice a terrible justice. Rome is aptly described by the prophet Daniel as the *iron kingdom:* "The fourth kingdom shall be strong as iron, forasmuch as iron breaketh in pieces and subdueth all things, and as iron that breaketh all these shall it break in pieces and bruise;" and again, as the *ferocious beast,* "dreadful and terrible, and strong exceedingly, with great iron teeth, which devoured and brake in pieces, and stamped the residue with the feet of it." It was justice practically omnipotent and omnipresent, and so neither to be resisted nor escaped, — justice which never dreamed of mercy until the work of conquest and consolidation was done. It made men long for mercy, because it demonstrated to them that there was no hope for them in righteous law.

The Total Result. So it came about that there was going up from all the world a wail for deliverance when the divine Deliverer appeared.

Says Neander: "The three great historical nations had to contribute, each in its own peculiar way, to prepare the soil for the planting of Christianity, — the Jews on the side of the religious element; the Greeks on the side of science and art; the Romans, as masters of the world, on the side of the political element. When the fullness of the time was arrived, and Christ appeared, — when the goal of history had thus been reached, — then it was, that through him, and by the power of the spirit that proceeded from him, — the might of Christianity, — all the threads, hitherto separated, of human development, were to be brought together and interwoven in one web." [1]

Regarding the subject from another point of view, human nature had exhausted itself in the efforts of the Gentile world to solve the problem of man's elevation and salvation. The Oriental had given the freest rein to human desires, in the most favorable circumstances, and was perishing in magnificence and luxury. The Greek had given fullest scope to reason and taste, in circumstances equally favorable, and was perishing in the very glory of his creations of thought and beauty. The Roman had made all the other powers subordinate to his executive energy, and conscience, with its insatiate justice, was crushing him, and all the world with him, even by his universal empire. There were no other powers in human nature to bring to the task. The world over, on the great and all-absorbing question of man's salvation, the oracles of heathenism were dumb.

It was only as Judaism had wrought with heathenism and for it, that hope remained for mankind. Along the line of the divine purpose of grace, Jew and Gentile had

[1] *Church History*, vol. i. p. 4.

wrought together, for the most part unconsciously, for more than a thousand years, and the final results were now to be reached.

When the Cæsars were firmly established on the throne of the Empire, and the three phases of civilization, in Judaism, Hellenism, and Imperialism, had in measure blended and reached out over the world from Gibraltar and Britain to the shores of the Caspian, the Messianic expectancy and longing reached the highest intensity. It was the fullness of times. Could the world endure longer without the coming of Christ?

CHAPTER II.

THE ADVENT AND THE WRITTEN GOSPELS.

Jesus Christ came in "the fullness of the time" (Gal. iv. 4), or at the hour appointed in the divine plan and prepared for by the divine providence, — the hour when everything was ready for his coming. He proclaimed the great truths of the Gospel, was rejected by men, and finished his sacrificial work on the cross. In due time, under commission from him, his Apostles gave that Gospel to the world, first in their oral preaching, and then in the permanent records known as the four Gospels.

SECTION I.

THE ADVENT OF JESUS CHRIST.

In the life of Jesus Christ is to be found the key to the history of the world. As the ages before were but the preparations for his advent, and replete with events and prophecies which turned all eyes toward that advent, so the ages since have often been shown to be but the unfolding of his true power and glory in the progress of his kingdom among men. With the historical verity of his person and career, Christianity stands or falls. The person of Jesus Christ constitutes Christianity in its highest and truest sense.[1]

It is natural, therefore, in these days, when radical infidelity is pushing its destructive criticism to the utmost, that the life of Jesus Christ should become the centre of the religious controversies which are agitating the world.[2]

To attempt a full discussion of this whole subject, or to give a detailed chronological exhibition of the life of Christ, would obviously lead beyond the scope of the present work. Nothing more can be done than to group the main facts and direct the attention of the reader — who wishes to consider the subject further — to some of the writers from whom he can obtain the needed guidance and assistance.

The Time of the Advent. According to the view long held and early indorsed by the Romish Church, Jesus Christ was born on Christmas, at the opening of the Christian Era, or about 754 years after the founding of Rome. A more accurate historical knowledge has made it evident that his birth was rather four or five years earlier, or about 750 or 749 after the founding of Rome, and most probably in the spring-time. This conclusion is based upon the fact that Herod the Great, in whose reign the birth of Christ took place, died in the fourth year before the commencement of our era, shortly before Easter.[3]

The important facts connected with the Advent may

1 See Schaff, *The Person of Christ*, p. 9.

2 See Tischendorf, *The Origin of the Gospels*, p. 23. Also, Row, *The Supernatural in the New Testament*, pp. 4–8.

3 See Matthew ii. 1; Josephus, *Antiquities*, xvii. 9, 3; Andrews, *Life of our Lord*; Robinson, *Harmony of the Gospels*.

be found in the opening chapters of the Gospels. That Christ came at just the right juncture in the unfolding of the divine plan is the main point for present consideration.

Lange has remarked, that the days of Herod form the centre of the world's history, and that every review of the state of the Jewish and heathen world, at the time of Christ's birth, confirms the truth of the remark of Paul to the Galatians, that he appeared when the fullness of the time was come.[1]

Many prophecies combined to fix upon just that as the time for the appearance of the great Deliverer.

Jacob, in blessing his sons, declared that the sceptre was not to depart from Judah, nor a lawgiver to cease from among his descendants, till Shiloh should come (Genesis xlix. 10). In Herod the Great, Judah still had a king, but perhaps in less than a month after the birth of Jesus, Herod died, and the kingdom as such came to an end.

A special period — marked according to the method elsewhere used in the Jewish Scriptures, of computing by heptads (weeks) of years — was fixed, from the going forth of the command to restore and to build Jerusalem, to the cutting off of Messiah (Dan. ix. 24–27). Starting from the time of the issue of the commission of Artaxerxes to Ezra (Ezra vii. 12–28), say about 457 B. C., the middle of the seventieth heptad reached forward 486½ years, to about 30 years after the opening of the Christian Era, as the date of the death of Messiah.[2] The same prophecy fixed with great accuracy the duration of Messiah's public work and the date of the destruction of the Holy City by the Romans.

The time of the manifestation of Christ in his public

[1] Lange, *Commentary on Luke*, p. 33.

[2] See *Prideaux*; also, Wordsworth, *Daniel and the Minor Prophets.*

work was also determined by prophecy. He was to come, the desire of all nations, to the second temple, and to impart to it by his presence a greater glory than that of Solomon's temple (Hag. ii. 7–9; Mal. iii. 1). A generation later than the death of Jesus the temple passed away and this prediction could not have been fulfilled after that date.

More definitely still, a herald was to appear before Messiah, a voice crying in the wilderness, making preparation for his coming (Isa. xl. 3; Mal. iii.; iv. 5). A few months before the entrance of Jesus upon his public mission, John the Baptist appeared, claiming to be such a herald, and in due time baptizing Jesus and introducing him to the Jewish nation as the Messiah (Matt. iii.; Mark i.; Luke iii.; John i.).

The Expectation of the World. These are only instances taken out of that great mass of prophecy which at the time of the Advent, through the temple and synagogue system, had brought the Jews into an attitude of hourly expectancy of the Messiah.

That there was a like expectancy, throughout the heathen world, of some deliverer or ruler to come forth from Judæa, is equally clear. It was thus that the Magi came, at the right hour, inquiring at Jerusalem after the new-born King of the Jews. Suetonius relates that "an ancient and definite expectation had spread throughout the East, that a ruler of the world would, at about that time, arise in Judæa."[1] Tacitus makes a similar statement.[2] Schlegel mentions that the Buddhist missionaries traveling to China met Chinese sages going to seek the Messiah about 33 A. D.[3]

The entire world was thus evidently in an attitude of

[1] *Life of Vespasian*, c. iv.
[2] *History*, v. 13.
[3] *Philosophy of History*.

expectancy. The Oriental had despaired of his material magnificence, the Greek of his reason and philosophy, and the Roman was despairing of his universal empire. God must interpose or the world must perish.[1]

SECTION II.

THE CAREER OF JESUS.

At just the right hour Jesus Christ came and accomplished his appointed task, in a life of probably a little over thirty-three years, about three and a half of which were devoted to his public ministry. The attempted chronological arrangement of all the recorded facts of his career may be consulted in the various Harmonies.[2]

I. *Outline of the Career.*

Without entering into the minute details of the harmonists, a fair working outline of the life of Christ may be constructed from the chronological data furnished chiefly by John and Luke. John, as is well known, narrates the whole period of our Lord's public ministry in connection with his journeys to Jerusalem to keep the different feasts, omitting no single passover occurring during this period, but even mentioning the one not kept by him at Jerusalem (John vi. 4). He has thus furnished the scheme of Christ's public ministry. Luke has not only supplied several special dates of the greatest importance,[3] but has in his preface intimated his intention of narrating the events of our Lord's life *in order*, — an order doubtless largely chronological.

Wieseler's Outline. Paying due regard to these data from John and Luke; admitting and emphasizing the

1 See Döllinger.
2 See Andrews, *Life of Our Lord;* Robinson, *Harmony of the Gospels.*
3 Luke ii. 1; iii. 23; Acts i. 1, 3; and particularly Luke iii. 1, 2.

impossibility of securing a perfect chronological arrangement of all the facts; and avoiding that fatal error of the harmonists, of attempting to secure chronological unity at the expense of the individuality of the Gospels, — Wieseler divides the Gospel History into six Sections.[1]

Section 1. The history of our Lord's childhood. Luke i. 5–ii. 52. Compare Luke iii. 23–38. Matt. i., ii.

Section 2. From the first public appearance of John the Baptist, and then of our Lord, to the imprisonment of the Baptist, and Christ's return to Galilee, after his journey to the Feast of Purim. Luke iii. 1–iv. 13; Mark i. 1–13; Matt. iii. 1–iv. 11; John i. 19–v. 47.

Section 3. From our Lord's return to Galilee to his journey to the Feast of Tabernacles. Luke iv. 14–ix. 50; Mark i. 14–ix. 50; Matt. iv. 12–xviii. 35; John vi. 1–vii. 1.

Section 4. From our Lord's journey to the Feast of Tabernacles to his last regal entry into Jerusalem. Luke iv. 51–xix. 28; Mark x. 1–52; Matt. xix. 1–xx. 34; John vii. 2–xii. 11.

Section 5. From our Lord's regal entry into Jerusalem to the day of his crucifixion and burial. Luke xix. 29–xxiii. 55; Mark xi. 1–15, 47; Matt. xxi. 1–xxvii. 61; John xii. 12–xix. 42.

Section 6. From our Lord's burial to his ascension. Luke xxiii. 56–xxiv. 53; Acts i. 1–11; Mark xvi. 1–20; Matt. xxvii. 62–xxviii. 20; John xx. 1–xxi. 25.

Simplified Outline. It will be observed at a glance that Section 2 takes in our Lord's early ministry in Judæa; Section 3, his public ministry in Galilee; and Section 4, his ministry in Peræa, after he was driven from his public ministry in Judæa and Galilee by the hostility of the Jews. This suggests, as more easily remem-

[1] See Wieseler, *Chronological Synopsis of the Four Gospels*, p. 24.

bered, the following statement of the divisions given by Wieseler: —

Section 1. The childhood and youth. Thirty years from 4 B. C. to 26 A. D.

Section 2. The inauguration and ministry in Judæa. About one year, from 26–27 A. D.

Section 3. The public ministry in Galilee. About two years, from 27–29 A. D.

Section 4. The public ministry in Peræa — beyond Jordan. About six months, from October, 29 A. D., to April, 30 A. D.

Section 5. The atonement by death. About one week, April 2d to 8th, 30 A. D.

Section 6. The burial, resurrection, and ascension. About forty days, from April 9th to about May 18th, 30 A. D.

II. *The Historical Reality of the Career.*

It is admitted on all hands that "the life of Jesus is the most momentous of all questions which the Church has to encounter, — the one which is decisive whether it shall or shall not live."[1] If his life be not a reality, then even the morality which is based upon the Gospels has its root in immorality, — in a lie. What then of the historical reality?

The direct knowledge of the life of Jesus is derived almost exclusively from the four Gospels. The other writings of the New Testament, however, furnish some additional facts.

After these comes the indirect knowledge from writings based upon the Sacred Scriptures, whether by the advocates or the opposers of the Christian system, and which attest the facts of Christ's life, because these writings must have originated in the facts.

[1] See Tischendorf, *Origin of the Four Gospels*, p. 24.

Finally, in two classical writers, Tacitus and Pliny, we possess incidental expressions which have a lasting interest. The former testifies that Christ, the founder of the religion which had gained so strong a hold even in Nero's time, had been punished with death, by the procurator Pontius Pilate, during the reign of Tiberius.[1] The latter asserts, in a communication to Trajan, that the Christians, already a numerous body in Bithynia, were in the habit of singing songs of praise to Christ as God.[2]

It is therefore easy to see why the Gospels are the main point of attack in the present age. They are the chief direct witnesses to the historical reality of the life of Jesus Christ.

Whether judged by the plain principles of common sense or by the formal canons of a scientific criticism, the argument for the historical verity of the life of Christ, as that life is presented in the Gospels, is of overwhelming force. It will only be proper, in this connection, to advert to some of its forms, chiefly in order to direct attention to some of those works accessible on the subject which may be consulted with profit.

From Common Sense. From the point of view of common sense, the history of the world, both before and since the beginning of the Christian era, is a Sphinx's riddle, if the historical truth of the life of Jesus Christ be denied. How was it that all the ages before reached out in type and prophecy and human longing and development toward the man of Nazareth, and found their fulfillment and completion only in him? How is it that all the ages since have been but the logical unfolding from the life of that central figure of human history? How could a myth —an impostor, a cheat, a lie—give to man all his highest blessings, and all his grandest civilization, and inspire all

[1] Tacitus, *Annal.* xv. 44.

[2] Pliny, *Epist.* x. 97. See Tischendorf, *Origin,* etc. p. 25.

his noblest purposes and achievements? The historical verity of the Christ-life in the Gospels is the only sufficient reason for the movements of the ancient ages, the only adequate cause for the developments of the modern ages and the Christian anticipations of the future ages.

In the view of common sense, a mythical Christ and no Christ at all are equally fatal to the rationalistic hypotheses.

1st. On the supposition that Jesus of Nazareth never actually existed, it is not within the range of rational belief that the *idea* of such a being was formed in that country, in that age, and in the minds of such men as the Evangelists are held to have been, and as in point of mental endowment and culture and social rank they certainly were. When it shall have been fully ascertained what that being who is presented to us in the Gospels really was, the evidence will be irresistible that this is not within the range of rational belief, but is so unlikely and unnatural as to be morally impossible. It would contradict all experience and all legitimate induction from experience, and be as utterly out of the course of human things as any miracle ever recorded.[1] The men of that age never could have conceived the life of Jesus unless they had first witnessed it; never could have conceived his sublime doctrine unless they had first heard it.

2d. On the supposition that Jesus of Nazareth did actually exist, and that the statements made by the Gospels concerning the facts of his humanity are *on the whole* what the writers saw and heard, then the facts concerning his divinity must likewise be true, and the entire record of the Gospels must be true.

It has been shown by various able writers, in pursuing this line of argument, that the life of Jesus stands out a mysterious exception to all the laws which ordinarily govern the destiny of men.

[1] See Young, *Christ of History*, p. 24.

The outer conditions of that life were most unfavorable. He was born in poverty, among the lowly and ignorant, wrought for most of his life as a carpenter, received no formal education, had only the companionship of peasants and fishermen, and no acquaintance with the great and wise, received no patronage of any kind from any one.

His public life was the briefest, — only a little over three years and this friendless young peasant of Galilee came to his death of shame by the cross. Even in that brief course he used no ordinary weapons or machinery or plans, but only the simple utterance of great spiritual truths which men hated, and the setting at work of invisible spiritual forces at which men scoffed. The moral condition of the age and place in which he appeared was eminently unfavorable. It was an age of awful corruption, as witnesses Paul, in the Epistle to the Romans, in his description of the state of the Gentile world, and as also witness the heathen historians of that age. The land of the chosen race, with its greater light, was the centre of moral perversity; Galilee was disreputable even in that; and Nazareth was the focus of intellectual as well as of moral darkness. There was nothing in those thirty years in that centre of darkness to develop such character, life, and doctrine as those of the Jesus of the Gospels. A righteous man could ask with pious horror, "Can any good thing come out of Nazareth?"

Yet out of Nazareth came forth Jesus, of his own free will, claiming to be the Messiah, yet wearing a form wholly different from that of the Messiah expected by his age, and possessed with an idea wholly original and totally different from that of his age, — he came forth to save not from earthly subjection but from sin, and to save not Judæa only, but all the lost world.

Just as evidently unique was he in his spiritual individuality, — in his constant and conscious communion with God; in his consciousness of sinlessness, of divinity and of the grandest of missions; in the universality, completeness, and unapproachable greatness of his manhood, attained and manifested by him without apparent cause and without conscious effort; in the entire unselfishness and boundless self-sacrifice of his life and in the sublime devotion of it to God and humanity; in his faith in God and truth and in his calm assurance of the triumph of his kingdom on earth. In all these he was absolutely alone among men.

In the centre of darkness he began a unique work with the revelation to men of their moral condition and with the call to repentance, and there he gathered the disciples who in his name should conquer the world. Mingling a terrible severity with a divine tenderness, and uniting the severest simplicity with the most absolute authority, he dealt with the corrupt age, sparing no wickedness, overlooking no sorrow, teaching in a form and clearness unattained by any other teacher the three great doctrines which are announced in the Gospels, — the doctrine of the soul, the doctrine of God, and the doctrine of the reconciliation of the soul and God by his sacrificial death alone.

Such a character, personality, work, in such outer conditions, are simply impossible, except upon the supposition of the Deity of Jesus Christ. They forbid — even if the supernatural elements are left out of sight — his classification with men as a mere man. The simple facts of his humanity, once admitted, irresistibly bear with them the undoubted truth of his Godhead.[1] The historical verity of the life of Jesus of Nazareth cannot be denied without abjuring common sense.

[1] See Young, *Christ of History*. Also, Bushnell, *Nature and the Supernatural*, ch. x., "The Character of Jesus forbids his possible Classification with Men."

From Scientific Criticism. It has been shown to be equally beyond the range of rational belief that the Apostles did their preaching and wrought the mightiest revolution of all ages without the actual existence and career of Jesus as presented in the Gospels. Without the verity of the history no adequate and rational motive for their conduct can possibly be pointed out.

"There never was such a being as Jesus of Nazareth!" Whence then this mightiest movement of time, which is seen in the origin, development, and world-wide sway of Christianity?

"He was but a miserable deceiver, at the best, himself deluded while misleading others!" How then this world of light out of such utter darkness? Who can believe that all the best blessings of the world could come from such a source? Is a lie more beneficent than the truth?

"The disciples were convinced that he was a failure, but they stole away his dead body and devoted themselves heart and soul to keeping up the work of deception which he had begun!" Can a sane man believe that? Do men naturally act from such motives? Would they keep up such a course, with no whisper of dissent or exposure of the base secret, through fire and blood, along all ages, until the world is converted to their lie? Imagine the poor fishermen and peasants, in deadly fear and in despair, stealing away that lifeless body of Jesus for such a purpose!

The conclusion of scientific criticism is in accordance with that of common sense, — that the Gospels are veritable history. Such criticism in its only proper form is simply the best rational application of common-sense principles.

The evidence bearing upon the genuineness and authenticity of the Gospels has been often and admirably presented by the scientific defenders of Christianity.

Tischendorf has exhibited in a simple and interesting, though not eminently systematic, manner, for the Christian public at large, and with a knowledge of the ancient authorities unequaled by any of his opponents, the main facts and arguments in favor of the Gospel claims.[1]

Professor Fisher has set forth, in his clear and compact style, for the more cultivated Christian public, a broad and complete view of the subject, in which he has not only established the claims of the Gospels by the principles of scientific historical criticism, but has also stated and refuted successively the various false hypotheses of the rationalists, — including those of Baur, Strauss, and Renan, and that of their chief American imitator, Theodore Parker.[2]

But perhaps the freshest, ablest, and most complete presentation of the latest aspects of this whole question may be found in "The Supernatural in the New Testament Possible, Credible, and Historical," by Rev. C. A. Row, prepared and published at the request of the leading British Society devoted to the work of keeping the subject of Christian Evidences before the public. The author was invited to undertake this important work, because in his previous publication he had shown himself peculiarly qualified to meet and answer the later skeptical writers on their own ground.[3]

What with the common-sense and the scientific criticism, the Christian may confidently conclude that there is nothing in the ancient history of the world more certain than — nay, nothing so certain as — the facts of the career of Jesus Christ. The probabilities in favor of the view that Jesus Christ was born, lived, suffered, died, and rose from the dead, as the Gospels represent,

[1] See *The Origin of the Gospels.*

[2] See *Essays on the Supernatural Origin of Christianity.*

[3] See Row, *The Jesus of the Evangelists.*

are overwhelmingly great, as against either the hypothesis of a mythical Christ or of no Christ at all. The Gospels are veritable history, or else no such thing as veritable history can be shown to have come down to us from the ancient times.

The deliverer came forth from Judæa, as the world expected, and by his life and death prepared the forces which were to renovate the race. How out of the shame and death with which his career ended could the longed-for life and glory arise?

SECTION III.

THE PREACHING OF THE APOSTLES.

There are two sources of information concerning the apostolic work: the Sacred Scriptures, and the facts and traditions preserved by the early Christian writers.

I. *Facts from the Scriptures.*

The Apostolic History, as given by the sacred writers, may be subdivided into two parts: a connected narrative, extending from our Lord's ascension to the second year of Paul's captivity at Rome, embodied in the Acts of the Apostles; and a body of detached and incidental statements, scattered throughout the other books of the New Testament.

Of the Acts of the Apostles, Dr. J. Addison Alexander has said, that the subject is "a special history of the planting and extension of the Church among the Jews and Gentiles, by the gradual establishment of radiating centres or sources of influence at certain salient points throughout a large part of the empire, beginning at Jerusalem and ending at Rome." [1]

The two central figures in the Acts are Peter and

[1] Alexander, *Acts of the Apostles*, vol. i., Introduction.

Paul, — the former in the first twelve chapters and the latter in the last sixteen. Yet the book is as far as possible from being a biography of these two men, either as individuals or as Apostles. The subject of the first part is not Peter, but the planting and extension of the Church among the Jews by the ministry of the Apostles, among whom Peter appears as a leader, often associated with the whole body, but sometimes especially with John. The subject of the second part is not Paul, but the planting and extension of the Church among the Gentiles by the ministry of Paul.

From the point of view of the present work, it will appear that the Acts of the Apostles furnishes a glimpse — an outline sketch — of the work of the Apostles in fulfilling the commission and giving the Gospel to the world. It describes its promulgation among those representing the three great world-wide phases of thought, — at Jerusalem, the centre of Jewish religion and influence in the early Church; at Antioch, the centre of Greek thought and influence; and at Rome, the centre of Roman power and influence. Along these three lines of apostolic effort, as will subsequently appear, the first three Gospels had their origin.

The book begins too late to take in the work done for the Jews during the life of Jesus, and recorded in the Gospels; and it ends before the later and more extended spiritual influence of John's work in Asia Minor and throughout the Church. Nevertheless, all the men connected with the four Gospels engage in its work, and, with the exception of one, are prominent in it; Matthew, as one of the Twelve, at the opening of the history; Peter and Mark, and Paul and Luke, as the chief actors in the early progress of the Christian movement; and John, as singled out from the rest at the outset.

From the remaining portions of the Sacred Scriptures — the Epistles and the Apocalypse — a body of detached and incidental statements is derived, which may be used to supplement and complete the account given in the Acts. Among other things, glimpses are given of the movements of Peter and John among the Gentiles, by which, after their work recorded in the Acts, they extended their influence over the Roman world; and it is suggested that Paul was probably released from prison at Rome, to push his mission work still farther among the heathen, and to be again at a later date placed in bonds to suffer martyrdom.

It is manifest to the careful reader of the Acts of the Apostles, that the same temple and synagogue system which had so long connected Jerusalem with all the world, and by means of which the universal expectancy of a coming deliverer had been awakened, was one chief agency employed by the followers of Jesus of Nazareth in disseminating his doctrine.

The early work centred in Jerusalem, and especially in the temple itself, as may be seen from the first five chapters of the Acts, which end with the declaration that, "daily in the temple, and in every house, they ceased not to teach and preach Jesus Christ." The influences, however, reached out almost immediately to the synagogues of the foreign Jews and Judaized foreigners. The sixth and seventh chapters of the Acts give a glimpse of the work in one of these synagogues, so numerous in the Holy City. In it the proto-martyr Stephen discusses the truths of the Gospel with the representatives of Europe, Asia, and Africa.

In their work abroad over the world the Apostles and other early preachers found the synagogues the great centres for influencing men, and the new faith was proclaimed in these throughout the Roman Empire in an incredibly short space of time. When Saul went on his journey of persecution to Damascus, it was with letters to the synagogues; and when he was converted he straightway preached Christ in the synagogues (Acts ix. 2, 20). It was in the synagogues that the way was prepared for reaching both Jew and Gentile, — as in the preaching of Paul and Barnabas at Antioch in Pisidia (Acts xiii. 14, 42); at Iconium (Acts xiv. 1); and at other places.

In the providence of God the same great system of intercourse which had been the means of preparing the world for the Advent became a most important agency in giving that world the Gospel.

II. *Facts from Tradition.*

It is true, however, that the work of the majority of the Apostles in spreading the Gospels throughout the world is not exhibited in the sacred writings. What is known of it is learned chiefly from the early ecclesiastical writers, — as Nicephorus, Tertullian, Eusebius, and others.

It is sometimes difficult to pick out the precise historical facts from the mass of statements, yet the current traditions, generally received at the time, doubtless had a basis of historic fact, and are worthy of some degree of credence. It is made clear that such were the zeal and success of the Apostles, that at the close of the first century Christianity had been preached and embraced throughout and even beyond the bounds of the Roman empire.

It is said that Andrew carried the Gospel through Scythia and the neighboring countries, and then over into eastern Europe; and that he at last suffered martyrdom on the cross at Patræa, a city of Achaia.

James, the brother of John, is said to have preached to the dispersed Jews in Judæa, Samaria, and Spain, and to have settled at last in Jerusalem, where the Acts assure us he was beheaded by Herod (xii. 2).

Philip, after preaching successfully for several years in upper Asia, went to Hierapolis, the centre of idolatry in Phrygia in Asia Minor, and perished by martyrdom in the attempt to overthrow that idolatry.

Bartholomew, or Nathanael, preached abroad as far as Hither India; then returned westward and labored with Philip in Hierapolis in the overthrow of idolatry; and, barely escaping martyrdom there, bore the message of his Master up to Albania, on the shores of the Caspian Sea, where he won the martyr's crown.

Simon, the Canaanite or Zealot, is said to have preached the Gospel in Egypt, Cyrene, Africa, and finally in Britain, where he was put to death on the cross.

Jude first preached in Syria and afterward throughout Judæa, Galilee, Samaria, Idumea and Arabia, Syria, Mesopotamia and Persia, and at last fell a martyr through the zeal of the Magi in the defense of the old Oriental faith.

Matthias, who took the place of Judas, first preached with great success in Judæa, and afterward in Ethiopia, where he was stoned and beheaded.

Tradition adds to the statements of the Scriptures much that is interesting and important concerning the lives of the men whose names are immediately connected with the Gospels. This will properly be brought forward in treating of the authorship of the Gospels.[1]

It is obvious from the Scriptures and tradition combined, that before the close of the apostolic age the Great Commission had already met its fulfillment, in spirit at least. This brought the crisis of that age, foretold by Christ in his last days. The Church, a spiritual

[1] See Kitto, *History of the Bible.*

kingdom, had now been firmly established the world over. The time had come when men could everywhere worship the Father in spirit and in truth. There was, therefore, no longer need of the great religious centre at Jerusalem and of the temple and synagogue system. Apostate Judaism had become only an influence for evil, everywhere interfering with the progress of the Gospel. The proclamation of the crucified Christ seems quickly to have sifted the false and the true; and then the rejecters of the new doctrine, still holding possession of the synagogues, became the agents of bloody persecutions. It was in this way that Stephen met with his death and that the first persecution arose (Acts vii., viii.). It was the apostate Jews in the synagogue at Damascus who sought to slay Saul of Tarsus (Acts ix. 22); and the Hellenistic Jews at the synagogue at Jerusalem who afterward attempted the same thing (Acts ix. 29).

It was largely out of the foreign element connected with the synagogues that the Church was gathered, while most of the Jews rejected the claim of Jesus to be the Christ, and organized persecution against the Christians; as was the case at Thessalonica (Acts xvii. 1–9). The synagogue at Berea is instanced as a marked exception to this general rule (Acts xvii. 10–12); but the Jews of Thessalonica, by their emissaries, extended the persecution even to Berea, and drove Paul out of it (Acts xvii. 13–15).

This inference from the Acts is confirmed by Justin Martyr, who affirms that "converts, in greater numbers and of more genuine character, proceeded from the body of the pagans, than from the great mass of the Jews." [1] It is still further manifest from the writings of Justin, that the more thoroughly Judaized this pagan element

[1] See Justin Martyr, *Apolog.* l. 2, f. 88. Neander, *Church History*, vol. i. p. 63.

had become, the more hopeless was the task of preaching the Gospel to it. Of the proselytes in the strict sense, he says to the Jews, that they "do not simply not believe, but they blaspheme the name of Christ twofold more than yourselves, — and they would murder and torture us, who do believe on him; for they strive in every respect to become like you." [1] It was from proselytes of the gate, or those who had adopted from the Jewish system the principles of theism and the hope of Messiah, without becoming wholly Jews, that the mass of converts to the Church came.

When these converts had been gathered into the Church, — the few Jews and the many pagans, — the work of temple and synagogue as a connected and world-wide system was done. They could henceforward be a source of only evil to the world-religion, — a source of terror in that age only less dreadful than Jesuitism with the Inquisition in a later age. The destruction of the temple by Titus, in 70 A. D., and the breaking up of the Jewish nation, destroyed at once the centre and the power of the old system, and brought the Christian Church into its true place of prominence and influence.

Thenceforward there were four distinct classes of representative men, and four definite and different phases of thought, recognized in the ancient world, — Jewish, Greek, Roman, and Christian.

SECTION IV.

THE ORIGIN OF THE WRITTEN GOSPELS.

While the great work of the Apostles and their co-laborers was still going forward in the full tide of its energy, the chief business was that of preaching the doctrine of Christ's life, crucifixion, and resurrection for

[1] See Neander, *Church History*, vol. i. p. 67.

the salvation of the world. In the early stages there was little need of written records, for there were the living and divinely inspired witnesses.

But as the work widened there came, in the various local churches, emergencies requiring special instruction on the varied topics of the Gospel as related to Christian life. Before the Apostles passed off the stage of action there arose the necessity for a permanent record of the story of the Gospel as they had proclaimed it to men. Hence were given to the Church the Epistles and the Apocalypse, and the four Gospels. The origin of the latter alone requires to be considered in this connection.

I. *Theory of the Origin.*

In a true theory of their origin is found the explanation of the number of the Gospels, their peculiarities, their agreements and differences. Such a theory must evidently be based upon and constructed out of the facts of the age and work of the Apostles.[1] It must run somewhat as follows: —

The Gospel for the World. The aim of the Great Commission and the common design of the four Gospels were to commend Jesus the Nazarene to all mankind as the great Deliverer from sin and its evil consequences. "Go preach my Gospel to every creature."

The Races of the World. As has been seen, there were three great races and three great phases of thought reaching throughout that world with which Christianity first came into contact, — the Jewish, the Roman, and the Greek. There was in addition the kingdom of Christ, the Church, constituted of those brought out of the three races of men and made spiritual by the preaching of the Gospel.

[1] See Westcott, *Introduction to the Study of the Gospels*, ch. iii., for a clear and valuable discussion of the origin of the Gospels.

The Preaching to the World. The Apostles went forth preaching the Gospel like common-sense men, presenting Jesus to each of the three great races or classes of mankind in the way best suited to the end in view, of leading those races to submit to him as the divine Saviour. The same presentation would not equally commend him to all the races. Each of them had its peculiarities which must be taken into account; each of them its side to be reached; each of them its own characteristic view of the evils of the world and of the qualities of the needed deliverer, of which, so far as it was right, the Gospel must take advantage. Those early preachers took wise account of all this, and preached to the Jew, to the Roman, and to the Greek, — from the three great centres, Jerusalem, Antioch, and Rome, as set forth in the Acts, — in a form suited to their needs.

After the Church had been founded and enlarged by converts made in all lands by the preaching of the missionary Gospel in its varied adaptation to the races, that Gospel which presents Christ as the light and life, for the purpose of leading men, already Christians, to higher attainments in the Christian life, became necessary and was preached throughout the world.

The Permanent Records for the World. But the Apostles could not be everywhere and always with men. Before they passed away there arose the desire in the various races of men, who had heard their Gospel, to have it embodied in permanent written form, that it might preach to them still when the early preachers were absent or dead.

This desire expressed itself among the Jews, and Matthew, by divine inspiration, gave them his Gospel to meet that desire. It was the Gospel which his long preaching to the Jews, the men of prophecy, had already thrown into the form best suited to commend to their acceptance Jesus as the Messiah.

The same desire expressed itself among the Romans, and Mark by divine inspiration gave them his Gospel to meet that desire. It was the Gospel which Peter, by his preaching to the Romans, the men of power, had already thrown into the form best suited to commend to their acceptance Jesus as the almighty deliverer of men.

The same desire expressed itself among the Greeks, and Luke by divine inspiration gave them his Gospel to meet that desire. It had its basis in the Gospel which Paul and Luke by their long preaching to the Greeks, the men of reason and universal humanity, had already thrown into the form best suited to commend to their acceptance Jesus as the perfect, divine man.

All these, the missionary Gospels, were given their final shape before the fall of Jerusalem, probably between 50 and 70 A. D.

It was later that the longing came, in the Church, for a spiritual Gospel, which should help the Christian to develop, strengthen, and perfect the life already begun, and John by divine inspiration gave his Gospel to meet that longing. It was the Gospel the materials for which he had gathered in the more intimate communion with his Master, and which, by his long preaching to the brethren, he had thrown into the form best suited to commend to the faith of Christians Jesus as the light and life of all who believe.

II. *Historic Basis and Adequacy of the Theory.*

Basis. That this is not a mere groundless hypothesis may readily be made to appear. It has a stable basis of fact.

That the aim of the Great Commission was to give the Gospel to all the world, appears upon its very face. The Gospel was to be preached to every creature.

That there were three great races and three corresponding phases of thought throughout the world has already been shown in treating of the preparation for the Advent.

That the Apostles went forth presenting the Gospel to these various classes of men in the way best suited to the nature of each, and with the view of winning them to Christ as the Saviour, has been seen in considering the preaching of the Apostles.

That the four Gospels actually originated in the manner stated will be shown in the subsequent chapters in treating of the origin of each of the Gospels.

Adequacy. If this be the true theory, it may readily be seen that it will furnish a most perfect and satisfactory explanation of the number and character of the Gospels, and of their otherwise unexplained agreements and differences. This will appear best in the course of the subsequent discussions, but a brief statement of some few points will help to make those discussions more intelligible.

1st. There are four Gospels, because Jesus was to be commended to four races or classes of men, or to four phases of human thought, — the Jewish, Roman, Greek, and Christian. Had not these exhausted the classes to be reached there would doubtless have been more Gospels; and had there not been so many classes, with essential differences in temperament and modes of thought, there would doubtless have been less. The world of that age must have been revolutionized and the nature of the races materially changed to admit of either more or less.

2dly. The very striking differences seen in the three missionary Gospels, Matthew, Mark, and Luke, and between these three and the Christian Gospel, John, are fully explained. While the resemblances of the three Synoptics originated in the common facts of the character and career of Christ, which all the Apostles went forth to preach, the differences originated in the adaptation of each by a different Apostle to a different class of men, — of Matthew to the Jew, of Mark to the Roman, and of Luke to the Greek. The fact that the first three Gospels were missionary Gospels, originally preached to unspiritual men with the view of bringing them to the faith in Christ and to the Christian life, accounts for their so marked variation from John, the Christian Gospel, originally preached to spiritual men already brought to faith in Christ and into membership in the true Church by the Gospel in its first three forms, and preached for the purpose of aiding them in making progress in the divine life. The impossibility of only one Gospel, the absurdity of four Gospels of precisely similar character, the insufficiency of the three missionary Gospels, and the completeness of the four Gospels as they are, all appear manifest from this point of view.

3dly. The force of the great mass of alleged discrepancies, as objections to the historical character of the Gospels, is utterly broken by the simple consideration — essential to the theory and based upon undoubted facts — that the productions of the Evangelists are not histories, but *memoirs* in a modified sense; in short, not at all biographical sketches of Christ, but records of the Apostles' practical preaching of Christ as the Saviour of men.[1]

The justness of this consideration is manifest, as has been shown by Mr. Row, from the statements of their object by the Evangelists themselves. The Gospels most distinctly affirm that they do not belong to the class of professed histories, but to that of memoirs. "They not only affirm that they are memoirs, but memoirs of a peculiar character, that is to say, religious memoirs, composed with a double purpose, namely, that of setting

[1] See Row, *The Supernatural*, etc. p. 475; and Westcott, *Introduction*, etc. ch. iii.

forth the events of a life and at the same time of teaching a religion."

Matthew's object appears in the opening line of his book, — to bring the Jew to faith in Jesus as the Messiah. Mark opens with "the beginning of the *gladsome message* of Jesus Christ the Son of God." Luke writes for the special and immediate purpose of communicating systematic instruction concerning the Gospel facts to Theophilus. John more distinctly declares that he has selected his materials out of a large mass and written them for a definite religious purpose: "Many signs truly did Jesus in the presence of his disciples, which are not written in this book, but these are written that ye may believe that Jesus is the Christ, the Son of God, and that believing ye may have life through his name" (John xx. 30, 31).

Even more definitely is the character of the Gospels presented in the traditions of their origin, not as histories but as records of the Apostolic preaching, — as will be seen in the subsequent chapters.

It follows, therefore, that it was no part of the design of the writers to secure that chronological accuracy of arrangement and of detail which is "essential to history, but which forms no portion of the plan of a memoir."[1] It is absurd to demand it of them. They nowhere propose to give it. It would have prevented the accomplishment of their great object; since religion and not chronology, conversion of men to Christ and not the writing of history, was the chief thing. In preaching to the various classes of mankind, those facts and truths were brought forward which suited the practical end in view, and they were put in that order which seemed best fitted to secure the one great result, the acceptance of Jesus as the Saviour. Where the order of time suited the preach-

[1] See Row, *The Supernatural*, etc.

er's purpose, it was freely followed, and it was as freely departed from where it did not suit that purpose.

In short, chronology is of comparatively little importance in the Gospel view of the life of Christ, — of so little, indeed, that from John only can be learned the extent and the successive periods of the public ministry of the Saviour. A rigid adherence to the order of time and a complete biography of Jesus would have been the worst of faults, a fatal fault, since by eliminating their practical features, it would have unfitted the Gospels for reaching the various classes of mankind.

The same point of view makes clear the object of the Evangelists in devoting so much space to the narration of the events connected with the death of Jesus. The cross is the capital fact of Christianity as a religion, the one upon which salvation and eternal life depend. Hence Matthew, Mark, and Luke give one third of their Gospels to it, while John gives it one half of his.

4thly. The theory presented explains the fitness of the Gospels for the world in all ages. Those classes were representative classes for all time. There are the same needs among men to-day, — one man needing, for conviction of the truth of Christianity, to hear an authoritative word of God in type or prophecy, in the Scriptures, and to be assured of its fulfillment as proclaiming the divine mission of Jesus; a second needing to see him as the divine power in his living activity, confirming his own claims; a third requiring a manifestation of God addressed to reason, through the perfect manhood of Jesus; a fourth demanding only the spiritual presence and teachings of Jesus to recognize in him the light and life. The Gospels appeal respectively to the instincts which lead men to bow to divine authority, power, perfection, and spirituality, and may thus be shown to exhaust the sides of man's nature from which he may best be reached and led to submission to the Saviour, and to completeness in him. The four Gospels given to men in the apostolic times are therefore the complete Gospel of God for the world in all ages.

III. *Object of the Present Work.*

The object of the present work is to verify this theory, while using it in the elucidation of the meaning of the four Gospels.

The Aim. The attempt will be made to show that all the Gospels, both in their general drift and in their special peculiarities, fall in with and confirm the theory which has been outlined, while the theory itself explains or renders significant much in the structure and matter of the Gospels that is otherwise inexplicable or without significance.

The subordinate part which the chronological order of events plays in the work of the Evangelists will be seen in the prosecution of this work. It will appear that there is a higher law of unity and arrangement than mere succession in time. Out of the vast array of facts and events which were crowded into the life of Jesus, the Holy Ghost leads each writer to select those which will best serve the special purpose of each; and to arrange them in accordance with his own design, now following the order of time and now departing from it. No one of them attempts a complete life of Christ after the pattern of the biographers. All of them together can scarcely be said to furnish the materials for such a life.

The Method. It will manifestly be necessary to consider in connection with each Gospel such questions as the following: —

What was the actual origin of this Gospel, and for whom was it especially designed?

What was the character and what were the needs of those for whom it was written?

How far does this Gospel itself agree with the answers to these questions, in its authorship, its point of view, its material, and its entire scope?

No one capable of duly weighing them will consider these inquiries unimportant. How important will best appear when they have been answered.

PART II.

MATTHEW, THE GOSPEL FOR THE JEW.

"One God, one law, one element,
And one far-off divine event,
To which the whole creation moves."
ALFRED TENNYSON.

"The book of the generation of Jesus Christ, the son of David, the son of Abraham."
MATTHEW i. 1.

"Primus omnium Matthæus est Publicanus, cognomento Levi, qui Evangelium in Judæa Hebræo sermone edidit, ob eorum vel maxime causam, qui in Jesum crediderant ex Judæis, et nequaquam Legis umbram, succedente Evangelii veritate, servabant." JEROME.

CHAPTER I.

HISTORICAL VIEW OF THE JEWISH ADAPTATION OF THE FIRST GOSPEL.

THE investigation of the Gospels for present purposes is either historical or critical. The former includes the inquiries into their actual historical origin and design, into the character of the class for whom they were intended, and into their authorship. The latter embraces the inquiries into their actual contents, and into their general and special adaptation to the classes for which they were prepared.

SECTION I.

ORIGIN AND DESIGN OF THE FIRST GOSPEL.

Two questions need to be answered, in accordance with the facts of history, if possible, before any complete and critical knowledge of the structure and drift of the Gospel can be attained. These questions are: What was the actual origin of the Gospel according to Matthew? For what class of readers was it primarily designed?

I. *Imagined Origin.*

The so-called scientific criticism, in the hands of the rationalist, has lost both its science and its criticism. It has exhausted the power of an ungoverned and ungovernable imagination in the attempt to account for the origin and form of the Gospels, while it has not given the least attention to the plain facts of history touching the points in question.

One has imagined an original Hebrew or Aramæan Gospel out of which the four were afterwards compiled in the most bungling and mechanical manner. By turns Matthew, Mark, and Luke have each been made to play the part of a fundamental Greek Gospel, on the basis of which the remaining ones have been constructed. Some have fancied that there was one primitive Gospel, and that the separate or remaining Gospels grew out of lesser evangelical essays representing single incidents in the life of Christ, or out of memoirs of Christ current in the early Church. Still others have assumed that the Gospels are the productions of the Evangelists whose names they bear, who do not however give plain historical facts, but "whose minds are said to have expressed in na ve fiction the consciousness of the Church."

A first fatal objection to all such hypotheses is, that

they are pure imagination, with just as considerable a basis of fact as "Baron Munchausen" or the "Arabian Nights." A second, and equally fatal, is that they do not in the slightest measure account for the free and beautiful originality and the wonderful and sustained unity found in each and all the Gospels. As a consequence of their utter baselessness and inadequacy, and at the same time furnishing a further proof of their falsity, these innumerable hypotheses have all alike failed to command the general assent of even the unbelieving world, while the most able and brilliant of them all have ultimately, and often speedily, failed to secure the abiding faith of their own authors, and have fallen into merited contempt and oblivion.

II. *Actual Origin and Design.*

The question to be asked by the seeker for truth is not, What possible origins of the Gospels can be conceived? but rather, What was their actual origin? Concerning the first Gospel the question is, What, as a matter of history, was the origin, and what the design, of the Gospel according to Matthew.

It must be manifest to any one of average common sense, that even second-rate tradition on this point, if no better can be obtained, is infinitely more valuable than the best conclusions of the uncertain rationalistic imagination. Of what use, then, the imagination, if the real historical origin of the Gospels can be clearly established?

Now the fact is that the investigator is not left to uncertain tradition, much less to pure conjecture, for it can be conclusively shown that Matthew wrote his Gospel for the Jewish race, the first of the three great representative races of which the civilized world of his day was made up.

Most Ancient Witness. The most ancient direct testimony concerning the Gospel according to Matthew is that of Papias. Papias was bishop of Hierapolis, in Asia Minor, a city which, according to the tradition already given, was evangelized by Philip and Bartholomew.

The testimony of Papias possibly reaches back to the end of the first century, certainly to the beginning of the second. Eusebius names him among the famous bishops of his age, makes him contemporary with Justus of Jerusalem and Ignatius of Antioch, in the first quarter of the second century; and speaks of him as "a man in the highest degree eloquent and learned and above all skilled in the Scriptures."[1] Irenæus writes, that he was said to be the disciple or hearer of John and the associate of Polycarp, who was bishop of Smyrna at the opening of the second century.[2] That he refers to John the Presbyter (or elder), the disciple of the Apostles, and not to John the Apostle, is evident from the statement of Papias himself, as quoted by Eusebius, in which he confesses that he heard the words of the Apostles from those who were their followers, especially from Aristion and John the Presbyter.[3]

The testimony of Papias was originally given in the fourth book of a work in five books, which he called, "Interpretations of our Lord's Declarations." From this work, — now no longer extant, but which still existed in the time of Eusebius, in the fourth century, — the early church historians have made copious extracts.[4]

In the preface to his work Papias makes known his object and method, declaring that he not only recorded

[1] *Hist. Eccles.* lib. iii. 36.

[2] Idem, lib. iii. 39.

[3] Idem.

[4] Euseb. *Hist. Eccles.* lib. iii. 39. Iren. *Against Heresies,* book v. ch. xxxiii. 4.

what he found in written form, but also made special effort to gather up such unwritten tradition as could be traced back to the Apostles. "Nor shall I regret," said he, "to subjoin to my Interpretations, also for your benefit, whatever I have at any time accurately ascertained from the Elders and treasured up in my memory, in order to give additional confirmation to the truth by my testimony. For, as it seems to me, I have never (like many) delighted to hear those who make a great show of words, but those who teach the truth, nor those who relate new and strange precepts, but those who give the commands of the Lord and things which came from the truth itself. Whenever, therefore, I met with any one who had been on intimate terms with the Elders, I used to make special inquiries touching what were the utterances of the Elders, — what Andrew, or Peter, or Philip, or Thomas, or James, or John, or Matthew, or any other disciple of the Lord, or what Aristion and John the Presbyter, also disciples, said. For I believed that the books would not be of so much profit to me, as the living word of men still surviving."[1]

In the course of his work, in a passage preserved by Eusebius, Papias recorded what he was able to learn in this way respecting the origin of the Gospels. His testimony concerning the first Gospel is, that "Matthew wrote the Oracles (of the Lord) in the Hebrew tongue, and every one interpreted them as he was able."[2]

The circumstances connected with this testimony are given thus in detail, in order that the full value of it may be seen. It is true that Eusebius elsewhere speaks of Papias as a man of inferior judgment;[3] but it is also

[1] *Hist. Eccles.* lib. iii. 39.

[2] Euseb. *Hist. Eccles.* lib. iii. 39. See Fisher, *Supernatural Origin of Christianity,* p. 160.

[3] Idem.

true that this was chiefly on account of the millenarian views of the latter, which were so offensive to the church historian. The latter opinion is therefore of little weight in comparison with the former high estimate already quoted. Papias was evidently a good man, and Professor Fisher has rightly said, that "however moderate his intellectual powers, he was justly regarded as an honest witness or reporter of what he had seen and heard. He reports what he had received from companions of the Apostles." It is likewise well to remember that the testimony of a man of narrow intellect may, in such circumstances, be even better than that of a greater man whose view of facts is warped by adherence to some favorite theory. Judged by his purpose, method, and opportunities, no better witness need be cited than Papias.

The statement of Papias is then that of a competent witness, made after devoting himself intelligently and diligently to the work of ascertaining the facts in question. He made his investigations less than a generation after the writing of the Gospels, or after an interval less than our present remove from the first Napoleon or even from the Duke of Wellington. He had the best of opportunities, for Polycarp, whose associate he was, had been the disciple and friend of John, and knew more about that Apostle than did any one else in that age, and more, doubtless, than any of the contemporaries of even Napoleon or Wellington knew of them. Such testimony can only be made to appear worthless by that destructive criticism which would sweep away all the facts of history and make Homer, Shakespeare, Napoleon, and Jesus all myths alike.

Later Testimony. But Papias is not alone in his testimony. Some of the ablest of the leaders of the early Church agree with him.

Irenæus — the pupil of the same Polycarp, and who was bishop of Lyons in the last quarter of the second century — affirms, that "Matthew issued a written Gospel among the Hebrews in their own dialect, while Peter and Paul were preaching at Rome, and laying the foundations of the Church."[1] His position in the Church and his wide acquaintance with it made him a most credible and competent witness. Still more explicitly: "The Gospel of St. Matthew was written for the Jews, who specially desired that it should be shown that the Christ was of the seed of David; and St. Matthew endeavors to satisfy this desire, and therefore commences his Gospel with the genealogy of Christ."[2]

Origen (disciple of Clement of Alexandria) — a man of extraordinary learning and of extensive travel, who was known throughout the entire Church during the first half of the third century — also declares, that "St. Matthew wrote for the Hebrew, who expected the Messiah from the seed of Abraham and David."[3]

Eusebius, bishop of Cæsarea, — a historian of great celebrity, whose veracity has never been questioned by any one except the infidel Gibbon, and who flourished during the latter part of the third century and earlier part of the fourth, — besides preserving the testimony of Papias, as already cited, gives the following definite statement of the facts concerning the origin of the first Gospel: "Matthew having in the first instance delivered his Gospel to his countrymen in their own language, afterward, when he was about to leave them and extend his apostolic mission elsewhere, filled up, or completed, his written Gospel for the use of those whom he was leaving behind, as a compensation for his absence."[4] It

[1] Irenæus, *Against Heresies,* book iii. i. 1.

[2] *Caten. in Matt.* Massuet, p. 347; *Against Heresies,* iii. 9, 1.

[3] Origen, *In Joann.* tom. i. 6.

[4] Euseb. *Hist. Eccles.* iii. 24.

is doubtless true that of all the men of his day Eusebius was the best acquainted with the historical records and the traditions of the Church.

Jerome — "the most learned of the Latin Fathers of the Church," who lived still later — says: "The Church, which according to the word of Christ is built upon a rock, has four evangelical rivers of Paradise. . . . . First of all is Matthew the publican, called Levi, who composed a Gospel in the Hebrew tongue for the special use of those Jews who had believed in Christ, and no longer followed the shadow of the Law, after the revelation of the substance of the Gospel."[1]

Gregory Nazianzen also affirms that Matthew wrote for the Hebrew.[2]

But there is scarcely need of further presentation of testimony on a subject upon which there was one harmonious tradition.

Pertinent Facts. While many points suggest themselves as worthy of discussion, only the main facts touching the origin and design of the first Gospel are related directly to the present investigation. These facts are: that Matthew wrote the Gospel for his Jewish countrymen; that it was the embodiment of the oral Gospel which he had preached to them; that it was intended to give that preaching permanent form for their benefit; and that it took advantage of the Jewish Messianic beliefs and was in this way fitted to commend Jesus as the Messiah to the Jews.

There is still another point that should be noticed, which bears indirectly upon the theory of the Jewish origin of Matthew and is confirmatory of it, but which is not essential to that theory. Patristic authority, represented in and by the witnesses already cited, is almost unan-

[1] Hieron. *Comment. in Evang. Matt. Prolegom.* 3, 4.

[2] *Carmin.* lib. i. sect. i. 12, vers. 31.

imous in asserting a Hebrew original of the first Gospel. The treatment which this testimony has often received at the hands of the critics illustrates well the ease with which a rash and dogmatic criticism can dispose of the plainest facts of history.

The testimony of these witnesses — the very men upon whom largely depend the establishment of the canon of the Scriptures and the settlement of the great questions of primitive church history — is declared to be false, because *if there had been a Hebrew original of the first Gospel it would have been preserved.* How utterly unwarranted the assumption may be made apparent by a fair presentation of the case.

These men of the highest character, and with the best opportunities for knowing the facts, declare it to be a fact, that Matthew first wrote his Gospel in the Hebrew. There is entire agreement in the matter, since no one in that age contradicts the statement. Aside from its being contrary to their acknowledged character to utter falsehood, they had in this case no conceivable motive for it.

Moreover, in the view of common sense it seems eminently natural and appropriate that Matthew should address the Gospel to his countrymen in the Hebrew. It was at once their sacred language and, in modified form, their vernacular tongue; and one of the best methods of allaying prejudices and conciliating them, would be to make use of it. Paul used the Hebrew, and with marked effect, for this very purpose, when, standing on the stairs of the castle above the temple at Jerusalem, he addressed the Jewish mob below: "He spake unto them in the Hebrew tongue, ... and when they heard that he spake in the Hebrew tongue to them, they kept the more silence" (Acts xxi. 40–xxii. 2). That Matthew, a native of Judæa, should address the native Jews in the Hebrew was, of course, still more natural and appropriate.

But the entire question of fact is set at rest by the best of direct testimony from those who saw the Gospel in its Hebrew form. Jerome, the most skilled of all the Fathers in the Hebrew tongue, and who lived in Palestine, declares that he himself saw the Hebrew Gospel, and had an opportunity of transcribing and translating it.[1] Epiphanius, one of the most learned among the Fathers of the Eastern Church, gives similar testimony.[2]

The disappearance of the Hebrew form of the Gospel is easily accounted for by a state of things peculiar to that age. Few of the early Christian writers were familiar with that language. They were accustomed to go to the Septuagint or Greek version for their knowledge of the Old Testament, and they therefore naturally turned to the Greek form in which Matthew's Gospel existed, and which was confessedly of divine authority. It is moreover true, as is affirmed by early Christian writers, that "the Hebrew Gospel of Matthew was used, and alone adopted of all the Gospels, by certain heretical sections of the ancient Church, the Ebionites, and the Nazarenes; and was mutilated and interpolated by them."[3] This abuse of it naturally led the early Christians to neglect and avoid it; while it also explains the fact that the authors of the Peschito, or Syriac version of the Gospels, translated the Greek Gospel of Matthew, instead of reproducing or modifying the apostolic original in Hebrew.

Or, if these causes were not sufficient to account for its disappearance, the great historic event of the age is certainly sufficient. The destruction of Jerusalem swept away the centre of Hebrew civilization, brought to an

[1] Hieron. *de Vir. Ill.* c. 3; *Contra Pelagianos,* lib. iii., etc.

[2] Epiphan. *Hæres.* xxx. de Ebionitis.

[3] See references to Epiphanius, Jerome, etc., in Wordsworth, *Greek Testament,* Introduction to St. Matthew's Gospel.

end the knowledge, among the scattered Jewish masses, of even the modified or Aramæan form of the language which had survived the wreck of the Babylonish captivity, and consigned to ultimate destruction most of the Hebrew literature save the Old Testament Scriptures. The Jewish historian Josephus furnishes an illustration of the fate of the Hebrew original of Matthew. Josephus himself informs us that he "wrote his great work, the History of the Jewish Wars, originally in Hebrew, his native tongue, for the benefit of his own nation; and he afterwards translated it into Greek. No notices of the original Hebrew now survive: it has perished; but the Greek version is often referred to by the early Christian Fathers, and is now extant."[1] Is it any wonder, then, that the Hebrew original of the first Gospel, with the strong prejudices existing in the Church against its use, soon perished?[2]

As already said, the theory of the present work does not directly depend upon the acknowledgment of a Hebrew original of Matthew's Gospel. Indirectly, however, it does; for if that original be admitted it furnishes another indication of the Jewish aim of the Evangelist. Besides, the same *à priori* critical methods that would sweep this Hebrew document out of existence would carry away with it all the most stable facts of history, leave the Gospels without any historical basis, and make all investigations concerning them worse than useless. As Archbishop Whately so admirably showed in his "Historic Doubts," this new and advanced mode of playing fast and loose with facts would annihilate all history.

In protesting against such reckless criticism, Principal Tulloch, in his "Lectures on Renan," says, on this very point: "It appears to us, however, that it is impossible

[1] Josephus, *Jewish Wars.*

[2] See fuller discussion in Wordsworth.

to disregard these statements (of the Fathers) altogether, especially while resting so confidently as we do on the testimony of the same Fathers to the genuineness of the Gospels. We regret, therefore, to notice that, in the last edition of his Greek Testament, Dean Alford goes the length of repudiating a Hebrew original of St. Matthew's Gospel, in the face of evidence which, with all possible deductions, seems irresistible."[1]

It may be confidently affirmed then, that, taking into account the number, credibility, and competency of the witnesses cited, it cannot be reasonably maintained that their statements on these points are not in the main in agreement with the historical facts, and that they did not arise out of those facts. Matthew undoubtedly prepared his Gospel for the Jews.

SECTION II.

THE CHARACTER AND NEEDS OF THE JEW.

If the first Gospel originated, as has been seen, in the preaching of the Apostles, especially of Matthew, to the Jews, and was designed to commend Jesus to the acceptance of the Jews, then the character and needs of the Jew must furnish the key to that Gospel.

The Jew must be understood before the Gospel for the Jews can be adequately appreciated and interpreted. What manner of man was he? What, especially, were his spiritual needs? The answers will cast light upon whatever has been prepared for the Jewish race, under the influence of the Holy Ghost.

I. *The Jews.*

There are certain characteristics which clearly distinguish the Jews from the other great historic races.

[1] *Lectures on Renan's 'Vie de Jesus,'* note, p. 119.

They were the chosen people of God, and were conscious that God was in a peculiar sense in their history. They had the oracles of God, the true world-religion. They had the only divinely ordained forms of religious worship. Above all, they had the promise of the Messiah, in whom all their blessings and privileges should attain perfection, and his coming was the central and absorbing thought in the mind of the race.

Out of these characteristics, which made the Jew an altogether peculiar man, came the needs of the Jewish race, — partly through a right development, partly through a wrong. Along the line of these peculiarities must, therefore, be sought the correct understanding of the Gospel requirements of the Jews in the time of Christ and the Apostles. A development altogether right would have produced the ideal Jew; a right and wrong combined produced the actual Jew.

The Chosen People. The Jews were the chosen people of God. They were elected to be the objects of his special care, the recipients of his special favor, and, notably, to be, in religion, the repository of God's revealed truth, the hope of the world, and the central race of the ages. No other people has ever occupied such a position.

Had the Jews made the most and the best of their election, they would doubtless have been to-day the most favored race of mankind. A sense of the distinguishing love of God did indeed lead the true Israel to humility, to thankfulness, to devotion to Jehovah, and to an appreciation of their high destiny. But in the days of Christ and the Apostles, as in the time of the Prophets, the true Israel was but a remnant. With the great mass of the Jews the election had resulted only in pride, conceit, arrogance. They were ever ready to cry, "We be Abraham's seed and heirs to the promise of God," — thus claiming as their own inherited and inalienable right what could be theirs only through the grace of God and fidelity to the covenant.

The Jews had the clear consciousness that Jehovah was in a peculiar sense in their history, as their God. This naturally resulted from their election and from their experience as a people. No other nation could point to such a miraculous career, to such deliverances in which God himself appeared in his omnipotence to save them from their bondage, from their adversaries, from their captivities. Jehovah was known throughout the world as the God of the Jews.

With the true Israel this consciousness of intimate union with God was doubtless a source of spiritual profit. It was a great comfort in prosecuting the ends of righteousness to feel assured that all the world existed for them, that its changes took place for them, that its real treasures were to be inherited and enjoyed by them, and that all the nations were to become submissive to their faith. It sustained them in sore trials and lifted them above disaster and defeat and all the accidents of time.

But with the mass of Jews it led to a national narrowness and exclusiveness, which had reached their height at the time of the Advent. Their selfishness had become extreme and proverbial. While they had forgotten that they were elect out of the world, not against it but for it, in order that all the world might be blessed in them, they had also forgotten that the world was not theirs for them to make the most of as Jews for their own selfish ends, but theirs to bring to the true faith through the oracles of God and the coming of the Messiah. Their selfishness naturally led to worldliness and covetousness. The old Mosaic enactments — such as that of the Sabbatic year and of the tithes to be used in the religious festivals and to be distributed to the poor — which were intended, negatively, to scatter the Jews' property and to check the cupidity of their nature, and, positively, to bring out a genuine and large benevolence, had long since become a dead letter, and through their haste to become rich the name *Jew* was becoming then, as it is now, "a by-word and a hissing."

The Evangelist who would reach and save the Jews must recognize their election and the presence of God in their history, and must at the same time aim to correct their errors.

The World-religion. The Jews had the oracles of God. The world-religion had been delivered to them. They alone had the written revelation of the true God. That revelation gave them the key to the character of Jehovah, to his works, to his providences, to his sublime and eternal plan. It cast the only clear light in the world upon the nature, character, condition, and destiny of man. It alone gave man a glimpse of the origin and end of the universe and the present earthly system of things. In short, the Jews had all the clear religious light in the world.

An Apostle has declared that the benefits of the election of Israel were every way great, and chiefly because to them were committed the oracles of God (Rom. iii. 2). The revelation of doctrine given to the Jew had in it all the germs of the fuller revelation by Christ; so that the true Judaism found its natural culmination in Christianity. As a fact that old revelation led the true Israel, along lines of thought and experience the most natural, directly to Christianity. It is likewise a fact that it led the most of the Jews to a knowledge of the true doctrine concerning God, a knowledge to which the Gentiles did not attain, and thus made it unnecessary for the Evangelist of the Jews to dwell upon these elementary doctrines.

At the time of the Advent, the masses had departed from the pure religion of the Law and the Prophets.

The great council, the Sanhedrim, the head of the Jewish system, had been brought, in large measure, under the influence of the heathen rulers of the nation, and secularized. There had sprung up a party, the Herodians, doubtless numerous, who had cut loose from Jewish hopes and aspirations as well as Jewish worship, and who "saw in the power of the Herodian family the pledge of the preservation of their national existence in the face of Roman ambition," — a party so entirely worldly that a Herod could meet all their longings for a deliverer. The remainder of the nation was divided into the two great religious sects, — the Pharisees and Sadducees (the Essenes or mystics were too few to be of importance), the traditionalists and the skeptics. The former class, embracing by far the greater number and reaching down among the common people, had added to the teaching of the Scriptures a mass of traditions which had completely overlaid that teaching, and taken its place, making their religion mere form and ceremony, mere theatrical show. The latter class, comprising the more scholarly and cultivated of the people, had not only discarded all tradition, and rejected every doctrine which was not plainly taught in the Scriptures, but had made free with the Scriptures themselves — very much after the style of the modern rationalists — receiving or rejecting as best suited them, and giving little or no attention to practical religion. In truth practical religion was at the lowest ebb.

Most of the Jews had lost sight of or perverted those great doctrines which are the proper regulators of human conduct. Their practical creed ran thus: "Thou shalt love thy neighbor and hate thine enemy." "Thou shalt not take interest from a Jew, but shalt exact usurious interest from all Gentiles." "Be scrupulous about outward forms, for God looks mainly at these." To each living truth they had conjoined the fatal error which destroyed it, or else had quite substituted the error for the truth.

The Evangelist who would reach and save the Jews must recognize their possession of God's oracles, and must seek to recall these lost principles and to correct the perverted ones. He must carry this apostatizing race back to the oracles of God.

The Divine Forms. The Jews had the only divinely ordained forms of religious worship. The Mosaic ordinances embodied the Mosaic truth. The Mosaic ritual embodied God's view of the best forms of the divine worship in that age of tutelage, when prescribed forms seemed necessary to a rude people who were under training for a later spiritual age and worship. The Jews alone had the true and God-given forms of worship.

These religious forms were doubtless very helpful to the true Israel in keeping the revelations of God before their minds, and lifting their thoughts heavenward. The ritual undoubtedly served as a perpetual object-lesson to the whole nation, keeping some of the main truths of Judaism always before them.

But the mass of the nation, long before the Advent, had lost sight of the substance in the form. Their religion had become intensely formal, a mere outward show, a procedure in which man only acted a part, played the hypocrite. The Pharisees could steal the possessions of widows and orphans, and then tithe the herbs and weeds in their gardens and make long prayers at the corners of the broad streets, and think themselves the patterns of the world in religion.

The Evangelist who would reach and save the Jews must understand the true import of these divine forms, as the changing shadows of an unchanging substance, and must aim to correct this awful, and, if uncorrected, fatal perversion of the truth.

The Messianic Promise. Above all, the Jews had the promise of the Messiah.

Acknowledging the divine authority of the Old Testament Scriptures, they read in them of a coming Deliverer. The promises and prophecies had grown clearer all along the centuries. He was to be the seed of the woman, the seed of Abraham, a prophet like unto Moses, the royal son of David, the child of a virgin. All the types found their explanation in him, all the sacrifices pointed to him, all prophecy centred in him, all the experience and history of Israel shadowed his coming and work. In person he was to be God and man, Emmanuel, the everlasting Father and the man of sorrows in one. Officially he was to be Messiah, or, as the Greek has it, Christ, the anointed of God; and as the anointing of the old dispensation was used in inducting into the three offices of prophet, king, and priest, he was to be a prophet, like the greatest of the prophets, was to be the legal heir to the throne of David, and was to bear the sins of his people. This great outline was filled in with a multitude of details, made up of circumstances and incidents connected with his birth, his life, and his death, and serving to mark his character and his work for the world. The Jews had daily access to this prophetic history of the Messiah, and were hourly expecting his advent when Jesus of Nazareth came and claimed to be the fulfillment of prophecy.

To the true Israel, the Simeons and Annas, the doctrine of the Messiah was the support and solace in the trial and sorrow which fell upon the later days of the old dispensation and made way for the opening of the new.

But the masses had departed from the correct teaching on this subject. They had not read the prophets aright. They had started out from the prediction of Christ as the son and heir of David, or as king, and had warped all their reading and interpretation to agree with their worldly notions of what was demanded by that. The Roman Empire dazzled them and they could only interpret prophecy in its light. David had conquered and imposed tribute on the surrounding nations, had led the armies and decided the great civil questions, had made Israel one of the powerful kingdoms of the earth. The Jew overlooked or explained away everything that did not accord with the temporal splendor of a king and kingdom after this model. He had cast away that grander idea of a spiritual, universal, and everlasting kingdom, which fills the books of the Prophets. He had lost sight of the part to be played by the prophet and priest in the Messianic work and character. His Messiah was to be the Jewish *Cæsar* of the world.

As the Messianic idea was the one in which all the other Jewish ideas of that age centred and culminated, the Evangelist who would reach and save the Jewish race must, above everything else, keep in view the true doctrine on that point, and must, most of all, give himself to correcting the otherwise fatal perversions of the truth by the degenerate Jews.

II. *The Key to Matthew's Gospel.*

Such being the character of the Jews, it is easy to see how it furnishes the key to the Gospel intended for them.

Clearly it would have been a fatal mistake to set forth Jesus of Nazareth — as Mark sets him forth for the Roman — simply as the Son of God, wielding almighty power in establishing a universal empire. It would not have commended him to the true Israel who had been holding out for ages, with brave heart and boundless endurance, against the material power of all the great nations of the world, and who ever bowed to Scriptures and prophecy, but never to mere power. It would have had little attraction for the apostate Israel, absorbed in their dream of a magnificent world-empire, except as it tended to foster their perverse view of the Messiah.

Equally vain would it have been to bring him forward as Luke does — as the divine-man, coming down from God out of heaven, passing through a perfect human development, entering into sympathy with all suffering and sorrowing humanity — for the Jew was not looking for the perfect man, the son of Adam, the son of God, but for a son of Abraham, a king descended from David by the royal line.

Still more fruitless would it have been to exhibit him as John does, — as the eternal Word, the very God, the light and life of the world, — for the veil was before the eyes of the Jew, and he could not discern the spiritual God as manifested in the Word. The light shone into the darkness and the darkness comprehended it not.

For the Jew the credentials of Jesus must be drawn from Moses and the Prophets. In his origin, human and divine, in the capital facts of his life, in his character private and official, in short, in his work and in his kingdom, he must be shown to meet the requirements of the Messianic Scriptures. Jesus must be set over against the prophetic Messiah, so that they shall both be seen to be one and the same. This work properly done, no Jew could escape the conclusion: Jesus of Nazareth is the Messiah.

SECTION III.

THE AUTHORSHIP OF THE FIRST GOSPEL.

There has been but one prevalent opinion concerning the authorship of the first Gospel. It has always been ascribed to a Jew, the Apostle Matthew. This authorship is sufficiently established by the witnesses already cited.

Like most of the Apostles of our Lord, he was a man almost without a biography. He takes occasion to mention but the fewest facts concerning himself: his call to become a disciple of Jesus; the feast which he made for his new Master; and his appointment to the Apostleship. The other Evangelists simply corroborate his statement of these facts. Tradition, as has been seen, makes some additions concerning the origin of the Gospel which bears his name, and concerning his later ministry outside of Judæa.

I. *A Representative Jew in Nature.*

From these facts and traditions in connection with the Gospel itself, the Apostle is seen to have been a representative Jew and eminently fitted by his nature, and by his experience, Jewish and Christian, for the work of preaching and embodying the Gospel for the Jewish race. What is known of his personal history marks him as a man appreciating the need for the Gospel most fully himself, and fitted to press it most earnestly upon the acceptance of his countrymen.

His own account of his call to become a disciple of Christ, and of the feast in his house, is as follows: "And as Jesus passed forth from thence, he saw a man, named Matthew, sitting at the receipt of custom; and he saith unto him, Follow me. And he arose and followed him. And it came to pass, as Jesus sat at meat in the house, behold, many publicans and sinners came and sat down with him, and his disciples" (Matt. ix. 9, 10). Mark, in his account, calls Matthew by his Jewish name, "Levi, the son of Alpheus," and represents the feast as occurring in his house (Mark ii. 14, 15). Luke names him Levi, and declares that "he left all," that he made Jesus "a great feast in his own house," and that there was "a great company of publicans and others that sat down with them" (Luke v. 27–29).

The account of his appointment to the Apostleship is given by himself, by Mark, and by Luke. All the catalogues place him in the fourth couple of the twelve Apostles along with Thomas; Mark and Luke place him first, "Matthew and Thomas" (Mark iii. 18; Luke vi. 15); but he places himself second, and writes, "Thomas and Matthew *the publican*" (x. 3).

The business of the tax-gatherer, from which he was called, had doubtless trained him to system. The public official is obliged to methodize his business, to use titles, headings, indices, to put things into such shape that they may be easily grasped and understood. Hence his eminent fitness to present to the Jew the claims of Jesus as Messiah, in a clear, systematic, and business-like manner.

It is obvious, likewise, that the business of the publican must have led him to an intimate knowledge of the Jewish character, especially of the covetousness and hypocrisy which were such marked features of it.

As a publican he was at variance with the Pharisaic party, and the Pharisaic disposition among his own people. By the orthodox Jew he must have been looked upon as unclean and often treated as an object of contempt. He may have been freed from the power of Pharisaism in either of two ways: by being overcome and carried away by the spirit of covetousness and extortion, which reached their height in the average tax-gatherer of the day; or by attaining to a more liberal piety and a more vital comprehension of the Old Testament, and so reaching a contempt for the common formality and hypocrisy which passed for piety.

It was in the latter way that Zaccheus attained to his emancipation from Pharisaism, and it has been suggeste that Matthew was a Jew of like spirit, and therefore an honest and upright publican. The readiness with which he left his vocation and his possessions to follow Jesus, and the necessity for some previous spiritual fitness on his part, have been urged in favor of this view.[1]

On the other hand, equally strong reasons may be brought forward for regarding him as belonging to the infamous rather than to the pious publicans. From the time of his conversion he seems to have regarded the publican on the one side, as he regarded the Pharisee on the other, as a representative Jewish sinner, each, in his place and way, the wickedest man of his race. It is remarkable that he has not recorded the story of Zaccheus, the honest publican, nor the parable of the Pharisee and the publican, nor anything else concerning the publicans which could raise our estimate of their character as a class. It is still more remarkable that he has recorded so much that blackens that character, and especially that memorable saying of our Lord, "Verily I say unto you, that the publicans and the harlots go into the kingdom of God before you" (xxi. 31). While he joins with the other Evangelists in connecting the publicans and sinners, he alone, in this passage, conjoins *publicans and harlots*.

II. *A Representative Jew in Experience.*

There is also enough in these facts, in connection with his Gospel, to show that Matthew's experience of the saving power of the Gospel was that of a representative Jew.

He arose and left all and followed Jesus. These words of Luke indicate, perhaps, that he had grown rich or was growing rich in the calling of the publican. He left behind him forever the gain and the means of gain,

1 See Lange, *Life of Jesus*, vol. i.

so dear to the man who is a *Jew* by nature, to follow him who had not where to lay his head. It was a complete revolution of character and life.

But if Matthew was one of the outcast publicans, justly regarded as infamous, then his conversion into an Apostle of the Lord, in whom he recognized the true and eternal king of Israel, must have been indelibly impressed upon his mind as a miracle of divine grace. He was despised in the eyes of the false theocrats of Israel, and the true Theocrat thus highly exalted him. He must have learned to feel the contrast between the true and the spurious kingdom of God in all their respective aspects. But even without taking into account the unreasonable contempt of the Pharisees, it is still manifest that his former doubtful calling, when compared with his present exalted vocation, his former associates, who consisted partly of the most degraded of men, when contrasted with the consecrated circle in which he now lived, and, finally, his former, when compared with his present, state of mind, must all have appeared to him in their darkest colors. He was translated from a condition of the deepest shame to one of the highest honor, from a most critical to a most advantageous position. Hence it would accord with such a state of things, that a strong feeling for contrasts should have been found in him,"[1] along with a profound appreciation of all the various aspects of life.

His many years of preaching the Gospel to his countrymen compelled him to study most diligently the great facts concerning the person and work of Jesus, and to throw them into the form best suited to commend him as Messiah to the Jews.

Recurring to the peculiar characteristics of the Jew, as already given, it will be seen that Matthew had meas-

[1] See Lange, *Life of Jesus*, vol. i.

ured the whole range of the Jewish character and experience. He was one of the chosen people, and understood their arrogant, self-righteous claims to the peculiar favor of God and to exclusive right to the world. He was familiar with the oracles of God and with their perversions. He had perfect acquaintance with the forms of the true religion, and with the formality and hypocrisy that had arisen out of them. He had been taught the true doctrine of Messiah and all the departures from it. All this is manifest throughout his Gospel.

Take him all in all, there was no man among the Apostles so fitted as Matthew to embody the Gospel in permanent form for the Jew. The impulse which led his countrymen to ask him to make a record of that Gospel for them, and that which led him to accede to their request, were doubtless both from the Holy Ghost, the Spirit of all wisdom. Doubtless, out of all the men of that age, the Holy Ghost chose the man best fitted, by his nature and experience as a representative Jew, to write the Gospel for the Jew.

CHAPTER II.

CRITICAL VIEW OF THE JEWISH ADAPTATION OF THE FIRST GOSPEL.

In examining the first Gospel in the light of its Jewish origin, design, and authorship, its very marked adaptation to the needs of the Jew of that age will become apparent as we consider the plan of the Evangelist, the central idea and general drift of his production, the characteristic omissions and additions, and the incidental variations and peculiarities.

SECTION I.

THE JEWISH ADAPTATION IN THE GENERAL PLAN OF THE FIRST GOSPEL.

It may seem strange, and requiring explanation, that at this late day inquiry should need to be made in order to ascertain the plan of the Gospels. Have we not the divisions of Matthew and its plan given in the twenty-eight chapters of the Gospel? Is not the same thing true of the sixteen chapters of Mark; of the twenty-four of Luke; of the twenty-one of John? Why, then, look any farther?

I. *The Plan of the Gospels.*

Even a partial investigation of the facts will convince any one that the outward history of the Bible is one continued record of marvels. Sometimes an accident, often a trifle, has, in the ordainings of Providence and through coöperation with some prevailing tendency of human thought or drift of human events, decided the way in which the great mass of men should regard the Word of God for centuries to come.

The mechanical division of its separate books into chapters and verses may be looked upon as one of these apparently trifling incidents, which has nevertheless exerted a vast influence upon the views taken of the connections of the Scriptures, from the time when the printed Bible first began to find a place in the Christian home until the present day. The work was done in a way, and at a time, to give it the greatest possible influence in hiding the structural harmony and unity of the Sacred Word. Prepared by a purely mechanical process, — as one would be led to conclude, without even the trouble of an examination, by the fact that Robert Stephens completed the division of the New Testament into verses during a *journey on horseback* from Paris to Lyons, in the troublous times of the middle of the sixteenth century; given to the Church ten years before the birth of Lord Bacon, while the mechanical philosophy still held undisputed sway in the world of thought; it was exactly fitted to meet the intellectual wants of the times. Commending itself as a convenient arrangement, in favor of which much may yet be said; completed in time to be attached to even the earlier English editions of the Bible (the earliest had been issued only sixteen years before, and King James's version was not issued till sixty years after), it was equally fitted to take advantage of the drift of events in extending and perpetuating its influence among the English-speaking peoples.

It does not fall within the scope of the present discussion to inquire, what may have been the design of God in ordering such a thing at such a time. One result of it has undoubtedly been to turn the attention to the great doctrines that everywhere lie upon the very surface of the Scriptures, and to reserve the development of the argument for the rhetorical unity of the various books of the Bible until this age, when the attack comes from that side. On the other hand, it can scarcely be denied that its tendency has been to lead the multitudes to read the Word of God very much as if made up of detached portions, having little or no logical or rhetorical connection with one another, and each composed of ten or twenty words, more or less; and to lead the popular expounders of the Scriptures to construct their commentaries very much in accordance with this view.

Perhaps the influence of this mechanical chopping up of the Scriptures, in preventing the recognition of a beautiful structural harmony, and in concealing most obvious and characteristic differences in aim and plan, has been nowhere more positive than in that portion so much read and commented upon — the Gospels. The common theory among the masses seems to accept the productions of the Evangelists as so many lives of Christ, more or less complete, but it assigns no peculiar sphere and attributes no special design to any one of them. It recognizes no existing reason why there should be more than one Gospel, or, since there are more than one, why there should not be three or five instead of four.

It follows naturally from this failure to recognize a specific aim in each Gospel, that the masses come to look upon them all as being without coherent plan or inherent harmony of structure. Nor could one even remotely infer from most of the works professing to expound them for the masses, that Matthew or Mark or Luke or John, whether consciously or unconsciously, each gave to the world a book with a definite plan, possessed of a harmony and unity entirely different from that which Cardinal Hugo and Robert Stephens together discovered so long ago, when the former divided the New Testament into chapters and the latter into verses.

These considerations will fairly justify the present inquiry after the plan of the Gospels.

II. *The Plan of Matthew's Gospel.*

It may be seen, in the light of a careful study of its origin, aim, and matter, that the Gospel according to Matthew is naturally divided into five parts, or, rather, into three principal parts, — presenting the successive stages of the work of Jesus as the Messiah in establishing the kingdom of heaven, — with an appropriate introduction and conclusion.

In these divisions the character and career of Jesus are unfolded in their connection with the appropriate Old Testament exhibitions of the Messiah. The historic personage is thus seen side by side with the prophetic ideal, and the exact correspondence of the two is made apparent.

It may not be wholly unnecessary to remark that an outline view is given first, in order that, by getting the contents of the Gospel fully and clearly before the mind, the way may be prepared for a better understanding of the more specific and interesting views that are to follow.

For the assistance of any who may desire to make a fuller comparative study of the characters of "Jesus" and "Messiah," the Messianic teachings of the Old Testament have been connected with the outline view given of Matthew's Gospel.

OUTLINE OF THE FIRST GOSPEL.

INTRODUCTION.

The Advent of the Messiah. Matthew demonstrates by way of introduction, that Jesus had the origin and official preparation of the Messiah of the Prophets. i. 1–iv. 11.

Section 1. Jesus had the origin of the Messiah. i. 1–ii. 23.

A. In his royal and covenant descent from David and Abraham. i. 1–17.

Prophetic References. For the prophecies suggested to the Jew by verse 1, see Ps. lxxxix. 35, 36, cxxxii. 11; Isa. ix. 6, 7; xi. 1; Jer. xxiii. 5, 6. For the scriptural basis of the argument of the genealogy, see the genealogies in Gen. xlvi.; Ruth iv.; 1 Chron. iii.

B. In his divine origin and human birth, as Immanuel, — begotten by the Holy Ghost and born of the Virgin Mary. i. 18–25.

Proph. Refs. For the prophecy fulfilled in this passage, and formally referred to in verses 22, 23, see Isa. vii. 14. For the prophecy that he shall save his people from their sins, and for the scriptural data for deciding that this was the precise time for the appearing of the Messiah, see Dan. ix. 24–26.

C. In the place of his birth, — not Nazareth, as the Jews supposed, but Bethlehem; in the circumstances of his early life in connection with the two places; and in the place of his residence and development, the secluded Nazareth. ii. 1–23.

Proph. Refs. For the prophecy of the star, ch. ii. 2, see Num. xxiv. 17. For the coming of the Gentiles, fulfilled in the Magi, verse 1, see Isa. xi. 10; xlii. 1; lx. 3. With the decree of the Sanhedrim, verse 6, compare Mic. v. 2. With the flight into Egypt, verses 13–15, compare Hos. xi. 1. With the murder of the innocents, verses 16–18, compare Jer. xxxi. 15. With the settlement and residence in Nazareth, verse 23, compare Ps. xxii. 6; lxix. 7, 12; Isa. xlix. 7; liii. 2, 3, etc.; and John i. 46.

Section 2. Jesus received the preparation and inauguration of the Messiah. iii. 1–iv. 11.

A. In the preparation of the Jews, by a forerunner, for his public appearance and ministry. iii. 1–12.

Proph. Refs. For the prophecy of the forerunner, referred to in verse 3, see Isa. xl. 3. For the garb of the forerunner, verse 4, see 2 Kings i. 8. For the prophetic character of Messiah, verses 10–12, see Isa. iv. 4; xli. 8–16; Mal. iii. 1–3.

B. In his external and public consecration for his work, in the baptism by John and in the recognition and anointing from heaven. iii. 13–17.

Proph. Refs. For the prophecy of the Messiah's subjection to the law of righteousness, verse 15, see Ps. xl. 6–10; Jer. xxiii. 6. For the promise of anointing by the Holy Spirit, verse 16, see Isa. xlii. 1; lxi. 1. For the prophetic recognition as the Son of God, verse 17, see Ps. ii. 7.

C. In his internal and private girding for the Messiah's work and his actual commencement of that work, as man for man, in his first bruising of the serpent's head, in the temptation. iv. 1–11.

Proph. Refs. Compare with this passage the Protevangelium, or first Gospel revelation, Gen. iii. 15. Also the promised obedience of the Messiah to the law of God for man, Ps. xl. 7, with the fulfillment in this passage, in verses 3, 4, of the law of self-renunciation, Deut. viii 3; in verses 5–7, of the law of trust in God, Ps. xci. 11, 12, and Deut. vi. 16; in verses 8–10, of the law of worship, Deut. vi. 13. Compare the experience of verse 11 with the promise of divine protection to Messiah, Ps. xci. 11, 12.

PART I.

The Public Proclamation of Messiah's Kingdom. Matthew demonstrates that Jesus did the public work and bore the public character of Messiah, the King and Prophet, in the period devoted chiefly to the proclamation of the coming Kingdom of Heaven, with divine power, in Galilee. iv. 12–xvi. 12.

Section 1. Jesus did this in his personal proclamation, unfolding the law and relations of his Kingdom, and demonstrating his own divine authority. iv. 12–ix. 35.

A. In his early and preliminary work, — in the place, message, and results. iv. 12–25.

Proph. Refs. For the prophecy of the place of beginning his mission, verses 12–17, see Isa. ix. 1, 2. With verses 18–22, compare the vision of holy waters, Ezek. xlvii. 9, 10. With verses 23–25, compare Isa. lxi. 1–3, etc.

B. In his proclamation of the Law of the Kingdom, — in its spirituality, as contrasted with Jewish views, — in t. e Sermon on the Mount. v. 1–vii. 29.

The Lawgiver presents the Constitution of the Kingdom of Heaven by exhibiting, —

a. The Citizens of the Kingdom. v. 3–16.

(a.) In their blessed character and experience. 3–12.

(b.) In their salutary influence upon the world. 13–16.

Proph. Refs. For the character of Messiah as King, Prophet, and Lawgiver, compare the promise to Judah, Gen. xlix. 10; and of a prophet like unto Moses, Deut. xviii. 15. Also such passages as Isa. ii. 2–4; ix. 6, 7; Mic. iv. 1–3, etc. For the prophetic basis for the spiritual character of the subjects of the kingdom, see the predictions and partial descriptions in Ps. lxxii.; Isa. lx.; Jer. xxx. and xxxi.; Ezek. xxxiv. 22–31; Dan. ii. 34, 44, etc. For the world-wide influence as the salt, compare Isa. lx. 21–22; Prov. x. 11; xi. 30; xii. 12, etc. For the light, compare Prov. iv. 18; Ps. xxxvii. 6; cxix. 105, 130; Isa. ix. 2; lx. 1–20, etc.

b. The teachings of the Kingdom, in its relations to Jewish Law and Life. v. 17–vii. 6.

(a.) To the old Jewish law: *first*, as revealed in the

Old Testament Scriptures (v. 17–19); *secondly*, as revealed in the doctrine of the Scribes and Pharisees, as given by the *literal* interpreter (v. 21–32), and by the *liberal* interpreter (v. 33–48).

(b.) To the Jewish life, as seen in the pattern saints of the day: *first*, in the religious life (vi. 1–18); *secondly*, in the worldly life (vi. 19–34); *thirdly*, in the conversation (vii. 1–6).

Proph. Refs. With the teaching of the Lawgiver concerning the mission of Messiah and the higher righteousness demanded in the kingdom of heaven, compare such prophecies as Isa. xxviii. 16–18; Dan. ix. 24, etc. With the condemnation of the literalist and the liberalist, compare the Law as given in Ex. xx; Isa. v. 18–25; Jer. xiv. 13–16; xxiii. 38–40, etc. With the contrast with the Pharisee righteousness, compare Ps. li. 16, 17; Isa. lvii. 15; lxvii. 1–4; Jer. vii. 1–28, etc. With the life of trust, as opposed to the Pharisee worldliness, compare Ps. xxxiv. 10; xxxvii. 3; xxiii.; and the various enactments requiring the Jews to hold and use their wealth as stewards of Jehovah.

c. The practical Way into the Kingdom. vii. 7–27.

(a.) The positive directions. Verses 7–14.

(b.) The warning against the two chief dangers. Verses 15–23.

(c.) The final urgent exhortation. Verses 24–27.

Proph. Refs. For teachings concerning the way of life, compare Ps. xxiv. 3–5; Prov. viii. 17; Isa. xlv. 19; lii. 13–15; liii. 1–12; Jer. xxix. 10–14, etc. For the fate of the rejecters of God, compare Ps. i. 4–6; Dan. xii. 2, etc.

C. In his establishment of his divine authority to set up such a Kingdom and proclaim its Law, — as shown by three series of miracles brought together and arranged for the purpose. viii. 1–ix. 35.

a. First series, exhibiting Jesus as the Messiah, in his relation to the Old Testament Law. viii. 1–18.

Proph. Refs. For special prophecy fulfilled, compare verse 17 with Isa. liii. 4.

b. Second series, exhibiting Jesus, the Messiah, as in

himself all-powerful, and as claiming absolute authority. viii. 18–ix. 8.

Proph. Refs. With "son of man," ch. viii. 18, compare Dan. vii. 13. With "Son of God," ch. viii., compare Ps. ii. 7. With the absolute divine authority, ch. ix. 2, compare the authority attributed to Messiah in Ps. ii; Ps. cx.; and throughout the Messianic prophecies, especially in Isa. ix. 6, 7.

c. Third series, exhibiting Jesus, the gracious Messiah, in his relations to lost men, — showing active mercy and requiring active faith. ix. 9–35.

Proph. Refs. With his character as Saviour of sinners, ch. ix. 10–13, compare Hos. vi. 6; Jer. xxxi. 33, 34; Isa. lii. 53, etc. With his character as the Healer and Lord of life, ch. ix. 22, 25, 30, 35, compare Isa. liii. 4 ix. 2, etc. With Jesus as the conqueror of the demons and their prince, rse 33, compare Gen. iii. 15.

Section 2. Jesus also did the public work, and bore the public character of the Messiah, in his labors, as associated with the Twelve Apostles, in the wider proclamation of the coming Kingdom in Galilee. ix. 36–xvi. 12.

A. In the choice, preliminary instruction, and mission of the Twelve. ix. 36–x. 42. This embraces: —

a. The occasion of the call and mission, — the spiritual destitution of Israel, — the general commission, and the catalogue of the Twelve. ix. 36–x. 4.

Proph. Refs. For the prophetic view of the condition of Israel and the work of Messiah, the compassionate Shepherd for the lost sheep, especially as seen in ch. ix. 36–38, and ch. x. 1, 6–9, compare Isa. liii. 6; Jer. l. 6; Ezek. xxxiv., etc.

b. The charge to the Twelve, or the law of associated effort in the Kingdom, and their exclusive mission to Israel. x. 5–42. Their instructions cover: —

(a.) Their work in preparation for the Kingdom, in heralding the coming of Jesus to the various cities of Israel. Verses 6–15.

(b.) Their work in the established Kingdom, or from

Pentecost on: *first;* to the destruction of Jerusalem, verses 16–23; and, *secondly*, to the end of time, verses 24–42.

Proph. Refs. For general character of Messiah's work, verses 6–9, compare Isa. liii. 6, etc., as just given. For the enmity shown to Messiah and his followers, compare the bruising of his heel by Satan, foretold in the Protevangelium; Gen. iii. 15; Ps. ii. 1–3; Isa. liii. 2, 3, etc. For the social estrangement resulting, verses 34–39, compare Mic. vii. 6; Exod. xxxii. 26–29.

B. In the awakening of doubt of his Messiahship, and consequent opposition, by the fuller revelation of the exclusively spiritual character of his Kingdom. xi. 1–xii. 50.

The antagonism as presented by Matthew, includes: —

a. The apparent expression, on the part of John the Baptist and his followers, of doubt of the Messiahship of Jesus, — giving Jesus occasion to present his credentials as the Messiah; to vindicate the faith and divine mission of his forerunner; to judge that childish generation, and the cities in which his mighty works had been done; to claim the divine authority and extend the gracious invitation of Messiah. xi. 1–30.

Proph. Refs. Compare verse 5 with Isa. liii. 4; xxxv. 5–10; viii. 14, 15. Compare verses 20–24 with Isa. i., etc. Compare the gracious invitation, verses 28–30, with Isa. xlv. 22; lv. 1–3, etc.

b. The appearance of open opposition. xii. 1–45.

(a.) Unorganized, on the part of the leaders of Israel, for a righteous and merciful act. Verses 1–13.

(b.) Organized, by the Pharisees and Scribes, resulting in the withdrawal and quiet work of Jesus. Verses 14–45.

c. The interference of his relatives, whose claims he rejects for higher. xii. 46–50.

Proph. Refs. Compare the acts which awaken the opposition, ch. xii. 1, 9–13, with 1 Sam. xxi. 3–6; Ex. xxix. 32, 33; Lev. viii. 31; xxiv. 9; Num. xxviii. 9, 10; Hos. vi. 6. See, also, Ex. xxiii. 4, 5; Deut. xxii.

4. For the quiet withdrawal and beneficent work, verses 15–21, see Isa. xlii. 1–4.

C. In his consequent substitution of parabolic for plain teaching, in presenting the mystery of the opposition to the Kingdom of Heaven. xiii. 1–53.

The parables of the Kingdom include: —

a. Four parables to the people, with explanations to the disciples.

b. Three parables to the disciples alone.

Proph. Refs. For the Messianic prophecy fulfilled in this phase of the work of Jesus, compare verses 10–16 with Isa. v. 4–7; vi. 9, 10; Ezek. xii. 2.

D. In the culmination of the opposition in his rejection by the representatives of all the leading classes. xiii. 54–xvi. 12. The exhibition of this rejection includes: —

a. His rejection by the synagogue of Nazareth, on account of his obscure origin, — resulting in the withdrawal of his works of power. xiii. 54–58.

Proph. Refs. For the obscurity of Messiah, compare Ps. xxii. 6; lxix. 7, 12; Is. xlix. 7; liii., etc.

b. His rejection as the heavenly King by Herod the earthly king, — resulting in his withdrawal, and furnishing the credentials of the Messiah, in his character and works. xiv. 1–36.

Proph. Refs. For proof that Jesus, in contrast with Herod, appears in the true character of Messiah, compare Isa. vii. 14–25; ix. 1–3; xi. 1–5; Mic. v. 1–5; Jer. xxiii. 1–6.

c. His rejection by the Jerusalem Scribes and Pharisees, the theological authorities and models, — resulting in his exposing their hypocrisy and wickedness; and his withdrawal into the Gentile world, where he furnishes anew the credentials of the Messiah, the deliverer of the world. xv. 1–39.

Proph. Refs. With the rejection, verses 7–9, compare Isa. xxix. 13. With his work in his retirement, verses 21–39, compare the prophecies of blessing to the Gentiles through Messiah, in Gen. xii. 3; Isa. xi. 10; xlii. 6, etc.

d. His rejection by the Galilee Pharisees and Sadducees, — the true Head of the Theocracy by the earthly heads, — resulting in withdrawal, and his condemnation of them. xvi. 1–12.

Proph. Refs. On the rejection compare with the same Scriptures as in the rejection by the Scribes and Pharisees.

PART II.

The Distinct and Public Claim of Messiahship. Matthew shows that, after the rejection and the retirement from the public ministry in Galilee, Jesus openly claimed to be the Messiah, and abundantly proved the righteousness of his claim both to his disciples and to the people. xvi. 13–xxiii. 39.

Section 1. Jesus did this with the Twelve, while correcting their false Jewish views of his priestly character and of his kingdom. xvi. 13–xx. 28.

A. In calling forth their explicit confession of his Messiahship and giving them authority in the kingdom of heaven (the Church), — thus preparing them for the lesson of the suffering and conquering Messiah. xvi. 13–20.

Proph. Refs. For prophecies of the authority here claimed, see Ps. ii. 6; xlv. 6, 7; lxxii. 8–11; Isa. ix.; Mic. v. 1–5; Dan. ii. 44, etc.

B. In teaching in its first form, the lesson of his sacrificial death at the hands of *the Jewish Sanhedrim*, and of his resurrection, — and then confirming their faith anew. xvi. 21–xvii. 21. This includes: —

a. The announcement of the death and its unwilling reception. xvi. 21–28.

b. The twofold confirmation of their faith, in the transfiguration and in the healing of the epileptic demoniac. xvii. 1–21.

Proph. Refs. For the doctrine of the suffering Messiah, compare all the sacrificial system of the Old Testament; and such passages as Isa. liii. 4–10; Dan. ix. 26, etc. For the rejection by Israel, see Isa. xlix. 7, etc. For the doctrine of the resurrection, see Ps. xvi. 10.

C. In teaching, in its second form, the lesson of his death, — through *betrayal by his own followers*, — and then unfolding the true spiritual relations of his followers in his kingdom. xvii. 22–xx. 16. This comprehends the unfolding of, —

a. The church relations and duties, — comprising the relation to the old religion and to worldly supremacy, and the law of church censure and of brotherly forgiveness. xvii. 24–xviii. 35.

b. The earthly relations and duties, — comprising those arising out of the family and earthly riches in their subordination to the heavenly mission. xix. 1–xx. 16.

Proph. Refs. For prophecy of the betrayal of Messiah by his own friends, compare Ps. xli. 9, with John xiii. 18. See also Ps. lv. 12–14, etc. For the unworldly character of the kingdom of Messiah, compare references under ch. v. 3–16.

D. In teaching, in its third form, the lesson of his death, — as a ransom for many, at the hands of *the Roman rulers*, — and then checking the rising spirit of worldly ambition. xx. 17–28.

Proph. Refs. For prophecies of the combination of many classes against Messiah, see Ps. xxii., etc. For the special rage of the Gentiles, or heathen, see Ps. ii. 1, in connection with Acts iv. 25. For the doctrine of the *ransom*, compare Ex. xxi. 30; Prov. xiii. 8; Isa. liii. 5.

Section 2. Jesus made this public claim before the people also, at Jerusalem, the city of the great King, — correcting the false Jewish notions and establishing his Messiahship by miracles performed in the Temple itself. xx. 29–xxiii. 39. This includes: —

A. The public claim to be the son of David, in Jericho; the triumphal entry into the city of David; the assumption of Messianic authority and performance of Messianic works in the Temple. xx. 29–xxi. 17.

Proph. Refs. With the healing of the blind men, ch. xx. 34, compare Isa. xxxv. 5–10. With the triumphal entry, compare Zech. ix. 9; Ps. cxviii. 24–26. With the cleansing of the temple, Isa. lvi. 7; Jer. vii. 11. With the miraculous credentials of Messiah, ch. xxi. 14; Isa. xxxv. 5–10. With the praises of the children, Ps. viii. 2.

B. The public conflict, defensive and offensive, as Messiah, with the hardened Jewish officials. xxi. 18–xxiii. 39. This comprises: —

a. The introductory sign of the nation's fate, in the cursing of the barren fig-tree. xxi. 18–22.

Proph. Refs. Compare the symbolic curse with that of Israel in Isa. v. 4–10.

b. The public conflict with the Sanhedrim, defensive and offensive, ending in their discomfiture and condemnation. xxi. 23–xxii. 14.

Proph. Refs. For the prophecy of the rejection of Messiah, compare ch. xxi. 42–44, with Ps. cxviii. 22, 23; also with such passages as Ps. ii. 9; xxi. 8, 9; Isa. lx. 12; Dan. ii. 34, 35, 44, 45. For the foreshadowed rejection of the nation, ch. xxii. 7–14, compare Dan. ix. 26; Zech. xiv. 1, 2.

c. The public conflict, defensive and offensive, with the leading classes of the nation, as tools of the Sanhedrim, ending in the judgment and casting off of themselves and the nation. xxii. 15–xxiii. 39.

Proph. Refs. With the argument against the Sadducees, compare Deut. xxv. 5; Exod. iii. 6; with that against the lawyer, Deut. vi. 5; Lev. xix. 18; with the discomfiture of the Pharisees, Ps. cx. 1. With the defining of the position of the Scribes and Pharisees, compare Neh. viii. 4–8; with the curse, Mal. ii. 7–9; with the judgment denounced upon Jerusalem, Jer. xxii. 5; Hos. iii. 4, 5.

PART III.

The Sacrifice of Messiah the Priest. Matthew demonstrates that, after his public rejection by the Jews, Jesus fully established his claim to be the Messiah, by fulfilling the Messianic types and prophecies in laying the foundation for the Kingdom of Heaven by his own priestly sacrifice. xxiv. 1–xxvii. 66.

Section 1. He represents Jesus as beginning his work, as the rejected and suffering Messiah, by preparing his disciples for his sacrificial death. xxiv. 1–xxv. 46.

A. In unfolding the true doctrine of his coming in glory, and of the end of the existing order of things. xxiv. 1–43.

Proph. Refs. For the fact of a coming judgment, compare ch. xxiv. 2, with 1 Kings ix. 7–9; Jer. xxvi. 18; Mic. iii. 12. For the time, compare ch. xxiv. 15, with Dan. ix. 27; xi. 31; xii. 11. For the suddenness of Messiah's coming, compare ch. xxiv. 27, with Zech. ix. 14. For the great events attending, compare ch. xxiv. 29–31, with Isa. xiii. 9, 10; Joel ii. 10, 30, 31; Amos v. 20; viii. 9; Dan. vii. 13, 14; Zech. xii. 10–12.

B. In teaching them the true posture of his followers in waiting for his coming, and in describing that coming in glory to the judgment of the world. xxiv. 44–xxv. 46.

Proph. Refs. For the terribleness of the final coming to judgment, ch. xxv. 31–46, compare Ps. i. 5; Isa. xxiv. 21–23; Dan. xii. 1, 2, etc.

Section 2. Matthew represents Jesus as consummating his work, as the rejected and suffering Messiah, by his priestly offering up of himself as the fulfillment of the Law and the Prophets. xxvi. 1–xxxvii. 66.

A. In preparing for the sacrifice and in putting himself in the place of the Paschal lamb; and in overcoming the terrors of death. xxvi. 1–46.

Proph. Refs. With the conspiracy of the rulers, ch. xxvi. 3, compare Ps. ii. With the price of betrayal, verses 14, 15, compare Ex. xxi. 32; Zech. xi. 12, 13. With the pointing out of the traitor, verses 20–23, compare Ps. xli. 9. With the predicted death as Messiah, verse 24, compare Gen. iii. 15; Ps. xxii.; Isa. liii.; Dan. ix. 26. With the assumption of the place of the lamb in the Passover, verses 26–29, compare Ex. xii. 21–29, etc. With the predicted forsaking by the disciples, verses 30–32, compare Zech. xiii. 7. With the experience in Gethsemane, verses 36–46, compare Ps. lxix. 20; Isa. liii. 3, 4; Lam. i. 12, etc.

B. In his betrayal by Judas, and in his trial and condemnation before the Sanhedrim and before Pilate, — or as the Messianic Priest in the power of his enemies. xxvi. 47–xxvii. 26.

Proph. Refs. For prophecies of the betrayal, with ch. xxvi. 47–50, compare Isa. xlix. 7; Ps. xli. 9, etc. With the unresisting surrender, verses 51–54, compare Isa. liii. 7, etc. For the general prophecy fulfilled, verse 56, see Isa. liii.; Dan. ix. 26, etc. With the bringing of false witnesses, ch. xxvi. 59–61, compare Ps. xxvii. 12; xxxv. 11. With the silence of Jesus, verses 62, 63, Isa. liii. 7; with the oath to the high priest, and the predicted coming, verses 63, 64, Dan. vii. 13, 14; with the abuse, verses 67, 68, Isa. l. 6; with the remorse and death of Judas, ch. xxvii. 3–10, Zech. xi. 13. With the experience before Pilate, ch. xxvii. 11–26, compare Isa. liii. 7, 9, 11, etc.

C. In his experience in the hands of his executioners, as the Messiah sacrificed for sin, — mocked, crucified, dead, and buried. xxvii. 27–66.

Proph. Refs. With the experience in the hands of his executioners, compare Isa. liii.; Ps. xxii.; Dan. xii. 2, etc.

CONCLUSION.

The Triumph of Messiah the Saviour and King. Matthew shows in conclusion that Jesus, after his death, fully established his claim to the Messiahship, as the risen Lord and Redeemer. xxviii. 1–20.

Section 1. By his rising from the dead on the third day, and furnishing abundant evidence, private and official, of his resurrection. xxviii. 1–15.

Proph. Refs. With the resurrection, verses 1–4, compare Ps. xvi. 8–11; Dan. x. 6; and Christ's own predictions.

Section 2. By his formal assumption of Messianic authority, and by sending forth his disciples to the spiritual conquest of the world. xxviii. 16–20.

Proph. Refs. With the assumption of Messianic authority, compare Ps. ii. 6–9; xxii. 27, 28; xlv. 6, 7; lxxii.; cx.; Isa. ix. 6, 7; xi. 1–10; Dan. ii. 44, 45; vii. 27, etc.

SECTION II.

THE JEWISH ADAPTATION IN THE CENTRAL IDEA OF THE FIRST GOSPEL.

The outline, as already given, is its own witness that the first Gospel was prepared by Matthew for the Jew. It also opens the way for showing how the central idea and general drift of the Gospel confirm the historical testimony touching the Jewish aim of the Evangelist.

I. *The Central Idea.*

A single glance makes it clear that Matthew seizes upon the one idea of the Jewish system which was most prominent in the Jewish mind of that age. He gives us the Gospel of Jesus, the Messiah of the Prophets.

The Messiah. His one subject, always and everywhere, is, Jesus is the Messiah. He opens with the origin of Jesus, the Messiah, and closes with his assumption of the universal authority of the Messiah, and from the beginning to the close never for a moment parts company with the Messianic idea.

It is patent to the reader that the first Gospel is that of the Messianic royalty of Jesus. It seizes upon the regal idea, as the one uppermost in the mind of the race, and takes advantage of it to open the way for the presentation of Jesus, under the most favorable aspect, to the Jewish soul. Its opening genealogy is that of Jesus, the Messiah, the Son of David (i. 1). He is the descendant of Joseph, the son and heir of David (i. 20). The Magi inquire, "Where is he that is born King of the Jews?" (ii. 2). John the Baptist announces him as the founder of the kingdom of heaven (iii. 2). Jesus himself begins and continues with the proclamation of the kingdom of heaven (iv. 17; v. 3, etc.). **Jesus is the Messiah, the King, throughout the Gospel.**

But the Evangelist takes special pains, as will subsequently appear more fully, to correct the false Jewish notions, at that day so prevalent, concerning the kingdom of Messiah, and to bring into their true place and rightful prominence the more important elements of his prophetic and priestly character, which had been so generally lost out of view. He accordingly exhibits the kingdom not as a temporal one, like the Roman Empire, but as theocratic, or as a spiritual reign of God himself, in the person of Messiah, in the hearts of men (v. 3–12; xii. 1–52, etc.). The prophetic glory of the Messiah is seen, as Jesus speaks for God the grand truths of this spiritual kingdom, in the Sermon on the Mount, in the parables, and in the other chief discourses, and as he foretells the events of the future, in the prophecies of his own death and in the revelation of the last things (ch. xxiv.). The priestly character of the Messiah is given its true prominence by various teachings throughout the Gospel, but especially by the three remarkable prophecies of his death, uttered during the period given to the instruction of his disciples in the much needed lesson of his sufferings and sacrifice (xvi. 21; xvii. 22, 23; xx. 17–19), and in his experience in his trial, condemnation, and death for the ransom of the world.

It should likewise be remarked that in pursuing his one central theme, the Evangelist never fails to take into account and attach due weight to the other ideas peculiar to the Jews. He regards them as the chosen people, their religion as the true world-religion, its forms as the only divine religious forms, and its promise of Messiah addressed first of all to the Jews. Every diligent reader of his Gospel will not fail to discern evidence of the constant aim of Matthew, while presenting his main theme, to press all these truths upon the attention, and at the same time to correct the erroneous and distorted views, which, as already seen, had arisen out of them.

Use of Prophecy. Out of his single central theme, so steadily pursued, arises Matthew's peculiar use of the prophecies of the Old Testament, so in contrast with the usage of the other Evangelists.

His references to the Jewish Scriptures, while more numerous than in all the other Gospels, are not, as in them, merely incidental, or for the sake of giving the knowledge of some doctrine involved, but rather to furnish the basis for the entire argument and to correct the practical errors into which the Jews had fallen.

Mark has perhaps, less than a score of such references, almost all of which are general. But three of them, at the most, are properly fulfillments of prophecy — Mark i. 2; i. 3; xv. 28, — and only the last of the three is distinctly presented as such.[1]

Luke has perhaps thirty references or allusions to the Old Testament Scriptures. Most of these are simple incidental citations of fact or law. The allusions to prophecy are given in the discourses embodied in the Gospel, — as in that of the angel (i. 17); of Mary (i. 55); of Zacharias (i. 69–75); of Simeon (ii. 32); in those of Jesus (iv. 17–21; vii. 22; xxiv. 25–28, 45–48). The argument of the book does not at all depend either upon the authority of the Scriptures or upon the fulfillment of prophecy.[2]

John has twenty or more references to the Old Testament Scriptures. These generally take for granted that the Church is acquainted with the revelation of the Old

[1] The references to prophecy in the Gospel according to Mark, are as follows: ch. i. 2, 3, 15; ch. ii. 25, 26; ch. ix. 12, 13; ch. x. 4, 19; ch. xi. 17; ch. xii. 10, 19, 26, 29, 36; ch. xiii. 14; ch. xiv. 27; ch. xv. 28.

[2] The references to the Old Testament Scriptures, in the Gospel according to Luke, are as follows: ch. i. 17, 55, 69–75; ch. iv. 4, 8, 10, 12, 17–21; ch. v. 14; ch. vi. 2–5, 6–10; ch. vii. 22; ch. x. 26–28; ch. xi. 29; ch. xiii. 14; ch. xiv. 1–5; ch. xvi. 16–18; ch. xviii. 20, 21, 31; ch. xix. 46; ch. xx. 17, 28, 37, 38, 42, 43; ch. xxi. 22; ch. xxii. 37; ch. xxiv. 25–27, 45–48.

Testament. In the first half of the Gospel, the references are chiefly incidental and confined to fact and law, — the words of the Baptist (i. 23) being an exception. In the second half, in which the teaching of Jesus in connection with his death is presented in its relations to the Christian life, all the references are occasioned by direct fulfillment of Messianic prophecies, well known to those who first heard these discourses of our Lord, and familiar to all intelligent Christians in all ages. The main argument of the Gospel does not, however, at all turn upon them as prophecies, but they are mainly introduced in order to bring out some hidden spiritual meaning, not brought out in Matthew and not needed for the purposes contemplated by him in his Gospel.[1]

Matthew, on the other hand, as has already been shown, rests his Gospel entirely upon a basis of Old Testament revelation. He presents one continued comparison of Jesus of Nazareth with the Messiah of the Prophets, a comparison which could not fail to have marvelous convincing power with any candid Jew. His argument is nothing, and his Gospel almost unintelligible without this, — in short, the Old Testament doctrine of the Messiah, as announced in the Protevangelium, in the opening of Genesis, and unfolded through all the ages till the final words of Malachi, is the only key to the first Gospel.

II. *The General Drift.*

The influence of the central theme of the Evangelist is everywhere manifest in the general drift of his Gospel, so different from that of the other Gospels.

[1] The references to the Old Testament Scriptures, in the Gospel according to John, are as follows: ch. i. 23; ch. ii. 17; ch. v. 9, 10; ch. vi. 14, 31, 45; ch. vii. 22, 23, 38, 42; ch. viii. 5, 17; ch. x. 34, 35; ch. xii. 14–16, 34, 38, 39–41; ch. xiii. 18; ch. xv. 25; ch. xix. 24, 28, 36, 37.

To follow the outward form, the Gospel opens with the origin and preparation of Jesus for the work of Messiah, and his induction into the office of Messiah. Part First presents the public proclamation by Jesus as Messiah of the kingdom of heaven, first by himself alone, and afterward as associated with the twelve Apostles. Part Second exhibits his public claim to be the Messiah, made and confirmed first to the Twelve and then to the people at large. Part Third sets forth his sufferings and death as the Messiah, first announced as being at hand, and then prepared for and endured as a ransom for many. The Conclusion exhibits the fact and proof of the resurrection of Jesus as Messiah from the dead, and his assumption of the royal Messianic prerogatives.

To follow the inward drift of thought, the Gospel takes the life of Jesus as it was lived on earth, and his character as it actually appeared, and places them alongside the life and character of the Messiah as sketched in the Prophets, the historic by the side of the prophetic, that the two may appear in their marvelous unity and in their perfect identity. The greatness of the Prophet like unto Moses is seen in the Nazarene, as he speaks for God the fundamental truths of the kingdom of heaven and foretells its future. The grandeur of the suffering Servant of Jehovah, "despised and rejected of men," "wounded for our transgressions," shines through all his words and acts that culminate in his vicarious death on Calvary. The sublimity of the King of whom Jehovah said, "I have set my King on my holy hill of Zion," appears in the Son of David, as he forms and gives law to a world-wide spiritual society, an everlasting state, the kingdom of heaven. Jesus and the Messiah are demonstrated to be in all respects one and the same.

All this was just what was needed to commend him as a Saviour to the Jews. It was a true view of the prophet of Nazareth, for whatever Jesus may have been besides, he was also and primarily the Messiah, the highest development of Judaism, — humanly speaking, the ideal Jew. He was not merely the accomplishment of Hebrew prophecy in an external sense, but the highest expression of all that was good in Judaism — the inheritor of whatever moral wisdom, whatever spiritual genius, survived in it.[1] This Jesus, at once the greatest among Jews, and the finisher of Judaism — the Messiah — is the Jesus represented by Matthew.

SECTION III.

THE JEWISH ADAPTATION IN THE OMISSIONS AND ADDITIONS OF THE FIRST GOSPEL.

The Jewish design of the first Gospel is still further manifest both from what the Evangelist omits of what is found in the other Gospels and from what he adds to what is found in them.

I. *The Omissions of the First Gospel.*

Matthew, in writing for the Jew, characteristically omits, as useless for his purpose, whatever is distinctively Roman, Greek, or Christian, in the presentation of the Gospel.

In General. The careful reader will note the entire absence of such explanations of Jewish customs, as that which Mark gives of the religious washing of the hands before eating, and of "the washing of cups, and pots, brazen vessels, and of tables" (Mark vii. 2–5), which were necessary for the stranger of Roman birth. There are no such explanations of Jewish topography, as that which Luke gives of the "village called Emmaus, which was from Jerusalem about threescore furlongs" (Luke

[1] Principal Tulloch, *Lectures on Rénan's 'Vie de Jésus.'*

xxiv. 13), and which were necessary to the strangers of Greek birth and philosophic turn of mind. There is an absence of such explanations of Jewish facts, as that which John gives of the enmity of the Jews to the Samaritans (John iv. 4), and which were necessary for the Christians over the world after the destruction of Jerusalem and the desolation of Judæa. For the Jew, at home in Jerusalem, or often visiting it, there was, at the date of Matthew's writing, no need of any of these things.

From Mark. The same careful attention will reveal the fact that the first Gospel uniformly omits those vivid details and scenic representations of events, which will be seen to abound in and to characterize the second Gospel, and which fitted it for the Roman, the man of power and action.

From Luke. Still more marked is the omission of those eminently human features, in which Luke's Gospel will be seen to abound; and of the facts of the ministry of Jesus in Peræa, with those universal aspects and relations of Christ's teachings and work, which furnish so large a portion of the third Gospel (ix. 51–xviii. 30), features and facts which fitted that Gospel for the Greek, the man whose ideal was the perfect man of human development, and who was the representative of universal humanity. To one who duly considers this omission by Matthew of what constitutes the very heart of Luke's Gospel, and of what has been to mankind at large the most precious of all the teachings of the first three Gospels, it will never cease to be regarded as a marvelous thing, and a thing which can be explained only by the consideration that the one Evangelist wrote for the Jew, the man of the covenant and of prophecy, and the other for the Greek, the man of world-wide sympathies and aspirations.

From John. Most remarkable of all is the absence

of the ministry in Judæa, to the true Israel, and those preëminently spiritual discourses which constitute the greater part of the fourth Gospel, and which fitted it for the Christian, the man already united to Christ by a living faith. One might at first suppose that these teachings were exactly suited to the wants of the Jewish race, since they were addressed directly to those who belonged to that race. But more careful consideration will make it plain that, as they were in the main addressed to that small class of Jews who held the advanced ground on the doctrine of the Messiah, and were possessed of more or less of the true spiritual insight, so they could have proved to the mass of the Jews only a stumbling-block, and were therefore fitted to form a part of that Gospel only which was prepared by John distinctively for the Christian.

All these things, had Matthew embodied them in his Gospel, would have done little toward commending Jesus to the attention and interest of the mass of the Jews, who were waiting for the advent of the Messiah of the Scriptures, and holding peculiarly Jewish and unspiritual views regarding the nature of his person, character, and coming. They could, therefore, properly have no place in a Gospel for the Jews.

But notwithstanding all these omissions, the Holy Spirit has guarded the first Gospel against being justly charged with presenting Jesus as exclusively the Saviour of the Jews.

He is the descendant of Abraham, but four Gentile women find place in the genealogy: Tamar of Timnath; Rahab of Jericho; Ruth of Moab; and Bathsheba of Gath (ch. i.). He is born King of the Jews, but those who first seek him to worship him are not Jews, but "wise men from the East," the first fruits of the Gentiles (ii.). He chooses twelve Apostles and sends them forth first to "the lost sheep of the house of Israel," but only one of them, Judas Iscariot, or Judas the *man of Kerioth*, is of Judæa, while all the rest are Galileans (x.). The final commission reads: "Go ye therefore and teach all nations" (xxviii.).

The Gospel, in Matthew's view, is first a Gospel for the Jews, that it may ultimately become a Gospel for mankind. In short, the omissions of Matthew, while they mark his production as distinctively for the Jews, do not by any means confine salvation to the Jews, but extend it to all the race.

II. *The Additions of the First Gospel.*

The first Gospel gives even better evidence of its special Jewish aim in what it adds to the records of the other Evangelists than in what it omits of that which is to be found in them.

Additions in Form. It has been remarked, of late, that Matthew adds an important feature to the form of his Gospel, in the careful and systematic grouping of his material, — a feature that especially adapted it to the Jewish mind.

There is scarcely a more systematic production to be found. This will appear clearly from an examination of the outline view given. With reference to this point, Lange has remarked, that "it is a characteristic of this Gospel, which is increasingly recognized, that a careful grouping of events prevails throughout."

This feature may be regarded as resulting from any one or all of three causes: the character of the contents of the first Gospel, as a comparison of the historic Jesus and the prophetic Messiah to establish their identity; the practical business training, already adverted to, of Matthew, the publican; or the characteristic needs of Jewish readers, who were trained to such systematic use of reason and memory by their entire religious system and practice. Doubtless all three influences had to do with the result under consideration.

This careful grouping may be observed in all the more characteristic portions of the Gospel: in the genealogy (i.); in the Sermon on the Mount (v.–vii.); in the three series of miracles (viii.–ix.); in the charge to the twelve (x.); in the parables of the kingdom (xiii.); in the series of rejections (xiii.–xvi.); in the three successive predictions of the death of Jesus (xvi. 21; xvii. 22; xx. 17); and in the final conflict of Jesus with the authorities (xxi.–xxii.).

It is not at all strange, considering the character of the rationalistic criticism, that this peculiarity has been made use of in the attempt to sustain the hypothesis, that the original Gospel of Matthew consisted only of a collection of fragmentary sayings; but in the outline view, already given, it may readily be seen that there was a rational motive in the mind of the Evangelist for grouping them as they are. Matthew has, in short, given us the most systematic of the Gospels, because his plan and purpose called for it. His arrangement fits his Gospel to appeal most powerfully to the Jewish soul and to fix itself permanently in the Jewish memory. Indeed, the Jew who once took its truths and facts into his mind could not get them out again, for it connected the name of Jesus of Nazareth indissolubly and forever with all the religious knowledge and hopes of the descendant of Abraham, and with all the glories of his past national history. Its system was, doubtless, divinely ordained to serve this very purpose. The rational aim, human and divine, leaves no place for the rationalistic conjecture.

Additions to Material. Still more clearly do the additions, which the first Evangelist makes to the material of the other Gospels, appear to be made to fit his production for Jewish readers.

By that mechanical analysis, which has always played so prominent a part in the study of the Scriptures, it has been shown that, if the Gospel according to Matthew be regarded as made up of 100 parts, 42 of these are peculiar to itself, and 58 common to this with one or more of the other Gospels. A much more important fact — and one that can readily be shown to be a fact, although it has been overlooked — is, that all the 42 parts peculiar to Matthew are precisely adapted to the Jewish aim of the Evangelist.

This may be shown by passing in review the narratives, discourses, and groups of events of which Matthew's additions are made up. They all have such a special Jewish reference as is not to be found in the material of the other Evangelists.

The origin of Jesus as Messiah (i.–ii.), is peculiar to Matthew.

The genealogy given (i. 1–17) is that of Jesus, through Solomon and Joseph, as heir to the throne of David; while that of Luke (Luke iii. 23–38) is that of natural descent through Nathan and Mary, which did not necessarily entitle him to the throne, but which was of interest to the Gentile world as giving his actual lineage. It should also be remarked that the first Evangelist traces back the line of Jesus only to Abraham, the father of the covenant people; while the third traces it to Adam, the father of the race.

The Jew would not listen to any one who had not the prophetic origin of the Messiah. The one line, of all possible opening lines, best fitted to attract and fix the attention of the Jew, was that with which Matthew opens his Gospel. The genealogy which it introduces gives the official pedigree of Jesus. It is documentary evidence, drawn from the Scriptures and from the public records, which the Jew could examine for himself. Its threefold division connected it with the greatest events of Jewish history, — the covenant, the monarchy, and the captivity.

The divine origin and human birth of Jesus (i. 18–25) is in accordance with prophecy, and distinctively for the Jew. The Anointed of God was to be "God with us," divine as well as human. Hence Matthew presents, in connection with the espousal of Mary and Joseph, the divine origin of Jesus by the power of the Holy Ghost, and his actual human birth of the virgin, — holding him up to the Jew, as not only the son and heir of David, but as named by God himself "*Jesus*," Jah-Hoshea, the Jehovah-Saviour, "Emmanuel." The families of Joseph and Zacharias were competent witnesses of the facts.

The narrative of events from the birth until the settlement in Nazareth (ii.) is given for the Jew, and was absolutely necessary for his conviction of the Messiahship of Jesus. The Jew would naturally and inevitably fall back upon the objection, that Jesus was from Nazareth of Galilee, and therefore had not the birthplace of the Messiah. Hence Matthew proceeds to establish the fact that Jesus was born in Bethlehem, and to show how and why the misconception had arisen. That he was actually born in Bethlehem and not in Nazareth, appeared from a train of events which had already passed into history, and which found their best and only sufficient explanation in his birth in the former place. When this Gospel was written, the notable coming of the Magi to Jerusalem, at the very time when Messiah ought to have appeared, was doubtless still remembered; the record of the meeting and the decree of the Sanhedrim called by Herod doubtless still remained; the flight into Egypt and the murder of the babes had still their living witnesses; and the residence in Nazareth is at last fully accounted for by the divine command to settle there and the prophecy that the Messiah should be called a Nazarene.

The Sermon on the Mount (v.–vii.), is peculiarly adapted to the Jew.

It is assumed here, in accordance with the view of many of the best authorities, that the Sermon given by Matthew was delivered on a different occasion and to a different audience from the so-called Sermon on the Mount of Luke (Luke vi. 17–49), which should rather be called the *Sermon on the Plain.* But the Sermon illustrates equally well on either supposition the point here to be kept in mind.

If the two are abstracts of the same address, then the fitness of Matthew's abstract for the Jew is seen in his preserving the Jewish features and references, which Luke so entirely omits.

But regarded as an independent discourse, it will be seen at once that the Sermon on the Mount, in presenting the constitution of the kingdom of heaven, keeps constantly in view the Law and the Prophets, and the condition and needs of the Jew of Christ's day. It might readily be shown in detail how it acknowledges the preeminence of the Jew by divine choice, and yet rebukes his unrighteous and arrogant pretensions, reveals his perversions of the Scriptures, tears off the mask of hypocrisy, and presses upon him the only way of righteousness and life by the most solemn and emphatic appeals to the issues of the final reckoning. Every sentence of it was aimed directly at the Jew.

The original mission of the Twelve (x.) was to the Jews (x. 6, 23), and in consequence of their spiritual destitution as witnessed in Galilee (ix. 35–38) ; and the charge given them had primary reference to their work for Israel, as may be seen by an examination of it.

The same peculiar features may be traced in the other

discourses of our Lord, added by Matthew, either wholly or in part, to the Gospel material: in the upbraiding of the cities of Galilee (xi. 20–30); in the answer to the Scribes and Pharisees who demanded a sign (xii. 38–45); in the divine compassion for the lost, and the law of Church censure and forgiveness (xviii. 10–35); in the judgment of the Scribes and Pharisees and of Jerusalem (xxiii. 1–39); and in the description of the day of judgment (xxv).

Besides the capital fact, emphasized by Matthew, that Jesus changed from plain teaching to parabolic because of the blindness and obduracy of the Jews (Matt. xiii. 10–16), it may be shown that most of the long list of parables contained in the latter half of the first Gospel are especially condemnatory of the Jews. This is true of the parable of the unmerciful servant (xviii.), which opposes the boundless forgiveness required in the kingdom, to the teaching of the Jew which confined the forgiveness of an offending brother to three successive offenses; that of the laborers in the vineyard (xx.), which lifts the Gentile to the same level of divine privilege with the Jew; that of the two sons (xxi.), which exalts the Gentile above the Jew; that of the marriage of the king's son (xxii.), which threatens that the kingdom shall be taken wholly from the Jewish people and given to the Gentiles; that of the ten virgins (xxv.), which contrasts true piety with Jewish formality; that of the talents (xxv.), which opposes productive spiritual activity to Jewish obduracy and barrenness.

The Jewish adaptation is also manifest in the great groups of events and teachings given by Matthew: in the three series of miracles (viii. 1–ix. 35); in the parables of the kingdom of heaven (xiii. 1–53); in the progressive stages of awakened doubt and opposition (xi. 2–xii. 50); in the series of rejections (xii. 54–

xvi. 12); and in the series of conflicts (xxi. 18–xxiii. 39).

The examination of all these various passages might be entered into with thoroughness, and extended to the most minute particulars, and always with accumulating evidence and increasing conviction that they were all added by the Evangelist, under the special guidance of the Holy Spirit, to commend Jesus of Nazareth to the Jews as the Messiah their Saviour. Everything bears the plainest marks of the Jewish aim.

SECTION IV.

THE JEWISH ADAPTATION IN THE INCIDENTAL VARIATIONS OF THE FIRST GOSPEL.

The adaptation of Matthew's Gospel to the Jewish needs appears in the incidental variations and peculiarities throughout the entire production.

I. *Incidental Variations.*

Different writers, in recording the same facts or events, under the influence of different aims, always exhibit their subject with manifold incidental variations. This feature is very marked in the Gospels, and in the case of each Evangelist it will be found that these variations always bear the marks of his special aim.

Narrative Changes. This will appear in comparing Matthew's mode of treating some portions of the evangelic facts with the mode adopted by the other Evangelists.

The mission of the Baptist is recorded or referred to in all the Gospels. In Matthew he heralds Jesus as the Messiah of the Jews, coming in fulfillment of prophecy. He who shall come after this heralding is to appear as the Lord Jehovah in person, to set up the kingdom of heaven among men, and the Jews are called to repentance as a preparation for his appearance. In Mark, the work of the Baptist is introduced to exhibit by contrast the mightier power of the Son of God, who comes to set up the kingdom of God. In Luke, the work of the Baptist brings Jesus forward as the one perfect man, placing himself on a level with all men by coming to be baptized "when all the people were baptized." In John, the Baptist witnesses to Jesus, before the Church and the world, as the divine, eternal, only-begotten Son of God, the Lamb of God sacrificed to take away the sin of the world, the life and light of men.

The temptation of Christ appears only in the first three Gospels, but in each of these with characteristic differences. Matthew, commending Jesus as king to the Jew, presents the temptations in one order of the threefold relation of Jesus: first, to human wants; secondly, to dependence on God; and, thirdly, to the sovereignty of the world, — closing thus by showing that the king, the second Adam, would win the kingdom by obedience to the law given to man and transgressed in the first Adam. Luke, commending Jesus to the world as the perfect man and Saviour, presents the temptations in a different order of the same threefold relation of Jesus: first, to human wants; secondly, to the sovereignty of the world; and, thirdly, to his human dependence on God, — closing thus with the preservation of the just relations of the divine-human Saviour to God. Mark, commending Jesus to the Roman, as the mighty God, the almighty worker and conqueror, gathers all up into a single sentence, and adds to the victory over Satan that over the terrors of the wilderness, thereby vastly increasing the impression of the power of the Son of God.

All the Evangelists set out from the Baptist in introducing their readers to the ministry of Jesus, but the differences in procedure are characteristic. Mark, keeping in view the Roman, merely makes the imprisonment of the Baptist the starting-point of a wonder-working ministry of Jesus in Galilee, into the marvels of which he hurries us at once, without even hinting at its prophetic relations. Luke, in tracing for the reasoning Greek the orderly development of the life and work of Jesus, opens with the ministry in Galilee, as the natural sequence of that of the Baptist, but does not emphasize the connection. John, writing for the Christian, sets out with the Baptist, as preparing the way for that private ministry of Jesus in Judæa which preceded the public ministry in Galilee, and which, as being directed to the true Israel and dealing with high spiritual themes, is passed over in silence by the other Evangelists, but brought forward in the Gospel for the Christian, the spiritual man, as eminently fitted to further its peculiar aim. Matthew, with his eye on the Jew, starts with the public ministry of Jesus in Galilee, — which, strictly speaking, could begin only when that of the Baptist, the forerunner, closed, — and presents Jesus at once and most prominently in his Messianic character, fulfilling prophecy.

Or, passing on to the scenes of Calvary, and the closing career, it will be observed that the only one of the seven sayings of Christ on the cross which is recorded by the first Evangelist is that from Psalm xxii. : " Eli ! Eli ! lama sabachthani ? that is to say, My God, My God, why hast thou forsaken me ? " That is distinctively the Psalm of the suffering Messiah. He may have repeated it all. At all events, it must have passed through his soul at that hour. Ages before the inspired psalmist had drawn the picture, and it was the one Scripture of all to bring home and explain that scene on Calvary to he Jewish soul. The agony, the forsaking by God, the coffing of men, the exhaustion and death, the piercing of hands and feet, the casting of lots for the garments, are all there in the Psalm as distinct as the reality itself. The triumph and the glory are there, too, just as distinct. "All the ends of the world shall remember and turn unto the Lord: and all the kindreds of the nations shall worship before thee. For the kingdom is the LORD'S, and he is the governor among the nations." So the Psalm (xxii. 27, 28) advances from the wail of the sufferer to the triumphant shout of the Messianic Conqueror and King. "All power is given unto me in heaven and in earth. Go ye therefore and teach all nations, baptizing them in the name of the Father, and of the Son, and of the Holy Ghost, teaching them to observe all things whatsoever I have commanded you." So the Gospel rises to the same triumphant Messianic note (Matt. xxviii. 18–20).

Such examples might be extended to cover all the facts and events which Matthew records in common with one or more of the other Evangelists, and would everywhere be found to exhibit the same characteristics.

Slighter Additions. But passing over these, there is a very large and important class of incidental additions, made by Matthew, in connection with materials common to two or more of the Gospels.

Matthew alone brings out the fulfillment of Messianic prophecies in connection with the great outward events of our Lord's life: in the place, time, and extraordinary circumstances of his public ministry (iv. 13–25); in the noiselessness of his work (xii. 17–21); in his rejection (xiii. 13–17); in his teaching by parables (xiii. 33–35); and in the miracles in the temple (xxi. 14–16).

It is from Matthew that we learn that the conflict of opinion, which resulted in the death of Jesus, had already begun as early as the healing of the two blind men and the dumb demoniac in Capernaum (ix. 27–34); that the

Sanhedrim plotted his destruction in public assembly (xxvi. 3–5) ; that the price given the traitor was that of a common slave (xxvi. 16) ; that Judas repented, returned the money, and committed suicide, fulfilling prophecy (xxvii. 3–10) ; that Pilate washed his hands of the blood of Jesus, and all the people said, "His blood be on us, and on our children" (xxvii. 24, 25) ; and that the enemies of Jesus made his sepulchre sure (xxvii. 62–66), and afterwards invented the report that his disciples stole his body away (xxviii. 11–15).

Matthew alone tells us that Jesus declared John to be the Elijah who was to come (xi. 12–15) ; that he characterized the Jew and the Gentile in the parable of the two sons (xxi. 28–32) ; that he forced the Jewish leaders to pronounce judgment upon themselves, and then added his own (xxi. 40–44) ; and that he predicted the connection of his death with the Sacrifice of the Passover (xxvi. 2).

It is to Matthew that we owe the fact that after the resurrection of Jesus many saints came forth from their graves in testimony of his divine mission and power (xxvii. 52, 53) ; and that he was worshiped by the disciples on the mountain in Galilee, and then assumed the divine authority of the Messiah (xxvii. 17–20).

Such variations have an increased importance from the fact that they furnish incidentally, and in way not to be resisted, just the credentials needed in presenting Jesus as Messiah to the Jews.

Word Changes. There is another class of variations, slighter, perhaps, but no less characteristic, often involved in the change of a single word, which deserves notice as illustrating the same Jewish reference of the first Gospel.

Only Matthew tells us, in narrating the temptation, that Jesus was led by the Spirit into the wilderness *for the express purpose* of being tempted by the devil (iv. 1). The Jew alone felt it to be a *necessity* that the second Adam, in his work of fulfilling the law and restoring man, should meet and overcome the tempter by whom the first Adam fell. So Matthew tells us that the devil, in preparing for the second temptation, takes Jesus to *the holy city* of the Jew (iv. 5), and there makes his second assault upon him. Luke says the devil brought him to *Jerusalem* (Luke iv. 9). To the Greek, the former expression would have been unintelligible without explanation; to the Jew it was the cherished form of speech, and his delight in Jerusalem was because it was the holy city.

Matthew's account of the triumphal entry of Jesus into Jerusalem bears like marks of the writer's aim. He alone tells us that the disciples brought *both a colt and an ass* to the Mount of Olives (xxi. 2, 5, 7); and this he repeats in three forms, showing that it was in exact fulfillment of prophecy (Zech. ix. 9). Mark and Luke speak of the *colt* only (Mark xi. 2; Luke xix. 30), as that on which Jesus rode; while John, in the language of prophecy, mentions the *ass's colt* (xii. 15). It is also worthy of remark that only the Evangelist who had a supreme interest in the Jews mentions the fact that all Jerusalem was moved at the entrance of Jesus the prophet of Nazareth of Galilee (xxi. 10, 11).

Or passing on to the arrest of Jesus in Gethsemane, could anything be more marked than the variations of Matthew's account from the accounts of the other Evangelists? Only he tells us of Christ's curse upon the use of the sword in his cause: "for all they that take the sword shall perish by the sword" (xxvi. 52). It was the needed caution to the Apostles, whose Jewish nature was always leading them to put the temporal in the place of the spiritual. And as Matthew had before taught the

Jew most clearly that the sacrifice of Jesus was entirely voluntary, as a ransom for sinners (xx. 28), so here that Evangelist alone represents Jesus as declaring, and that with the most solemn emphasis, that he made it voluntarily to fulfill the law and the prophets, when all the forces of heaven were at his command (xxvi. 53, 54).

These are but instances of those slighter changes found throughout the first Gospel, and everywhere showing its Jewish aim and coloring.

II. *Other Peculiarities.*

From the entire survey, as pursued thus far, it is further obvious that the first Gospel exhibits certain other marks, in matter entirely peculiar to itself, which can only be explained by its Jewish aim.

Jewish Assumptions. Matthew assumes, and everywhere acts upon the assumption of what have been shown to be the characteristics of the Jews as distinguished from the other men of that age.

He acknowledges the Jews the chosen people of God, as in the words concerning the faith of the centurion (viii. 10–12); in the charge to the Twelve (x. 5, 6); and in the words of the Canaanitish woman (xv. 24); while, in the very same connection, he rebukes their exclusiveness and wicked pretensions.

He assumes that to them belonged the oracles of God, while he everywhere exhibits, corrects, and denounces their perversions of the great practical doctrines. He admits that they possess the only true forms of religious worship, while he unveils and denounces with merciless severity their hypocritical formalism. He proceeds, as has been abundantly shown, upon their familiarity with the doctrine of the Messiah, while he exposes their carnal and worldly views of his kingdom, and presents it in its true spiritual aspects.

Jewish Expressions. There still remain certain expressions and features of the first Gospel which may be noticed as bringing out for the Jew with peculiar clearness the spiritual character of Messiah and his kingdom. Here was the one most insidious dream of the age, which needed, therefore, most of all to be dissipated.

The first of these expressions is *the kingdom of heaven*, or *of the heavens*, as the original has it. Matthew uses it no less than thirty times. He alone of all the Evangelists uses it. The Baptist's call was, "Repent ye, for the kingdom of heaven is at hand" (iii. 2). The opening proclamation of Jesus was, "Repent, for the kingdom of heaven is at hand" (iv. 17). So throughout the Gospel the phrase is used.

The phrase clearly expresses the idea that it is a kingdom distinct from all those kingdoms of this world after which the Jew had fashioned his idea of Messiah's dominion. Its origin is in the heavens where God dwells: its throne, the seat of its king, is there; its highest present and prospective glories are there.

This simple phrase taught that the kingdom of Messiah was to be a spiritual and heavenly kingdom, unlike the old theocracy with its temple and throne in Jerusalem; unlike the magnificent empire patterned after Rome, which the worldly Jew was dreaming of; wholly unlike the temporal empire of the Papacy long after established.

Matthew uses the equally significant and spiritual expression, the *Church*. The other Evangelists never use it.

The Church, *the ecclesia*, is the body of Christ's followers, called out from the unspiritual world, from the kingdom of darkness, and brought into spiritual obedience to him as their head. Matthew represents Jesus as identifying the Church with the kingdom of heaven, and giving it his divine authority: "And I say also unto thee, that thou art Peter, and upon this rock will I build my church, and the gates of hell shall not prevail against it. And I will give unto thee the keys of the kingdom of heaven ; and whatsoever thou shalt bind on earth shall be bound in heaven ; and whatsoever thou shalt loose on earth shall be loosed in heaven " (xvi. 18–20). This authority of the Church is also reaffirmed in connection with the statement of the law of offenses in the kingdom (xviii. 18–20). The kingdom of heaven, as manifested in the Church, is thus clearly seen to be a spiritual organization, independent of all temporal and worldly organizations.

Lest there should still be room for the dangerous Jewish error of confounding the kingdom of Messiah with the kingdoms of this world, Matthew represents Jesus as still more clearly distinguishing between the two by his plain teaching that the two are distinct, — each being supreme in its own sphere. When the Herodians and Pharisees tempted him to teach sedition, by the crafty question, " Is it lawful to give tribute unto Cæsar or not ? " Mark and Luke represent him as saying " Bring me a penny ; " and it has been alleged that his admirable reply, when it was brought to him, " Render therefore unto Cæsar the things which be Cæsar's, and unto God the things which be God's," was only an ingenious evasion of the question put to him ; but as Matthew puts it, he said, " Shew me *the tribute money*," so that it was with the penny in his hand as tribute money that his reply was given ; and accordingly it was no evasion, but an explicit inculcation of the duty of payment.[1]

If there is still doubt, let it be remembered that Jesus actually paid tribute, and on one occasion wrought a miracle to provide the means of paying it (xvii. 24–27), — a fact which Matthew alone records.

[1] For a suggestive summary of facts on this and other points, see *The Four Evangelists*, by Rev. Edward A. Thomson, pp. 41–46.

Still further, it will be found by examination, that in the first Gospel only is the authority of Pilate, the civil ruler, distinctly recognized. In this Gospel alone he is the *governor*. Moreover, in this Gospel only, as has been shown, is there added to the rebuke to the unlawful resistance of Peter, recorded also by John, "Put up thy sword into his place," the significant words, "For all they that take the sword shall perish with the sword."

The foundation of the kingdom upon righteousness rather than force, its existence in the midst of the kingdoms of this world, its rejection by the great leaders and rulers of men, complete the evidence of its spirituality, and give the death-blow to all the carnal expectations of the Jews. It is to be a universal kingdom established by the preaching of the Gospel throughout the world (xxviii. 18-20).

SUMMARY.

To one casting a final glance back, from the point now reached, over the entire course of investigation pursued, the Jewish adaptation of the Gospel according to Matthew cannot fail to appear clearly.

It has been shown to be a historical fact that Matthew, a Jew eminently fitted for the task, wrote this Gospel for the Jews, the men chosen by God to be the custodians of both the doctrines and forms of the true and divine world-religion, and the men from whom and to whom the prophets had ages before declared that the Messiah was first to come. This is the historical foundation of the true theory of the Gospel.

It has also been shown that the first Gospel itself everywhere bears the marks of its Jewish origin and aim. This appears in its entire plan, which is the unfolding of the central idea that Jesus is the Messiah of the Prophets. It appears likewise in the omissions and additions made by the Evangelist, both of which have been shown to have been made to adapt it to the Jewish soul and its needs. It appears no less clearly in all its incidental variations from the others, and in all its incidental, at first view almost accidental, peculiarities, — the entire production being moulded and shaped and colored, in its narratives, sentences, and words, by its Jewish reference and adaptation.

It is not, therefore, too much to claim, that the historical and critical views of the Gospel combine to establish the theory that Matthew was originally the Gospel for the Jew, and to demonstrate that this theory is the true key to the Gospel.

PART III.

MARK, THE GOSPEL FOR THE ROMAN.

"Sole victor from th' expulsion of his foes
Messiah his triumphal chariot turn'd;
. . . .
Son, Heir, and Lord, to Him dominion given,
Worthiest to receive."

JOHN MILTON.

"The beginning of the Gospel of Jesus Christ, the SON OF GOD; as it is written in the Prophets, Behold, I send my messenger before thy face, which shall prepare thy way before thee. The voice of one crying in the wilderness, Prepare ye the way of the LORD; make his paths straight."

MARK i. 1–3.

"Secundus Marcus, interpres apostoli Petri, et Alexandrinæ ecclesiæ primus episcopus, qui Dominum quidem Salvatorem ipse non vidit, sed ea quæ magistrum audierat prædicantem, juxta fidem magis gestorum narravit quam ordinem."

JEROME.

CHAPTER I.

HISTORICAL VIEW OF THE ROMAN ADAPTATION OF THE SECOND GOSPEL.

SECTION I.

ORIGIN AND DESIGN OF THE SECOND GOSPEL.

FOLLOWING the order laid down in the investigation of the Gospel according to Matthew, it becomes necessary to ask and answer the questions: What was the actual origin of the Gospel according to Mark? For what class of readers was it immediately designed?

The latter question has seldom been asked, but a vast amount of time and effort has been expended upon the construction of *à priori* and imaginative theories of the origin of the second Gospel.

Perhaps the most popular of these theories is that of the critics who would have us believe that this Gospel is only a very awkward rehash of that according to Matthew, with the occasional addition, no less awkward, of some statement from Luke. The remarkable resemblance of the first and second Gospels seems at first sight to give probability to the theory, but it will be shown subsequently that this resemblance is to be accounted for in a different manner. The hasty and sometimes shabby treatment of the second Gospel by many of the commentators has done not a little to foster, in the minds of common readers, a view too closely allied to that of these critics.

A careful study of the Gospel itself, with a wise reference to the age in which it was produced and to the actual history of its origin, will reveal the fact that it has a distinct aim and an independent unity of its own. Such study will scarcely fail to convince the candid mind that Matthew is quite as likely to be a rehash of Mark, as Mark is of Matthew. At the same time, much more accordant with a due reverence for the four Gospels, as produced by the inspiration of the Holy Ghost and forming together one part of a great plan of that Being who never really wastes material, is the theory that each one of the Evangelists, in writing what he wrote, was directed by infinite wisdom to perform an essential and distinct service for the world.

From the historical point of view, it can be shown conclusively that the second Gospel was written for the Romans, the second of the three great representative races of which the civilized world of Mark's day was made up.

Witnesses. The most ancient direct testimony here, as in the case of Matthew, is that of Papias, as preserved by Eusebius. Papias recorded what he learned by inquiry from the disciples of the Apostles. "Mark, the interpreter of Peter, wrote carefully down all that he recollected, but not according to the order of Christ's speaking or working. For, as I think, he neither had heard Christ, nor was a direct follower of him. But with Peter, as already said, he was afterward intimate, who used to preach the Gospel for the profit of his hearers, and not in order to construct a history of the sayings of the Lord. Hence Mark made no mistake, since he so wrote some things as he was accustomed to repeat them from memory, and since he continually sought this one thing, — neither to omit anything of those things which he had heard, nor to add anything false to them." [1]

The character of Papias, his method, and the value of his testimony, have already been considered under the origin and design of the first Gospel. The considerations there adduced apply with equal force here. Irenæus confirms the testimony of Papias. He states that, after the departure of Peter and Paul from Rome, "Mark, the disciple and interpreter of Peter, did also hand down to us in writing what had been preached by Peter." [2]

Tertullian of Carthage, who wrote later, agrees with Irenæus, declaring incidentally that the Gospel "which Mark published may be affirmed to be Peter's, whose interpreter Mark was." [3]

Clement of Alexandria, who flourished in the latter

[1] Euseb. *Hist. Eccles.* iii. 39.

[2] Irenæus, *Against Heresies,* iii. 1; iii. 10; Euseb. *Hist. Eccles.* v. 8.

[3] Tertullian, *Against Marcion,* iv. 5.

part of the second century, brings out more explicitly the Roman aim of the second Gospel. His scholarly attainments, wide acquaintance with the Church, and nearness to apostolic times, all combine to make him a most valuable witness in this matter: his scholarly attainments, for, having studied first with the various philosophers, and afterwards with the distinguished Christian teachers, in Syria, Palestine, Greece, Italy, and Egypt, and having profited in all, he had scarcely an equal in his century, and so had readiest access to all the written opinions of the age; his wide acquaintance with the Church, — for his travels and studies brought him into contact with well-nigh its whole extent from east to west, and gave him opportunity to learn the traditions on all such points; his nearness to apostolic times, — for his life reached back so far as to need but a single link to connect it with the passing away of the last of the Apostles. With these facilities for arriving at the truth on that point, he makes his statement touching the aim of Mark's Gospel as an undisputed fact, and does it at a time when, if contrary to fact, it would have been the easiest thing conceivable to expose its falsehood.

His statement was originally made in the sixth book of his Institutions, a writing not now extant but quoted by Eusebius. It is to the effect, that when the Gospel was preached to the Romans "such a light of piety shone into the minds of those who heard Peter that they were not satisfied with once hearing, nor with the unwritten doctrine that was delivered, but earnestly besought Mark (whose Gospel is now spread abroad) that he would leave in writing for them the doctrine which they had received by preaching; nor did they cease until they had persuaded him, and so given occasion for the Gospel to be written which is now called after Mark. The Apostle, understanding this by the inspiration of the Holy Spirit, was pleased with the earnest desire of these men, and commanded this Gospel now written to be read in the churches."[1]

Clement elsewhere specifies some "Roman knights" as having made this request.[2]

Origen, the pupil of Clement, agrees with his master in his statement of the origin of the second Gospel. In the first book of his Commentaries on the Gospel of Matthew, in giving the catalogue of the New Testament Scriptures, he writes: "As I have understood from tradition, respecting the four Gospels, which are the only undisputed ones in the whole Church of God throughout the world; the first is written according to Matthew, the same that was once a publican, but afterwards an Apostle of Jesus Christ, who having published it for the Jewish converts, wrote it in the Hebrew; the second is according to Mark, who composed it, as Peter explained to him, who also acknowledges him as his son in his general Epistle, saying, 'The elect church in Babylon salutes you, as also Mark my son;' the third is according to Luke, the Gospel commended by Paul, which was written for the converts from the Gentiles; and last of all is the Gospel according to John."[3]

At a later date, Eusebius the historian sums up the unvarying testimony of those who have gone before, and gives his own indorsement to the statement that Mark wrote his Gospel under the direction of Peter, at the request of the brethren at Rome, and with a special view to circulation in Italy and among the Romans generally.[4]

Gregory Nazianzen confirms the main point in this testimony, in his Theological Poems, for the instruction

[1] Euseb. *Hist. Eccles.* ii. 15.

[2] *Adumbrat. in* 1 *Pet.* p. 1007.

[3] Euseb. *Hist. Eccles.* vi. 25; Orig. *Comm. in Matt.* i.

[4] Euseb. *Hist. Eccles.* ii. 15; vi. 14; vi. 25.

of the Church, declaring that Mark wrote his account of the miraculous works of Christ for Romans.[1]

Jerome writes that "the second Evangelist is Mark, the interpreter of Peter, and the first bishop of the Church of Alexandria, who did not himself see the Saviour, but related those things which he had heard his master preaching, and according to the belief of the reporters rather than in strict order."[2]

The veracity of these witnesses on this point has never been fairly impeached. No reasonable motive can be assigned for their making the main statements in which they agree, except the conviction that those statements were founded in fact.

Pertinent Facts. We are therefore justified in accepting as undoubted facts, that Mark wrote the second Gospel; that it was substantially the preaching of Peter to the Romans; that the Gospel was written at the request of Romans, and was intended to give the preaching of Peter a permanent form for them; and that it took advantage of the Roman peculiarities, and was fitted to commend Jesus, as the Saviour, to the Roman soul.

The theory advanced in the present work does not directly depend for its verification upon the establishment of the fact that Peter was actually at Rome and had to do with the founding of the church there; for the Gospel was preached to the Romans all over the ancient world. The ease with which many writers throw aside, as unworthy of belief, the Patristic traditions concerning the connection of Peter and Mark with Rome, is, however, to say the least, exceedingly marvelous. It appears all the more so when it is remembered that the Church rests upon the testimony of these same ancient writers for the most of her knowledge of the historic origin of the

[1] Greg. Naz. *Carmin.* lib. i. sect. i. 12, vers. 32.

[2] Hieron. *Comment. in Evang. Matth.* proleg. 3, 4.

canon of the Scriptures and of the Christian religion. The influence of the modern criticism is at present manifesting itself in the tendency to treat slightly the unvarying Patristic traditions touching the connection of Peter with the Gospel of Mark. The methods, scientific value, and inevitable results of such criticism have already been adverted to, in considering the origin and design of the first Gospel. The common-sense view, which is always in accordance with the truly scientific one, undoubtedly is that expressed by Principal Tulloch: "If the testimony of the Fathers is good for anything at all, this connection (of Peter with Mark's Gospel) is as certain as any historical fact can be, and not less important than it is certain."[1]

Indirectly, therefore, as was seen in discussing the fact of a Hebrew original of Matthew's Gospel, the theory of the historic origin of Mark does depend, in some measure, upon the acceptance of these facts so clearly and unmistakably stated by so many of the Fathers of the early Church; for the same false principles of criticism must sweep away the entire basis of history and leave the present swinging loose from all the past.

The clearly ascertained historical facts concerning the origin of the second Gospel, furnish the true starting-point in seeking an adequate understanding of the Gospel.

SECTION II.

THE CHARACTER AND NEEDS OF THE ROMAN.

If the second Gospel originated, as has been shown, in the preaching of Peter, and was prepared through the agency of Mark for Roman readers, the character and needs of the Roman must furnish the key to this Gospel.

[1] *Lectures on 'Vie de Jésus,'* p. 109.

The questions to be asked and answered here are: What manner of man was the Roman? What were his spiritual needs? The answers to these questions will cast light upon whatever has been prepared under the influence of the Holy Ghost for the Roman race.

I. *The Romans.*

Certain characteristics clearly distinguish the Romans from the other great historic races of the age of Christ. They represented the idea of active human power in the ancient world. They embodied that idea in the state or empire, as the repository of law and justice. They came in process of time to deify the state as the grandest concrete manifestation of power. With the consciousness of being born to rule the world, they pushed the idea of national power to universal empire.

Out of these characteristics, which made the Roman an altogether peculiar man among men, came his spiritual needs. Those needs were deepened and intensified by the ultimate failure of the Roman race in its attempted work for the world. Along the line of the peculiarities of this race must accordingly be sought the correct understanding of their Gospel requirements in the time of Christ and the Apostles.

Active Human Power. The Romans represented the idea of active human power in the ancient world.

The liberty is here taken of assuming that, under Providence, the history of each nation is, either consciously or unconsciously, the embodiment and working out of some grand idea. That idea once seized upon furnishes the key to the nation's character, conduct, and mission, and shows what is needed, humanly speaking, in order to commend Jesus Christ to that nation as the divine deliverer of men.

This key to the character, career, and wants of the Romans is found in the idea of power. In writing to the Christians at Rome, therefore, Paul is "not ashamed of the Gospel of Christ, because it is the *power* of God unto salvation to every one that believeth" (Rom. i. 16). What, then, was the Roman idea of power, in its essence, modifications, and developments?

The horizon of Rome, broad as it was, was yet limited to this world. The Roman was not, like the Jew, the representative of supernatural and divine power, but of power natural and human. Even this lower and narrower domain he did not wholly appropriate, but leaving human power, as power of reason expressing itself in thought, to the Greek, seized upon power of will, expressing itself in action, as his peculiar governing idea. The Roman, as such, cared little for distinctively supernatural and spiritual power such as moved the Jew; he cared as little for the logical and æsthetic power of the Greek; his was the power of will, his the beauty of action, his the logic of deeds. He became, accordingly, the mighty worker of the world, casting up the highways across empires, and leaving behind him public improvements in every form and of a grandeur fitted to astonish the race to the remotest ages.

Power in State and Law. The Romans embodied their peculiar idea of power in the state as the repository of law and justice. The will of the individual was lost in the will of the state, the Roman lost in Rome. Rome regarded the race as being in a condition of anarchy, so to speak, out of which it was her mission to bring it. Her power was power ordered and organized, taking the form of law and government, directing and controlling.

Law, and duty, or obedience to law, were ideas common to both Jew and Roman. But the Jew taught the world law in its statical, divine, and eternal relations. With him it was a divine precept revealed from heaven, pointing out the only way of blessedness and perfection for man here and hereafter, waiting patiently for man to come up to its requirements, and depending for its enforcement, not so much upon a present hand of power, as upon divine sanctions drawn from prophecy and all the working of providence and from the distant future. It said to men: "God is long-suffering and can afford to wait; but his law must be obeyed, for though the punishment of rebellion and evil-doing may be long deferred it will surely come at the last, since God is supreme." The Roman, on the contrary, gave the world law in its dynamic, governmental, and temporal aspects. With him it was not a precept waiting for man to fall in with it, but the expression of a present force, the organized and martial might of Rome, demanding submission and remorselessly crushing men and nations into its iron moulds. It said to men: "Rome is all-powerful and does not choose to wait; therefore yield on the instant or die." The career of the Roman was, therefore, one of conflict and control; war and law were necessary results of his nature. We are accustomed to say that he had a genius for war and government.

The State, divine and universal. In time the Roman deified the state as the grandest concrete manifestation of power. It is easy to see how it came about. The Jew had only the one God of revelation, Jehovah; the Greek had as many gods as there were qualities good and bad in human nature, and forces productive and destructive in physical nature; the Roman, at the first, accepted the gods of the Greek, but afterwards remade them to suit his own notions. With the growth of his power he outgrew them. Jupiter, Apollo, Bacchus, *et id genus omne*, became either insignificant or dead to him. The day came when an active, mighty embodiment of force, working triumphantly in the world's great changes, alone could claim his submission; and then Janus, the god of war, was exalted to the high place. As the last phase of the worship of Olympus, Rome herself became the god of the world in virtue of being the mightiest thing in it, and Victory became the embodied symbol of national power and success. Rome thus became to the Roman at once the kingdom of god and god.

The Roman had the consciousness of being born to rule the world. Under the special protection of his national divinities he pushed his way to universal empire.

The Embodiment of Natural Justice. In carrying out this mission the man of power became the representative of natural justice in the world. In the early history of the republic he was narrow and unpractical. His rule was then essentially one of caste, for it was only the Roman who was in compact with heaven, only the Roman to whom the gods of Rome vouchsafed special protection. It is true that the broader and more humane doctrines of Plato, and the marked providences which prepared for the Advent, modified and somewhat mollified his views at a later date; yet it must still be admitted that, at the time of Christ, with something of the same tenacity with which the Jew clung to the notion that he had exclusive claim to the blessings of the covenant with Jehovah, the Roman clung to the opinion that he alone was privileged and ordained of heaven to rule mankind.

As his ideas broadened through contact with many nations and by long experience, his entire system of laws came to be mainly controlled by those principles of natural justice which come out so clearly in the divine administration of the world. It was thus that in pushing forward the conquest of the world he became fitted to consolidate those conquests, and appeared at the last as the great organizer of the world into a single empire.

The Ideal Roman. The grandest Roman, the ideal man of the race, was therefore the mightiest worker, conqueror, organizer, and ruler, — the man who as *Cæsar* could sway the sceptre of universal empire. Cæsar and Cæsarism were the inevitable last result of Roman development.

II. *The Key to Mark's Gospel.*

If the Roman was, as thus shown, the man of action, of law and justice, of state worship, of universal empire, these characteristics must furnish the key to the Gospel intended for him.

Setting apart from all other men this man of power, — in the day when his splendid visions of empire had begun to fade, when disappointment and unrest were taking possession of his soul, and when he had been made to feel most deeply that natural justice in the hands of a human despot is a dreadful thing for sinful men, — the Holy Ghost proposes to commend to his acceptance Jesus of Nazareth as his Sovereign and Saviour, the expected deliverer of the world.

How shall it be done? Evidently — according to that law of divine fitness manifested everywhere in God's working — in that way which is best suited to the character and antecedents of the Roman. A Gospel for the Roman must be moulded by the Roman idea.

Scriptures and prophecy, so potent with the Jew, would count for little with the Roman; he was ignorant of both. Reason and philosophy, so convincing to the Greek, would be scoffed at by the Roman; he had no appreciation of either. Before the beginning of faith he was blind to the grand doctrines so precious to the Christian. The Gospel for him must present the character and career of Jesus from the Roman side, or point of view, as answering to the idea of divine power, work, law, conquest, and universal sway. It must exhibit Jesus as adapted, in his power and mercy, in his mission and work, to the wants of the Roman nature and world. To the Roman these are the credentials of Jesus, no less essential than prophecy to the Jew, or philosophy to the Greek. Without them there could not even be a reasonable hope of arresting his attention.

At the same time, while making the most of everything correct in the Roman idea, the Gospel must aim to correct the errors in it, and lift it to the level of the divine idea.

SECTION III.

THE AUTHORSHIP OF THE SECOND GOSPEL.

The divine adaptation of the second Gospel to the Roman race is seen in the selection of its author and in his preparation for his task.

I. *Mark.*

John Mark was the chosen instrument, in connection with the Apostle Peter. He was the son of an influential Christian matron of Jerusalem, named Mary, in whose house the believers at Jerusalem were wont to assemble (Acts xii. 12). He was evidently already known and esteemed in the Church and identified with it, when Luke wrote the Acts of the Apostles, or that Evangelist would not have introduced the mother to notice by naming the son.

Career and Character. He early devoted himself to the missionary work, accompanying Paul and his uncle Barnabas on their return from Jerusalem to Antioch (Acts xiii. 25). He also set out with these two men on their joint missionary journey (Acts xiii. 5), but turned back when they came to the more difficult and dangerous part of their work, and returned to Jerusalem

(Acts xiii. 13). When they were about to set out on a second journey to strengthen the churches, and extend the Gospel, Mark was at Antioch, and his uncle proposed that he should again accompany them, but Paul, remembering his former ignominious desertion, refused to allow it, and separated from Barnabas when he insisted upon it (Acts xv. 37).

This so pointed and vigorous rebuke seems to have had a salutary effect. We find Mark afterward at Rome with Paul during the imprisonment of the latter. The Apostle sends salutations from him to the Colossians (Col. iv. 10). In the second Epistle to Timothy he sends for him because he has found him a valuable assistant (2 Tim. iv. 11). In his Epistle to Philemon he mentions him among his fellow-workers and sends greeting to him (Philemon 24).

The same Mark is also found associated, probably at a later period, with the Apostle Peter. He sends greeting by Peter from Babylon (1 Pet. v. 13). The traditions of the early Church affirm that he afterward accompanied the same Apostle to the westward, and even to Rome. After the death of Peter, he is said to have preached in Africa, especially at Alexandria, where he suffered martyrdom in the most terrible manner.

In these facts are found clear indications of the character of the Evangelist. Although the son of a Jewess, and bearing a name of special significance to the Jew (John, *gift of Jehovah*), it may, perhaps, be justly inferred from the prevailing use of his Roman name, Mark, that he was preëminently Roman in his nature and development. He was, like Peter, originally a man of action rather than of deep and abiding principle, a man of fervor and enthusiasm rather than of persevering effort; but he was transformed, by the power of the same Christ who transformed Peter, into the man of rapid, continued and effective effort in the missionary work of the Church.

The change in character for the better is very manifest in what is known of his history. If, as has been supposed, the young man who followed Jesus into the city, having a linen cloth about him (Mark xiv. 15) was Mark, the hasty and impulsive character appears in both the following and the flight. It appears again in the ready entrance upon the missionary work, with Paul and Barnabas, and in the equally ready desertion. But the old enthusiasm revives and brings him back to Antioch again, and he engages anew in the work and makes such progress in energy and principle and steadfastness as to become one of Paul's most trusted and successful helpers. After endearing himself still more to the Apostle Peter in their mutual work across the Roman world, he at last bravely dares and endures the martyr's fate.

Special Training. It is certain that his training was eminently adapted to prepare him to exert an influence on the man of power and action.

Three men had to do chiefly with the shaping of his character after the Roman ideal. He was made to feel the influence of the gentle and merciful spirit of Barnabas, whose fellow-worker for Christ he was in his early life. He received the impress of the tremendous sustained energy of Paul, whose companion he was in the Apostle's earlier ministry, and again at Rome during his captivity (Col. iv. 10 ; Philemon 24). He was moulded by the restless, unwearying activity of Peter, whose convert he probably was (1 Pet. v. 13), whom he accompanied in his mission to Babylon (1 Pet. v. 13), and whose interpreter he was (according to the Fathers) in the mission to Rome in which the Apostle suffered martyrdom.

While being thus fashioned in character by these great

Apostles and preachers, he was providentially brought into the widest and most varied contact with the Empire, in its customs and language, in its law and legions, from the centre of authority at Rome to its remotest limits.

It likewise seems strikingly providential that one who had come so largely under the influence of the two men, Peter and Paul, who represented the Christian idea of the conquest of the whole world for Christ and the establishment of his universal kingdom (Gal. ii. 7–9), should be chosen to write the Gospel for the Roman, the man of universal empire.

II. *Peter.*

But the instrument, so fitted in character and training for the work of commending Jesus to the man of power, needed still to be supplemented. Mark was probably not personally cognizant of the facts of the Gospel, save perhaps the later ones. Peter, the man of deeds rather than words, was therefore appointed to supply in his preaching, out of his vivid memory, and after his striking manner, the materials for the Gospel, while Mark was appointed, under the influence of the Holy Spirit, and in accordance with his character and training, to give it final shaping.

Career and Character. No more remarkable character appears in Gospel history than Simon Peter. Nor is there a more remarkable instance of the transforming power of Jesus Christ.

The first words addressed to him by Jesus laid open his character, as he was at that time, and predicted what he should become through his acknowledgment of the Messiah (John i. 42): "*Thou art* Simon the son of Jona," the hearkening, timid one, *the unstable man;* "thou shalt be called," and, according to the Hebrew idea, *shalt become,* "Cephas," rock, *the stable man.*

Peter had the prime quality of the man of action, — his thoughts had the closest possible connection with the nerves of voluntary motion. With him for a thought to come into his mind was to have it express itself on the instant, at the end of the tongue, in the hand, or by the feet. He was the impulsive man.

But in the earlier part of his career he had also a marked defect, which went far toward making his activity mere unprincipled and irrational motion instead of rational, noble action, — the want of a settled purpose and grand governing motive pervading and controlling all the workings of his mind. Jesus, the Christ, was to furnish him with that, and thus to change the unstable *Simon Jona* into the stable *Cephas*.

In his early course instability, fickleness, was his most prominent characteristic. When Jesus came to the disciples, walking on the water, it was Peter that made haste to meet him, but whose faith failed on the instant (Matt. xiv. 28–31). It was Peter who, in Christ's extremity, declared that he would die rather than forsake his Master, but who in the midst of peril denied him thrice and with added profanity before the cock crew (Matt. xxvi. 33–35, 69–75). It was the impulsive Peter who ran to the sepuchre, at the report of the women, and rushed past John into the tomb to examine the burial vestments (John xx. 3–10); but it was also Peter who in ten days was ready to propose a return to the old occupation on the Lake of Tiberias (John xxi. 3), as if despairing of anything from Jesus of Nazareth. When Jesus came to the shore of Tiberias where the disciples were fishing, it was Peter who, seeing his Lord, jumped into the sea and swam ashore to him. After his Master, thrice addressing him as *Simon Jona*, to fix the old sin and fickleness in his heart, had restored him to the place of grace and apostleship from which he had fallen, it was

Peter who almost immediately asked that prying question, "And what shall this man do?" which called forth again the sharp rebuke of the Saviour. Even long after he had entered upon the full work of an Apostle, when the question of the circumcision of the converted heathen came up, Peter was the waverer and Paul was forced to withstand him to the face (Gal. ii. 11; Acts xv. 7–11).

Special Training. Nevertheless one cannot run in thought along his career without the growing conviction, that he made constantly increasing progress in stability of character and fixedness of purpose all the way to the last. It was Peter who stood up at Pentecost, and in that recorded sermon distinctly accused the Jews of murdering Jesus of Nazareth, and boldly proclaimed his resurrection and Messiahship (Acts ii. 22–36). It was Peter who in the days of persecution dared to defy the magistrates, at the peril of his life, in that noble assertion of liberty of conscience: "Whether it be right in the sight of God to hearken unto you more than unto God, judge ye" (Acts iv. 19). It was Cephas of whom Paul wrote as one of the *pillars* of the mother church at Jerusalem (Gal. ii. 9). According to tradition, Peter, when about to be crucified, besought that it might be with his head downward, since he who had once denied the Master was unworthy to die as the Master had died. So fully did Jesus, the Christ, infuse into his soul that one grand purpose which came to control all his life.

The remarkable development of his faculty for practical work and organization is equally manifest. His quick, impulsive nature prepared him to be a leader of men. The infusing of a grand governing principle was also a requisite for leadership. It is evident that Christ took advantage of these characteristics and made him, in a sense, a leader in the early Church. The natural impulse to leadership comes out in such instances as Peter's proposal to build tents on the Mount of Transfiguration (Matt. xvii. 4), and to elect a new Apostle in the place of Judas (Acts i. 15–22); and in many of the incidents just referred to as illustrating his original character. The divine calling to leadership appears from the representative place given to Peter in conferring upon the Church the power of the keys (Matt. xvi. 18, 19); from the prominent place accorded him in the wonderful events of Pentecost (Acts ii. 14, 38); and from the inspired acknowledgment of his relation to the Jewish world by Paul (Gal. ii. 7–9). It is therefore manifestly true that, as the Head of the Church has in all ages since selected and trained men for the special work of organizers, so in the apostolic age he selected and trained Peter for such a work. It was in this way that Jesus completed the character of Peter, the man of action. His thought still remained so closely connected with the power of action, the man the quick impulsive man still; but the profound Christian principle which had been infused brought the thought to be always true, the impulse to be always right, so that consistent and continued action at length made him in large measure the genuine representative of the unwearying, all-conquering, all-organizing Roman.

It was this Apostle, who loved action better than logic, who saw deeds rather than heard doctrines, who felt the need of earnest and consistent activity more than of a profound and harmonious creed, — this Apostle whose intense personal affection for Jesus had made him watch every act and gesture and look and word of his divine Master, — that was chosen to preach that Gospel which Mark was commissioned to record for the Romans.

These two, Mark and Peter, formed the one perfect instrument, the one complete medium for introducing Jesus to the favorable consideration of the Roman race of that age. No other men, equally fitted for embodying the Gospel in permanent form for the man of action and control, can be pointed out in connection with the apostolic body. Neither of these men could have accomplished the work alone; for, even if Mark was of Roman birth and nature, he had not the facts of the Gospel; and even if Peter was a man of action and trained as such, he was at the same time of Jewish birth and nature. The two were indispensable. The impulse which led the Romans to ask for the permanent record of the Gospel, and that which led Mark and Peter to accede to their request, were both from the Holy Ghost, the Spirit of all wisdom and power. Doubtless, out of all the men of that age, the Holy Ghost chose the men best fitted in their character and experience to prepare and write the Gospel for the Roman world.

CHAPTER II.

CRITICAL VIEW OF THE ROMAN ADAPTATION OF THE SECOND GOSPEL.

In examining the second Gospel, in the light of its ascertained origin, design, and authorship, its peculiar adaptation to the needs of the Roman of that age will become apparent. The order adopted in treating of the first Gospel will be followed in treating of the second.

SECTION I.

THE ROMAN ADAPTATION IN THE GENERAL PLAN OF THE SECOND GOSPEL.

The propriety of seeking for a plan of the Evangelist, different from that given by the division into sixteen chapters, has already been shown, in preparing the way for the analysis of Matthew's Gospel.

By examining the second Gospel with the aid of its known origin and aim, it will be seen that it may be naturally and conveniently divided, as that of Matthew was divided, into three principal parts, — presenting the successive stages of the work of Jesus, the Divine Conqueror, in establishing his universal empire, the kingdom of God, — with an appropriate introduction and conclusion.

In these divisions the character and career of Jesus are unfolded, not from the Jewish point of view, but in those aspects which are peculiarly Roman.

OUTLINE OF THE SECOND GOSPEL.

INTRODUCTION.

The Advent of the King and Conqueror. The Evangelist brings forward the Almighty King in his Divine Person and Kingdom. i. 1–ii. 12.

Section 1. Jesus is exhibited as being the Divine Son of God. i. 1–13.

A. In his name and heralding. 1–8.

B. In his divine recognition at the baptism, and in the subjection of Satan, the wild beasts, and the angelic world, at the temptation. 9–13.

Section 2. Jesus is exhibited mightily proclaiming the kingdom of power. i. 14–ii. 12.

A. In his opening proclamation of the kingdom of God in Galilee, and the call of the first subjects. i. 14–20.

B. In his opening works of power in Galilee, rising gradually to the authoritative pardon of sin, foreshadowing the future of the kingdom, and rousing the people. i. 21–ii. 12.

a. The authoritative teaching in the synagogue at Capernaum, the manifold works of power there, and the rising fame. i. 21–34.

b. The morning of solitary prayer, followed by the circuit of Galilee, with innumerable works of power, resulting in blazing abroad his fame. i. 35–45.

c. The subsequent return to Capernaum, the preaching of the word, the assumption of the divine prerogative of forgiving sin, amazing the people and leading them to glorify God. ii. 1–12.

PART I.

The Conflict of the Almighty King. The Evangelist exhibits Jesus in the teaching, work, and conflict of the period of public ministry devoted to the continued proclamation of the coming Kingdom of Power. ii. 13–viii. 26.

Section 1. He presents the teachings of Jesus concerning the foundations of the kingdom of God. ii. 13–v. 43.

A. In the subjects and law of the kingdom. ii. 13–iii. 35.

a. They are sinners, and not formalist Pharisees. ii. 13–iii. 12.

b. The first subjects are called out of all classes, and include all those whose law is the will of the Father. iii. 13–35.

B. In the law of growth and development in the kingdom. iv. 1–34.

a. By the quiet outgrowth of truth in the heart (the Sower). 1–25.

b. Yet independent of the will and effort of man (the Seed-corn). 26–29.

c. And destined to fill the whole earth with its greatness (the Mustard-seed). 30–34.

C. In the power of the King, who is omnipotent. iv. 35–v. 43.

a. Power over nature, in stilling the storm. iv. 35–41.

b. Power over the world of spirits and of irrational beings, in healing the Gadarene demoniac and destroying the swine. v. 1–20.

c. Power over the kingdom of disease and death, in healing the woman with the issue of blood, and in raising the daughter of Jairus. v. 21–43.

Section 2. He presents Jesus, in the activity of the work of the kingdom, passing through a series of conflicts and withdrawals. vi. 1–viii. 26.

A. Conflict in Nazareth with his old neighbors, leaving them in unbelief. vi. 1–6 (a).

B. Conflict in Galilee, in connection with the mission of the Twelve, and resulting in withdrawal across the Sea of Galilee. vi. 6 (b)–52.

a. The mission and work of the Twelve. 6 (b)–13.

b. The terror of Herod at the report of it, and the reason for that terror. 14–29.

c. The return and withdrawal of the Twelve, with the symbolical miracles of power and mercy, — the loaves and fishes and walking upon the storm-tossed lake. 30–52.

C. Conflict renewed in Galilee (in Gennesaret), resulting in rejection by Jerusalem Scribes and Pharisees and withdrawal to Gentile borders. vi. 53–viii. 9.

a. The return to Gennesaret, the miracles, and the controversy concerning unwashen hands. vi. 53–vii. 23.

b. The withdrawal to the Gentiles, and the miracles of grace, in healing the daughter of the Syro-Phenician woman in the borders of Tyre and Sidon, and in restoring the deaf and dumb man and feeding the four thousand beyond the Sea of Galilee. vii. 24–viii. 9.

D. Conflict renewed in Galilee, in Dalmanutha, with

the local Pharisees, and the withdrawal and work of mercy on the blind man in Bethsaida Julias. viii. 10–26.

PART II.

The Claim of the Almighty King. The Evangelist exhibits Jesus, the Almighty Conqueror, as distinctly claiming the right to the Kingdom of Power, to be won through suffering and rejection, and both explaining and maintaining his claim. viii. 27–xiii. 37.

Section 1. He presents Jesus teaching his followers that the kingdom is to be won by triumph over suffering and death. viii. 27–x. 45.

A. In a first revelation, occasioned by the confession of Peter, foretelling *the rejection of "the son of man" by the Jewish Sanhedrim*, followed by exhibitions of divine glory, and by exertions of divine power which are traced to the secret source of all power. viii. 27–ix. 29.

B. In a second revelation, foretelling *the treachery of his own followers*, and followed by a period of instruction in the duties of subjects in the kingdom. ix. 30–x. 31.

C. In a third revelation, foretelling *his death by the Roman rulers*, and followed by instruction concerning the way for the subjects to rise to power in the kingdom. x. 32–45.

Section 2. He presents Jesus claiming the right to the kingdom of power, in the city of David, and establishing his claim, although rejected by the Jews. x. 46-xiii. 37.

A. In his public advent as the almighty heir of David, and in the accompanying works of power. x. 46–xi. 26.

a. At Jericho listening to the appeal of Bartimeus. x. 46–52.

b. At the triumphal entry into the Holy City. xi. 1–10.

c. In cursing the fig-tree and assuming royal authority in the temple, and in revealing anew the source of all true power. xi. 11–26.

B. In his conflict with and overwhelming triumph over the various leading classes. xi. 27–xii. 44.

a. Jesus on the defensive, — against the Sanhedrim, the Pharisees and Herodians, the Sadducees and the Scribes. xi. 27–xii. 34.

b. Jesus taking the offensive, warning against the doctrine of the Scribes, and contrasting with their religion the genuine piety of the poor widow. xii. 35–44.

C. In his prophetic unfolding, for his disciples, of both the near and remote future of Jerusalem and his kingdom. xiii. 1–37.

a. The events preceding the future coming. 1–23.

b. The coming of the king in power and glory and the urgent call for watchfulness and prayerfulness. 24–37.

PART III.

The Sacrifice of the Almighty King. The Evangelist exhibits Jesus, preparing for the setting up of the Kingdom of Power through his sacrificial sufferings and death. xiv. 1–xv. 47.

Section 1. He presents the preliminary preparation for his death. xiv. 1–41.

A. In the plotting of the Sanhedrim, the anointing for the burial, and the treachery of Judas. 1–11.

B. In the Passover supper, when Jesus puts himself symbolically in the place of the paschal sacrifice. 12–26.

C. In the sorrow over the foreseen desertion, and in the struggle with the terrors of death in Gethsemane. 27–41.

Section 2. He presents Jesus in the hands of his enemies, the sinful leaders and rulers of the Jewish nation. xiv. 42–xv. 47.

A. In his betrayal and apprehension. xiv. 42–52.

B. In his trial before the Sanhedrim. 53–72.

C. In his trial and delivering up by Pilate. xv. 1–15.

D. In the hands of the executioners, the Roman soldiers, — in the Prætorium, on the way to Golgotha, and on the cross. 16–41.

E. Under the power of death. 42–47.

CONCLUSION.

The Universal Empire established. The Evangelist exhibits Jesus, the Almighty King, conquering death and taking the universal Kingdom. xvi. 1–20.

Section 1. He presents him as rising from the dead and convincing his disciples of his identity. xvi. 1–14.

Section 2. He presents him as actually establishing the universal kingdom. xv. 15–20.

A. In the Great Commission with its promise of grace. 15–18.

B. In the assumption of divine authority in heaven. 19.

C. In coöperating with his disciples in the fulfillment of the Great Commission. 20.

SECTION II.

THE ROMAN ADAPTATION IN THE CENTRAL IDEA OF THE SECOND GOSPEL.

The outline thus given may be left to witness for itself that the second Gospel was prepared by Mark for Roman readers. In connection with its systematic exhibition of the material of the Gospel, it may more readily be shown how the central idea and general drift of Mark's production confirm the historical testimony regarding the Roman aim of the Evangelist.

I. *The Central Idea.*

It is a principle, now coming to be generally admitted, that in all literature the organic idea will give shape to the characters, incidents, metaphors, diction, and phraseology, — to the entire tone and tenor of a production, — a principle that holds not less clearly in Matthew's or Mark's Gospel than in Shakespeare's Hamlet. One of the very first inquiries, therefore, must be: What is the central or organic idea of the second Gospel?

The central idea of the Gospel according to Mark is found in the opening verse: "The Gospel of Jesus Christ the Son of God (Mark i. 1). The Evangelist, accordingly, presents Jesus, not as the fulfillment of a past divine revelation, as does Matthew; nor as the satisfaction of present human yearning, as does Luke; nor as the foundation of the future Church, as does John; but as the personal embodiment of the Son of God, in the fullness of his present, living energy, demonstrating himself the Son of God by his divine working. Everything, from the opening with the mission of the Baptist to the closing vision of Jesus exalted to the throne of God, is so shaped as to deepen the impression of his almighty power.

This Gospel represents him as proclaiming and establishing a kingdom, but it is a kingdom of power, and not of prophecy. While, therefore, Mark has so much in common with Matthew that many insist that he is a mere copyist or abridger, there is yet this wide difference, that whereas Matthew rests wholly on prophecy, Mark is so entirely independent of prophecy that, after the opening verses, he never even records the words of a prophet, except as he quotes from the mouth of Jesus.

For the Roman, the mighty worker and conqueror of the world, Jesus is held up as the divine almighty worker and victor. While Matthew furnishes us with the ancient types of Christianity, Luke with its inmost connection with the unchanging heart of humanity, and John with its deeper spiritual mysteries, Mark holds up "the picture of the sovereign power of Jesus, battling with evil among men swayed to and fro with tumultuous passions."

Lange, in the Introduction to his Commentary on this Gospel, has attempted — and with success — to show that the Gospel may be divided into "a progressive series of victorious conflicts," beginning with the conquest of the four chosen Apostles and ending with the final subjection and possession of the whole world. Through perpetual victory — victory even in seeming defeat, — the King, the incarnation of almighty power, moves on to realize the Roman ideal of universal dominion. It is therefore the almighty conqueror, and not the servant (symbolized by the *ox* of prophecy) as the allegorical interpreters would have it, that appears in Mark's delineation of Jesus.

But since the Roman had felt the crushing power of *the iron kingdom* and the remorseless cruelty of *the ferocious beast* of prophecy, Mark presents with peculiar distinctness the diviner aspects of the kingdom of God, — its spirituality and mercy no less than its power and righteousness. This great world-conflict and conquest, so realizing the Roman idea and yet so surpassing it, is everywhere represented as carried on with spiritual forces and weapons, and for spiritual ends. In retirement from men and in communion with the heavenly world the king is girded for the battle. No noise of spear or battle-axe is heard, for the contest is waged against the devil, his demons and his human agents in the world. The removal of the miseries of the world is sought through the forgiveness and eradication of sin. The Conqueror crushes into fragments the old social world, but he crushes it in mercy; and he reconstructs it not as the Roman has done — in the moulds of resistless and savage justice, — but by the law of righteousness and charity. The false Roman idea of power, weapons, conflict, victory, and empire are discarded, and true spiritual ideas made increasingly prominent from the opening of the Gospel to the close.

There are suffering and death in the kingdom, as in the earthly kingdom, but they are transformed. The suffering is not inflicted upon the vanquished, but endured by the victor for the sake of the victory of mercy and blessing. The death is borne by the conqueror to furnish the foundation and the beginning of a higher life of blessedness for all the king's subjects. To the Roman, with his deepening sense of misery under the stern reign of natural justice, as imperfectly embodied in Rome, Mark makes his exhibition of the kingdom of God in the fullest signification a *Gospel*, by portraying the career of the King and his conquering hosts as subordinately a career of humble service, of kindly ministrations, of boundless sacrifices, of cheerful suffering, and even of voluntary death, in order to save the perishing race from its heavy woes. The complete triumph is reached in the final conquest of death and the world.

In the great features of both character and career, Jesus eclipses all that is mightiest and best in the old Roman ideal, while at the same time correcting and exalting it.

II. *The General Drift.*

The influence of this central Roman idea is manifest throughout the second Gospel, in a general movement and drift quite unlike that of the other Gospels.

Rising above all the details of the Gospel according to Mark, Da Costa has clearly pointed out certain peculiarly Roman and soldierly features that characterize it as a whole. By a deliberate comparison he finds that its style bears a close resemblance to that of Cæsar's Commentaries, — both exhibiting the same emphatic repetition combined with the same rapidity of movement, the same copiousness of description with the same dramatic effect, so that even the word *straightway* (εὐθέως) — which is so characteristic of Mark, being employed in his Gospel about forty times — appears in the writings of the great Roman captain in the ever-recurring *celeriter*. No work of old Roman, in short, was ever more Roman in its rhetorical movement than the Gospel according to Mark.

With an aim differing from that of the present work, and yet in a form suited to the present purpose, the same distinguished author has called this Gospel, "The brief and terse narrative of that *three years' campaign*, so to speak, of the supreme Captain of our salvation — whose name from of old was *Warrior* as well as *Prince of Peace*, — carried on and completed, for the deliverance of our souls, the bruising of Satan, the glorifying of the Father, in his labors, his sufferings, his death, his resurrection and final triumph." [1]

This moulding of the entire material by the Roman aim of the Evangelist may be traced through the Gospel.

In the Introduction, Jesus is brought forward at once as the Son of God, and by a few rapid and graphic strokes is exalted to the very throne of the God of power.

To follow these rapid strokes in detail: a mighty prophet appears to herald the coming of one infinitely mightier, *the Lord;* at the baptism of that mightier One the heavens are rent open in acknowledgment of his Divinity; and when the Spirit has driven him into the wilderness three worlds gather round him. John is cast

[1] *The Four Witnesses*, pp. 111, 135.

into prison, and the wonder-working activity of this Son of God begins at once. He proclaims the kingdom of God at hand. He calls men, and they *straightway* follow him. He enters the synagogue at Capernaum on the Sabbath, and *at once* begins to teach ; the audience is astonished at the authority of his teaching; a demon recognizes his divinity and proclaims it, and is expelled by his power. Men are amazed at the omnipotence of his command, and his fame *immediately* spreads through Galilee.

And in this same life-like manner he is hurried from miracle to more notable miracle, from fame to more general fame, and from power to still greater power, until, in the space of forty-four verses, we find him exalted to the place of *God*, the righteous, moral Governor of the universe, *forgiving the sins* of the poor paralytic, while the people, in their amazement, glorify *God*, who is revealed there as they had never seen before.

Although all the main facts of this Introduction appear in the other Gospels, yet it is as different from them all as if every one of its facts were new. Everything in it is familiar as possible, and yet the delineation is as vivid as if everything were strange as possible. Throughout there is just the logic to attract the attention and arouse the interest of the man of power, who is too much given to making history to stop to interpret prophecy, too much engaged in rapid doing to pause for slow philosophizing, and too much absorbed in reorganizing and remoulding the present visible world to be disposed directly to give heed to the facts of an invisible and spiritual world, — just the logic for the Roman.

Part First of Mark's Gospel, exhibiting the foundations of the kingdom of God, may be looked upon as corresponding in part to Matthew v. 1–ix. 35, to Luke vi.–vii., and to John iii. Comparing it with these, there is noth ing in it of that reference to Judaism as the basis of the law of the kingdom, in which Matthew abounds; nothing of the philosophic presentation of the world-embracing law of charity to which Luke — writing for the universal man — devotes his space; nothing of the theology of the new life in which John delights. In short, Mark drops entirely the form of connected discourse in which the other Evangelists present the fundamental ideas of the kingdom and gives the character of the subjects, the law of growth and the power of the King, by a rapid succession of incidents, parables, and miracles, in what, for ease of execution and vividness of effect, must be acknowledged an incomparable picture.

In the Introduction and Part First, Jesus appears as the Son of God, wielding almighty power *in its most tangible forms*, in the former exercising the prerogatives of God himself, and in the latter demonstrating himself Lord of the universe. The Roman, the man of power, is thus as irresistibly attracted toward him, as the Jew, the man of prophecy, is by the genealogy of Messiah and other opening features of Matthew, and as the Greek, the world-man, is by the philosophic development of the life of the marvelous divine man by Luke, and as the Christian, the man of faith, is by the different opening, concerning the eternal Word, by John.

Part Second, in delineating the kingdom of power in the activity of its conflict, still holds the attention of the Roman by miracles second in grandeur to none of those which have preceded; yet, in the fourfold withdrawal from enemies, — from Nazareth, from Herod, from the Jerusalem Scribes and Pharisees, and from the local Pharisees of Dalmanutha, — it gives rising prominence to the spiritual weapons and influences by which the victory is to be gained, and which in the remainder of the Gospel are to hold the chief place.

Part Third, with its lesson of conquest by suffering, records in its opening section, after the confession of the Twelve, the transcendent miracle of the transfiguration with its divine recognition of the Son of God, and also the healing of the dumb demoniac at the foot of the mountain; but the spiritual element, exalted in the consequent revelation of the secret source of power in the kingdom in prayer and fasting, predominates from this point onward.

The presentation of the public claim of the King in Jerusalem has at the outset the restoring of sight to Bartimeus and the symbolic cursing of the fig-tree; but from that point forward the miracles of power, — the healing in the temple, the healing of the ear of Malchus, and all the wonders that gathered about the cross except the rending of the temple veil, — disappear from Mark's record, leaving only the miracles of foresight. The scenes of the last days are left to depend for their impressiveness upon the power of the naked facts of the final struggle with the Jewish authorities and the death upon the cross, — facts depicted with the life-like touch of an eye-witness, and fitted to draw from every true Roman the exclamation of the centurion at the cross, "Truly this man was the Son of God!" The narrative thus makes manifest that this Son of God, who wields at pleasure almighty power, is not to establish his kingdom by that, but by the ministrations of love, and the suffering of death in the sinner's stead, — thus conquering by a new power infinitely mightier than that embodied in old Rome.

It only remains at this point for the Evangelist to sketch the victory over death and the doubts of the amazed disciples, and the establishment of the universal kingdom by the new spiritual forces and weapons; and this Mark does in the final chapter, the appropriate conclusion of this Gospel, in which the almighty King is enthroned and the work of conquest organized and pushed to its completion.

All this was just what was needed to commend Jesus as a Saviour to the Romans. It was, moreover, a true view of the man of Nazareth, in whose many-sided character was found not only the Messiah, the ideal Jew, but also the universal Conqueror and King, the ideal Roman. This Jesus, the inheritor of all the true power and manhood found in the Roman nature, and adding to this a divine power and manhood, is the Jesus represented by Mark.

SECTION III.

THE ROMAN ADAPTATION IN THE OMISSIONS AND ADDITIONS OF THE SECOND GOSPEL.

The Roman design of the second Gospel is manifest as well from that which the Evangelist omits of what is found in the other Gospels, as from that which he adds to what is found in them.

I. *The Omissions of the Second Gospel.*

It will be seen on examination, that Mark omits whatever is distinctively Jewish, Greek, or Christian, and would therefore be of little if any service in his work of presenting his Gospel to the Roman. Any one even tolerably familiar with the evangelical records will remark how very extensive these omissions are.

From Matthew. As compared with Matthew's Gospel, which it most resembles, the omission throughout the second Gospel of the Jewish features will at once appear even to a cursory reader.

The long discourses which make up so large a part of Matthew are not found in Mark. According to the testimony of Papias, Mark gives an account of "things both said and done"[1] by Jesus; but the "things said" were rather incidental or brief sayings than systematic and extended discourses. The sermon on the Mount (Matt. v.–vii.); the charge to the Twelve (Matt. x.); the discourse to his disciples exhorting them to watchfulness and activity in waiting for his coming to judgment (Matt. xxiv.–xxv.), are not in the second Gospel. Aside from the fact that the Roman appreciated deeds rather than discourses, these discourses would have been to him peculiarly devoid of interest, since they deal so largely with Jewish ideas, and aim so directly to correct Jewish errors or to guide Jewish life.

But besides these great omissions, it has been remarked that there is in this Gospel a general freedom from Jewish references, and from everything that the Jew alone could fully understand and appreciate.

There is almost nothing in Mark of the Messianic origin and prophetic preparation of Jesus, to which Matthew devotes his entire introduction of more than three chapters (Matt. i. 1–iv. 11); and even that which does appear is with a different aim from Matthew's, — to give an impressive picture of Christ's opening work. John the Baptist comes forward in the wilderness in picturesque garb as the herald of Jehovah, the mighty coming Conqueror; Jesus appears at the baptism and is acknowledged by God as his "beloved Son;" and is then immediately driven into the wilderness, where Satan appears to tempt him, the wild beasts to terrify him, and the angels to minister to him (Mark i. 1–13).

Mark omits the parables of special Jewish significance.

Of the series of seven, delivered on the sea-side, only two are retained: that of the sower (Mark iv. 1–25), as containing a truth equally applicable to all men concerning the proclamation of the Gospel and the growth of the

[1] Euseb. *Hist. Eccles.* iii. 39.

kingdom of God; and that of the mustard-seed (Mark iv. 30–34), which exhibits, in a peculiarly Roman aspect, the world-wide growth of the kingdom. The remaining five, as meant especially for the Jew, are passed over; that of the tares (Matt. xiii. 24–35), as representing the field of the Messiah's work as not confined to the Jews as they suppose, but as extending to the whole world; that of the leaven (Matt. xiii. 33), as exhibiting the influence of the Gospel not as Jew-transforming merely, as the Jews thought, but as world-transforming; that of the hid treasure (Matt. xiii. 44), and that of the pearl (xiii. 45), as representing that the kingdom of heaven is not to be found and won easily by the king as something embodied in the Jewish institutions, as the Jews vainly believed, but rather as something concealed from the gaze of men, to be sought diligently by the divine King and to be purchased by him at the greatest cost (John i. 11); and that of the draw-net (Matt. xiii. 47–50), as teaching a mixed condition of things in the kingdom, rather than the exclusiveness of their own national election, of which the Jews boasted.

The reader of Mark's Gospel will also note the absence of the numerous parables condemnatory of the Jews, found in the latter half of Matthew's Gospel. The Jewish lessons of these parables would have been lost upon the Romans. There is doubtless the further reason for their omission, that, as the parabolic form of instruction was adopted by our Lord for the purpose of partially hiding the truth from the blinded Jews (Matt. xiii. 10–16), it could scarcely have been at all intelligible to Romans, who were entirely unaccustomed to deal with highly figurative forms of speech.

The same thing is illustrated by Mark's treatment of the first of the three series of miracles, given by Matthew to confirm the authority of Jesus as the Messiah, — the series designed to show the relation of Jesus to the Jewish ceremonial law (Matt. viii. 1–17). The first miracle, the healing of the leper, is recorded by Mark (i. 40–45) in bringing out the wonderful power and fame of Jesus, the Roman aspect of his work. The second, the healing of the centurion's servant, is omitted, as it chiefly presents the contrast of Gentile faith with Jewish unbelief. The third, the healing of Peter's wife's mother, with the added works of power, is recorded by Mark (i. 29–34), as exhibiting the excitement in the city and the marvelous power of Jesus over diseases, demons, and men; but the reference which Matthew (viii. 16, 17) makes to prophecy is omitted.

A notable exception to the general freedom of Mark from Jewish references appears, however, in the record of the conflicts of Jesus, with the disciples of John and the Pharisees, at the feast of Levi, about fasting (Matt. ix. 10–17; Mark ii. 15–22); and with the Pharisees about the desecration of the Sabbath (Matt. xii. 1–14; Mark ii. 23–iii. 6). It has been already seen, in the portraiture of the Roman character, that the genuine Roman-born man was, on his religious side, the Pharisee of the empire, considering himself — as did the Pharisee of Judæa — the only favored child of heaven. It was true of *his* religion, that it was a mere empty form and tradition, nay, more, an acknowledged hyprocrisy, for the priests of the Pantheon could not look each other in the face without laughing outright at the farce they were enacting. The Roman needed, therefore, to be taught, by Christ's treatment of Jewish caste, the true doctrine of equality on the basis of manhood, in the kingdom of God, and, by his treatment of Jewish formality and hypocrisy, the true doctrine of the spirituality and sincerity of the religion of the kingdom. Yet it must be observed that even these incidents are stripped of everything that a

Jew only could understand, and the passage in which they occur is completed by Christ's demonstration, in the healing of the withered hand, of his Lordship over the Sabbath.

From Luke. As compared with the third Gospel, the omission of the merely Greek features is equally apparent.

There is nothing in Mark of the marvelous coming down of heaven to earth, and of that human development of Jesus as the divine and perfect man, to which the introduction of Luke is devoted (Luke i. 1–iv. 13). These matters, which will be seen to be of such absorbing interest and such eminent appropriateness for the Greek, were not in place for the man of deeds.

The part of this material which Mark uses has reference to the baptism of John and the temptation, and is all comprised in ten verses. In the record which Matthew makes of the Baptist's mission, the fulfillment of prophecy is the prominent feature; in that of John, the testimony of the Baptist to the Lamb of God, the light and life of men; in that of Luke, the salvation of God for all flesh is the new thought brought out; in that of Mark, the mighty herald before Jehovah, the almighty conqueror. Equally characteristic is the omission by Mark of the human experience of Jesus in the temptation, as given by Luke and Matthew, while he only aims to bring out for the Roman reader, in the most graphic manner, the situation of the Saviour in the wilderness.

Indeed, the absence of those universal and human features, which will be shown to be so essential to the third Gospel, cannot fail to be noted throughout the second.

The successive stages of the life of Jesus, upon which Luke dwells, are not even mentioned by Mark. Jesus appears at once with his powers full-summed and at their highest, and engages without delay in his work as the almighty Victor. For the Roman there is but one stage in his career.

The entire ministry in Peræa, constituting almost one half of Luke's Gospel, and presenting the divine mercy in its most tender aspects to universal humanity, has no place in Mark. That which was fitted to move and mould the gentle Greek, with his thoughtful and beautiful soul, was not suited to influence the stern and martial Roman, who had in his nature as little as possible of beauty and sentiment. There are therefore wanting in the second Gospel the great parables of Luke, the favorites of all ages : the two debtors, the good Samaritan, the friend at midnight, the rich fool, the barren fig-tree, the great supper, the lost sheep, the lost piece of money, the prodigal son, the unjust steward, the rich man and Lazarus, the unprofitable servants, the unjust judge, the Pharisee and the publican, and the pounds ; besides the other rich instructions addressed to the heathen people in Peræa, or the country across the Jordan (Luke ix.–xix.), and suited to the man of universal sympathies.

From John. As compared with the fourth Gospel, the omission of the distinctively Christian features is apparent everywhere in the second.

Strictly speaking, Mark gives nothing of the great Christian discourses that make up the Gospel according to John. In a missionary Gospel aiming at the conversion of the Roman, they would have utterly failed to be appreciated.

These two Gospels have little in common save a few striking facts. These appear in Mark as facts in the wonder-working power of the conqueror, or as facts centring in the cross and essential to redemption. The former kind comprises the feeding of the five thousand (Mark vi. 32–44 ; John vi. 1–14), and the walking of Jesus on the water (Mark vi. 45–56 ; John vi. 15–21).

The latter kind embraces many of the incidents of the last Passover week, and some of those after the resurrection. It will be seen, however, that the great Christian lessons, which John connects with or draws from these facts, do not find place in Mark's Gospel.

II. *The Additions of the Second Gospel.*

The Gospel according to Mark gives equally conclusive evidence of its Roman aim in what it adds to the records of the other Gospels.

A mechanical criticism has shown that, if the Gospel of Mark is regarded as made up of one 100 parts, 7 of these are peculiar to itself, and 93 common to it with one or more of the other Gospels. Substantially the same fact appears in the statement that there are but twenty-three or twenty-four verses in Mark which are not found also in Matthew or Luke.

The historical origin of the Gospels, as already exhibited, opens the way to an explanation of the resemblances as well as the differences of the first three Gospels. Both Matthew and Peter were Apostles and familiar with the facts of the career of Jesus of Nazareth. Luke and Paul doubtless learned the facts and discourses either directly or indirectly from the Apostles, except so far as Paul was taught by Christ himself (Gal. i. 12).

The verbal coincidences between the first three Gospels, which have led to the many ingenious hypotheses regarding their common origin, can better be accounted for without these elaborate imaginings. Mr. Westcott has observed that " they occur most commonly in the recital of the words of our Lord or of others, and are comparatively rare in the simple narrative. Thus, of the verbal coincidences in St. Matthew about seven eighths, of those in St. Mark about four fifths, and of those in St. Luke, about nineteen twentieths, occur in the records of the words of others."[1] The recitative portions — discourses, parables, etc. — came from the lips of Jesus himself, were fixed in the minds of the Apostles, were reproduced in their preaching and embodied in the Gospels, which therefore could not fail to be alike in these respects. The narrative portions were given their shape in each case by the individual Apostle or Evangelist, and therefore could not but be different. There is, therefore, no call for any elaborate hypothesis.

The extraordinary resemblance of Mark's Gospel to that of Matthew has led to three hypotheses of their connection: a first, that Matthew is an enlargement of Mark; a second, that Mark is an abridgment of Matthew; a third, that both had a common basis in an oral Gospel which existed in the Church at the time of their origin and from which they alike drew their material.

But there is hardly a necessity for arbitrary conjecture in accounting for this most extraordinary resemblance, since history with the aid of common sense furnishes a far better explanation of the facts. Matthew and Peter were both personally cognizant of the great facts which they recorded, and they both first entered upon the work of preaching the Gospel to the Jews in Judæa. There is doubtless so much of truth in the theory of a common oral Gospel. The idea of power had its attractions, as has been seen, for both the Jew and the Roman. When Peter went abroad to proclaim the Gospel over the world, it was therefore natural that he should retain the exhibitions of the miraculous power of Jesus with which the preaching in Judæa had made him so familiar. It was equally natural and necessary that, in seeking to reach and influence hearers moulded by the Roman civilization, he should drop the references to prophecy which were un-

[1] Westcott, *Introduction*, p. 203.

intelligible to the Romans, and give to everything that increased vividness and picturesque effect without which their attention could not be won and retained.

From the small additions and large subtractions of the second Gospel, the mechanical critics have inferred the want of any great special significance of this Gospel. In their view it is the least important of all, in fact, of almost no value to those who have Matthew's Gospel. The inference warranted is, rather, that the criticism which sees so little difference and is content with looking only at outward dissimilarity is itself insignificant and worthless.

A true and worthy criticism cannot fail to demonstrate that the number of verses in which Mark's Gospel outwardly differs from the others is no proper measure of the real and essential difference. The score of verses, more or less, which he adds to the records of the other Evangelists, forms the least of all his contributions to the Gospel treasure. The greater additions will appear under the incidental changes and variations of this Gospel.

But even the slighter and less important direct additions may be shown to have aided materially in adapting the second Gospel to Roman readers.

The portions usually reckoned additions to this Gospel are the following: the parable of the seed-corn (Mark iv. 26–34); the healing of the blind man of Bethsaida (viii. 22–26); the healing of the deaf man of Decapolis (vii. 31–37); and the form of the last commission (xvi. 15–18).

The longest of all these is the parable of the seed-corn, occupying nine verses. Mark has altogether only four parables, and this is the only one peculiar to his Gospel. One of the four, that of the wicked husbandmen (xii. 1–12), is introduced by Mark, as also by Matthew and

Luke, in its proper place in connection with the series of conflicts in which Jesus engaged with the leading classes. The remaining three constitute Mark's group of parables.

The three can best be understood together. They have nothing to do with portraying the world-wide mercy to which Luke's parables, occurring later in his Gospel, are devoted; nor with the spiritual truth and the blessed relations of Christ to his people, which those of John exhibit; nor with the inward, subjective influences, to the setting forth of which a part of those in Matthew's first great group are devoted; but are all employed in unfolding the growth of the kingdom as an *outward, objective thing*. The first (the sower) contradicts the false Roman idea, by putting the invisible, spiritual power of truth in the place of the visible, material power of the Cæsars; the second (the seed-corn) presents a development as independent of human will and as inevitable as that of Rome herself according to the most Roman conception; the third (the mustard-seed) completes the sketch of the development of the kingdom, by depicting its rapid growth into that universality which Rome, alone of all the worldly empires, had even imperfectly realized.

The next addition, the healing of the deaf and dumb man of Decapolis (vii. 31–37), comprises seven verses. There is another, the healing of the blind man of Bethsaida (viii. 22–26), which is not unlike it. The two are among the most striking of the miracles of Jesus, and, through the symbolical acts connected with them most eminently fitted to make a deep impression on the man of deeds. In the former miracle, the great Healer put his finger into the ears of the man, and spitting touched his tongue with the spittle, by these signs to awaken the faith of the man and arouse his expectation of blessing.

In the latter miracle, Jesus performed a progressive cure, — first spitting upon the blind man's eyes and putting his hands upon him, thereby bringing him to "see men as trees walking;" and afterward putting his hands again upon his eyes, and making him to "see every man clearly." Both miracles furnish striking symbols of the dealings of divine grace with sinful man; both picture Christ's saving power for the easy comprehension of the man of action.

The last of these added passages in the second Gospel, the great commission, in a form quite peculiar (xvi. 15–20), presents not only the warrant of the followers of Christ for the conquest of the whole world, — the orders of the army of the great conqueror for its marching and action, — but also the promise of miraculous, divine coöperation, through the exaltation of the risen and ascended Son of God with his Father on the throne of the universe. It closes with the record of the actual pushing out into all the world, by the followers of our Lord, of the work of universal conquest (verse 20). It is the true Gospel commission for the man of action and of universal empire, the Roman.

Both the omissions and additions of the Evangelist were eminently fitted to commend Jesus to the Roman world of that age.

SECTION IV.

THE ROMAN ADAPTATION IN THE INCIDENTAL VARIATIONS OF THE SECOND GOSPEL.

The adaptation of Mark's Gospel to the Roman needs appears even more clearly in the incidental variations and peculiarities throughout the entire production. In these features, as already intimated, are to be found Mark's most important contributions to the Gospel treasure. He has added something of value to almost every line which he has given in common with the other Evangelists. By variations of incident, by touching, shaping, or coloring, and by new and fresh grouping of the facts, he has produced out of apparently old material an original Gospel, into the entire tone and movement of which he has infused, by the aid of the Holy Spirit, a living energy born of Jesus, the divine and almighty worker and conqueror.

I. *Incidental Variations.*

It has often been noticed that Mark's is the Gospel of minute and vivid details.

Through Peter, whose amanuensis or interpreter he is, in a sense, to be regarded, the Evangelist takes the position of an eye-witness and ear-witness, and renders everything life-like by the thousand varied and delicate touches fitted to make past events become present realities again. In recording ordinary occurrences, while he omits much of the didactic matter preserved by Matthew and Luke, he adds some circumstance of condition or of place. In picturing the extraordinary events, he alone of the Evangelists dwells upon the looks and gestures and, in general, upon the outward expressions of feeling on the part of Jesus. In describing the miracles, he dwells upon the instrumental or accompanying acts. By these processes which the careless reader may pass over almost without observing them, the plain narratives of the other Evangelists are transformed by Mark into living pictures. In truth, he must be acknowledged as being, among the Gospel authors, the "exclusive master of the pictorial and scenic in describing what took place."

Narrative Changes. This peculiarity of the second Gospel may be illustrated by any of the narratives given by it in common with some other Gospel.

The meeting of Jesus with the rich young man and what occurred in immediate connection with it are recorded by the first three Evangelists (Matt. xix. 16–30; Mark x. 17–31; Luke xviii. 18–30). Only Mark brings out the earnestness of the young man by mentioning that he came **running and kneeled to** Jesus when he asked him the momentous question concerning eternal life. The touching incident, that Jesus, before pronouncing the decisive words given by the three Evangelists, *One thing thou lackest*, looked upon him **and loved him**, without in any wise softening the severity of his declaration on account of this natural amiability, is recorded only by Mark. He alone adds, immediately afterwards, to the *follow me*, which he has in common with Matthew and Luke, the important words, **taking up the cross.** As only Mark relates that **Jesus looked round about**, when he uttered those terrible words: *How hardly shall they that have riches enter into the kingdom of God!* — so he alone follows this up with an account of the astonishment of the disciples, and the Master's *repeated* yet *explanatory* saying: **And the disciples were astonished at his words.** *But Jesus answereth again, and saith unto them, Children, how hard is it* **for them that trust in riches** *to enter into the kingdom of God!* And when our Lord adds that *it is easier for a camel to go through the eye of a needle, than for a rich man to enter the kingdom of God*, and the still more astonished disciples *say* **among themselves**, *Who then can be saved?* it is Mark who records, in the most forcible yet simple manner, that saying so full of comfort to the heart truly in search of salvation, in *repeating* the expression of God's almighty power in man's salvation, *for with God* **all things are possible.** When, shortly afterwards, Jesus promises to the disciples, that whatever any one shall have forsaken on earth for his sake he shall have restored to him an hundred-fold, and that he shall receive eternal life in the world to come, Mark adds what might have been but too easily forgotten, that this recompense, in so far as this life is concerned, shall be coupled **with persecutions.**

The account of the poor widow's mite is found in Mark (xii. 41–44) and Luke (xxi. 1–4). In the four verses of his Gospel Mark adds to the parallel account of Luke: that Jesus **sat over against the treasury**; that he saw **the people** cast in their gifts; that **many that were rich cast in much**; that the widow's two mites **make a farthing** (**a quadrant**, a well-known Roman coin); that **he called unto him his disciples** and told them that the poor widow had cast more in **than all they which have cast into the treasury.** Add to this the constant repetition of the words, **cast in,** and there is furnished the material which makes all the difference between the sober statement of Luke, designed to be read by the thoughtful Greek, and the vivid picture of Mark, designed to make the active Roman see the event itself.

These examples might be extended to cover all the events which Mark records in common with one or more of the other Evangelists, and would exhibit throughout the same characteristic features that so adapted this Gospel to the man of action.

Slighter Additions. The same distinguishing feature of the second Gospel may be illustrated by a large class of incidental additions made by Mark in connection with materials common to two or more of the Evangelists.

He usually gives the names and surnames, and mentions the relations, of the persons whom the other Evangelists mention more generally. The blind man restored near Jericho is Bartimeus, the son of Timeus (x. 46). The high-priest from whom David received the shew-bread as food is Abiathar (ii. 26). The Jewish name of the publican Matthew is Levi, and he is the son of Alpheus

(ii. 14). The sons of Zebedee are surnamed by Jesus Boanerges, which is the sons of thunder (iii. 17). Simon of Cyrene was the father of Alexander and Rufus (xv. 21), one of whom seems to have been a well-known person in the circle of Roman Christians (Rom. xvi. 13).

He takes peculiar pleasure in giving the identical Aramæan words used by Jesus. In the accounts of the young woman's restoration to life, Matthew mentions the bare fact, Luke gives our Lord's words in Greek, but Mark tells us (v. 41) that our Lord said to her: "*Talitha, Cumi*, which is being interpreted, Damsel, I say unto thee, arise." So in the account of the healing of the deaf and dumb man in the region of Decapolis (vii. 34), we have the word of Jesus: "*Ephphatha*," and have it interpreted for the Gentile reader, — "that is to say, Be opened." In Gethsemane we have the Syriac "*Abba*" (xiv. 36); and, in answer to the Jerusalem Scribes and Pharisees, the Hebrew "*Corban*," caught from the lips of Jesus (vii. 11.) The cry of agony on the cross is given by Mark in the precise Aramæan words in which it was doubtless uttered: "*Eloi! Eloi! lama sabachthani?*" By Matthew it is given in the original Hebrew — then already a dead language — "*Eli! Eli!*" etc.

But this point is perhaps best illustrated by some of those characteristic details by which Mark casts a flood of light upon the daily life of our Lord.

The account of the storm on the Sea of Galilee is found in Matthew (viii.), Mark (iv.), and Luke (viii.). Mark alone tells us, that "they took him *even as he was* in the ship" (iv. 36), — that is, exhausted by his labors and without any preparation for the comfort of the voyage. All three of the Evangelists tell us that while the terrible mountain storm was sweeping down over the waters, Jesus lay sleeping in the little ship. But Mark adds a circumstance equally picturesque and significant: "And he was *in the hinder part of the ship* asleep *upon the bench*," — for so, as is now generally admitted, must the last word be translated. He lay sleeping upon the bench covered with leather, on which the rowers were accustomed to sit, and not upon a *pillow*. "No convenience brought on board for that purpose, but only what the place itself offered, served for some moments as a couch to him who otherwise, on his own earth, had not where to lay his head."

Da Costa, who has given a detailed account of the characteristic differences of the Gospels, brings out another very striking feature in connection with Nazareth, the town in which Jesus was brought up. All the first three Gospels show that his doctrines and miracles had given rise to great astonishment and offense among the Nazarenes. Luke (iv.) tells us that they became so enraged that they thrust him out of the city and attempted to cast him headlong from the precipice on which the town was built. Matthew (xiii. 54, 55) records the questions of amazement, skepticism, and contempt: "Whence hath this man this wisdom and these mighty works? Is not this the *carpenter's* son? Is not his mother's name Mary? And his brethren, James, and Joses, and Simon, and Judas? and his sisters, are they not all with us?" But Mark (vi. 3) writes, "*Is not this the* carpenter, *the son of Mary?* This difference between the Gospels, apparently so unimportant, clearly reveals to us two striking circumstances in the private life of Jesus: *first*, that he himself, along with his father, and apparently until his baptism in Jordan, followed at Nazareth the trade of a carpenter; *secondly*, that in those days Joseph, the husband of Mary, must have long been dead. And thus it is that the Lord from heaven, he by whom the heaven and the earth were created, is found in his human nature exercising a trade on this earth, and by that trade, that labor of his own hands, providing, as a son and support, for Joseph's widow, the daughter of David, whose eldest son he was according to the flesh."

Word Changes. The word changes, occurring in every paragraph of the second Gospel, bear the same characteristic mark of adaptation to the man of deeds. By means of these the expressions of the other Evangelists are strengthened and intensified and their bald statements transformed into living realities.

Matthew and Luke tell us that at the baptism of Jesus the heavens were *opened* unto him; Mark tells us that Jesus **saw** the heavens **rent open** (i. 10). Matthew and Luke tell us that after the baptism Jesus was *led up*, or *led*, into the wilderness for the temptation; Mark says that the Spirit **driveth him** (i. 12). In describing the feeling awakened by the healing of the paralytic, Matthew (ix. 8) says *they marveled;* but Mark (ii. 12) says **they were all amazed** (literally, **beside themselves**). In the description of the storm at sea, Matthew (viii. 24) says *the ship was covered with the waves;* Mark (iv. 37), *the ship was* **full.** Matthew (xxvi. 37) says that in Gethsemane our Lord *began to be sorrowful;* Mark (xiv. 33) uses a stronger expression: **to be sore amazed.**

Mark likewise makes use of that repetition of words which is a form of figurative energy so common in the Latin tongue. This may be illustrated by such expressions as that used concerning the disciples, after the storm on the sea (iv. 41), "and they feared exceedingly" (literally, *they feared with a great fear*); that used concerning the people when the daughter of the ruler was restored to life (v. 42), "and they were astonished with a great astonishment;" and that used in speaking of the sin against the Holy Ghost (iii. 28), "blasphemies wherewith soever they shall blaspheme." This usage may be even better illustrated by the emphatic repetition of the exact words and phrases. In this way the Evangelist uses the words *cast in* seven times, in giving the account of the widow's mites (xii. 41–44). In like manner he repeats *the Gospel* and *the kingdom of God* (i. 14, 15); the words *eat* and *publicans and sinners* (ii. 16, 19); and the word *sea* (iv. 1).

These are only specimens of the variations that are to be found throughout the entire Gospel. The possessor of an English Harmony of the Gospels — still better, of a Greek Harmony — can readily examine them in detail for himself. They will everywhere be found to bear the Roman stamp.

II. *Other Peculiarities.*

The survey taken of the second Gospel brings to light other and incidental variations, not to be classed with those already referred to, but which can only be explained by the Roman aim of the Evangelist.

Roman Assumptions. As already indicated, Mark has furnished the Gospel of action, and especially of the divine activity of Jesus. This assumes the point of view of the Roman, the man of action.

Although so much the shortest of the Gospels, it has nearly as many miracles as Matthew. It deals but little with logic save the logic of facts. Mr. Westcott has called it "a series of perfect pictures;" and again, "the living portraiture of Christ in the clearness of his present energy." The teaching of mighty fact everywhere outruns that of verbal statement.

Its very brevity, resulting from these characteristics, would, as Canon Wordsworth has suggested, "commend it to the acceptance of a great body of the Roman people, especially of the middle classes, engaged in practical business, legal affairs, commercial enterprises, and military campaigns, and migrating in frequent journeys from place to place. Such an Evangelical manual as this would be particularly appropriate and serviceable to them." [1]

It is true that Mark nowhere represents Jesus as being addressed as *Lord* — as the other Evangelists so often do — but *the authority* of Lord and God is exhibited in all his career as it is not by any other Evangelist. It is Mark that has given us the God speaking out most clearly through the man in all the relations of life. Tangible forms, material symbols, were a necessity in a Gospel for the matter-of-fact Roman. To him an abstract God was no God at all. While Luke, writing for the so-human Greek, dwells upon the perfect humanity of Jesus as it appears exalted into union with the Divinity; Mark, for the Roman, strives to make visible through the manhood of Jesus, the invisible and Almighty God.

The fact has been often signalized, that the second Gospel gives with special fullness many of the events in the experience of Peter.

There are throughout abundant indications of the intimate connection of Peter with its authorship. It begins with Peter's first acquaintance with Jesus, at the preaching of the Baptist. Simon Peter is incidentally seen to be a central figure in it, as may be shown by comparing statements of Mark with those of the other Evangelists. Where Luke (iv. 42), writes: "And when it was day, he departed, and went into a desert place; and *the people* sought him, and came unto him, and stayed him, that he should not depart from them;" Mark (i. 35, 36) says: "And in the morning, rising up a great while before day, he went out, and departed into a solitary place, and there prayed. And *Simon*, and *they that were with him*, followed (Greek, *hunted*) after him." In the narrative of the fig-tree that was cursed, Matthew

[1] *Introduction to St. Mark's Gospel.*

(xxi. 20) represents *the disciples* as exclaiming, "How soon is the fig-tree withered away!" but Mark (xi. 21) represents *Peter* as first calling to remembrance the curse and making the exclamation. Matthew (xxiv. 3) writes that *the disciples* asked our Lord about the time when the temple should be destroyed; Luke (xxi. 7), that *some* asked him; Mark (xiii. 3), that *Peter*, James, John, and Andrew asked him privately. While Mark alone adds that strikingly significant circumstance that the cock *crew twice* before the Apostle's conscience was aroused;[1] he alone adds to the expression of Matthew (xxviii. 7), in the message of the angel after the resurrection, that equally striking and significant closing name of the denier: "But go your way, tell his disciples *and Peter* that he goeth before you into Galilee (Mark xvi. 7).

It is a still more striking fact, that things recorded in the other Gospels, which reflect peculiar honor upon Peter, are modestly passed over in this. Matthew alone records the attempt to walk upon the sea (Matt. xiv. 28–32). There is nothing said of the *bitterness* of Peter's weeping after his denial of his Master.[2] But most remarkable of all — considering the fact that Mark wrote for the Roman, and that the later Rome built its pretentious and inquisitorial hierarchy chiefly upon this one statement — is the absence of the benediction given to Peter on the occasion of his explicit confession of the Messiahship and Divine Sonship of Jesus: "Blessed art thou, Simon Bar-jona; for flesh and blood hath not revealed it unto thee, but my Father which is in heaven. And I say also unto thee, that thou art Peter, and upon this rock I will build my Church; and the gates of hell shall not prevail against it. And I will give unto thee the keys of

[1] Compare Matt. xxvi. 34, 75; Luke xxii. 34, 61; John xiii. 33, xviii. 27; with Mark xiv. 30, 63, 72.

[2] Compare Mark xiv. 72, with Matt. xxvi. 75, and Luke xxii. 62.

the kingdom of heaven; and whatsoever thou shalt bind on earth, shall be bound in heaven; and whatsoever thou shalt loose on earth shall be loosed in heaven."[1] Could anything more clearly mark the guidance of inspiration? It seems like a divine protest and provision against the Papal perversion of the passage with its doctrine of the keys, that it should have been omitted in the very Gospel for the Roman.

It is likewise worthy of note that Mark, in his treatment of themes connected with the geography of Palestine and with Jewish rites and customs, seems always to assume such a reader as the Roman undoubtedly was.

It has already been made evident, that there is, in general, in the second Gospel as compared with the first, a paucity of references to all matters that would require a Jewish reader, or copious explanations for the Gentile reader, in order to make clear the point and drift of the narrative; and as compared with the third, an absence of the accurate geographic and historic statements so necessary to the reasoning Greek, whose character would impel him to the mental reconstruction of the history and topography, but so useless to the Roman, intent only on the incidents themselves as exhibiting the power of the almighty conqueror.

With Mark the full impression designed to be made is not ordinarily dependent upon a minute and accurate acquaintance with Jewish peculiarities and places. When explanations of such things are introduced it is rather to add vividness to the impression than merely to give information. But that he does not entirely withhold such explanations because of the familiarity, either partial or entire, of his readers with matters essentially Jewish — as some one has asserted — may be seen at once from his record of the discourse about *unwashen hands* (vii.

[1] Compare Matt. xvi. 13–20, with Mark viii. 27–30, and Luke ix. 18–21.

1–5), as compared with the parallel account of Matthew (xv. 1–3). Evidently the reader for whom Mark wrote that account was not familiar with Jewish customs; and in this we have an unanswerable argument against the hypothesis which represents the usual absence of explanations as arising from such familiarity. The explanation is too elementary and superficial for the Greek; it was not needed by the Jew; but it exactly met the needs of the Roman.

Roman Expressions. While all the features thus far noticed are best explained by the supposition that the second Gospel was written, as history affirms, for the Romans, there are certain expressions and forms of expression which are, if possible, still more decisively Roman.

Of this nature is the employment by Mark of Latin words in Greek form, a thing which is nowhere else found in the New Testament. The paralytic when healed is commanded to take up his *bed*. Here Mark (ii. 12) uses the word κράβαττον, the Greek form of the Latin *grabatum;* instead of the pure Greek work κλίνη (Matt. ix. 6), or κλινίδιον (Luke v. 19, 24). In recording Herod's sending for the head of John the Baptist, Mark (vi. 27) uses the word σπεκουλάτωρ, which is translated *executioner* in our English version, but which means a soldier of the *body-guard* rather. It is the purely Latin word *speculator* spelled with Greek letters. The word ξέστης (Mark vii. 4), translated *pots*, is doubtless simply a corruption of the Latin *sextus* or *sextarius*, meaning the sixth part of some larger measure, and nearly corresponding to the English pint measure, mug, or bowl. Mark, and he only, explains the *two mites* of the widow, λεπτὰ δύο (xii. 42), by the word κοδράντης, a Greek spelling of the Latin *quadrans*, the fourth part of the well-known Roman coin, the *as*. The *centurion* who had charge of the crucifixion is called by Matthew and Luke, in pure Greek, ἑκατοντάρχης, but Mark (xv. 39, 44) calls him κεντυρίων, which is the Latin *centurio* in Greek letters. These Latin words would have been unintelligible to readers of a purely Greek culture.

Of like character is Mark's use of the Roman division of the night into four watches, — evening, midnight, cock-crowing (Latin, *gallicinium*), and morning. An examination and comparison of the various Gospels will show that this is peculiar to Mark, the other Evangelists retaining the ordinary Jewish division into three watches.[1]

Such incidental features, the consideration of which might be extended indefinitely, can only be satisfactorily explained by the theory that the second Gospel was written for Roman readers.

SUMMARY.

From the point now reached, taking into account not only the weight of the separate indications of a Roman aim, but also the combined force of all the considerations adduced, the Roman adaptation of the second Gospel cannot reasonably be denied.

It has been seen to be a historical fact, that Mark, a Roman in character and probably by birth, prepared this Gospel from the preaching of Peter, for Roman readers, the men who were the workers, conquerors, and rulers of the world. This is the stable historical basis of the theory.

It has also been shown that the second Gospel itself everywhere bears the marks of its Roman origin and aim. This is manifest in its entire plan, which involves the presentation of the divine power and activity of our Lord, and which views his life as one career of conflict and conquest ending in the universal sway of the kingdom of God. It is no less manifest in the omissions and

[1] Compare Matt. xxiv. 42–46 with Mark xiii. 35, and Luke xii. 38.

additions made by the Evangelist, all of which have been shown to be explained by his Roman design. It is equally clear in all the incidental variations of the Gospel, everything in it receiving its tone and color from the Roman aim with which it was produced.

It is not, therefore, too much to claim that the historical view combines with the critical, that Irenæus and Clement and Jerome join with the general plan, the particular scope, and the minute details of the Gospel itself, in establishing the theory that Mark was originally the Gospel for the Roman; and not too much to affirm that this theory furnishes the true key to the Gospel.

PART IV.

LUKE, THE GOSPEL FOR THE GREEK.

"Thou seemest human and divine,
The highest, holiest manhood thou."
ALFRED TENNYSON.

"Forasmuch as many have taken in hand to set forth in order a declaration of those things which are most surely believed among us, even as they delivered them unto us, which from the beginning were eye-witnesses, and ministers of the word; it seemed good to me also, having had perfect understanding of all things (rather, having traced down everything) from the very first, to write unto thee in order, most excellent Theophilus, that thou mightest know the certainty of those things, wherein thou hast been instructed." LUKE, i. 1–4.

"Tertius Lucas medicus, natione Syrus Antiochensis (cujus laus in Evangelio), qui et ipse discipulus apostoli Pauli, in Achaiæ Bœotiæque (Bithyniæque) partibus volumen condidit (2 Cor. viii. 18, 19), quædam altius repetens, et ut ipse in prooemio confitetur, audita magis, quam visa describens." JEROME.

CHAPTER I.

HISTORICAL VIEW OF THE GREEK ADAPTATION OF THE THIRD GOSPEL.

SECTION I.

ORIGIN AND DESIGN OF THE THIRD GOSPEL.

WHAT was the actual origin of the Gospel according to Luke? For what class of readers was it originally designed?

Manifestly the third Gospel was immediately addressed

to the same Theophilus (Luke i. 3) to whom the Acts of the Apostles was addressed (Acts i. 1). The name is Greek, meaning *lover of God.* Who he was can only be conjectured. Some have supposed, from the meaning of the name, that it was used, not to represent any particular person, but Christians in general; others have concluded that he was probably an honored Greek with whom the Evangelist had been at some time intimately associated; while most have agreed that he was only the representative of a large class to whom the Gospel had been preached, and with whom Luke, under the influence of the Holy Ghost, desired to leave it as a permanent treasure.

But although the Gospel was addressed immediately to Theophilus, yet, when the subject is investigated from the historical point of view, the statements of most trustworthy witnesses make it sufficiently clear that Luke wrote it for the Greek, the representative of the Gentile world at large.

Witnesses. The first witness to the fact is Irenæus, who flourished in the second century, and was, in his day, the most celebrated teacher in that school of teachers in Asia Minor, which may be traced back to the labors of the Apostle John, and which was at once the most intelligent and orthodox of the early schools of Christianity. Irenæus is a most competent and credible witness. His teacher was Polycarp. He received the great facts concerning our Lord and his Apostles as Polycarp had received them from the lips of the Apostle John.[1]

Irenæus, in the same passage in which he states the origin of the first and second Gospels, declares that "Luke, the companion of Paul, put down in a book the Gospel preached by him (Paul)."[2] Farther on, Ire-

[1] Iren. *Against Heres.* iii. 3–4; Euseb. *Hist. Eccles.* v. 20.

[2] Iren. *Against Heres.* iii. 1.

næus states that "Luke, who always preached in company with Paul, and is called by him 'the beloved physician,' and with him performed the work of an Evangelist, and who was intrusted to hand down to us a Gospel, learned nothing different from him (Paul)." [1] This testimony is confirmed by Eusebius." [2]

Origen, who flourished, as has been seen, in the first half of the third century, and whose wide and familiar acquaintance with the churches of Palestine and Asia Minor, gave him ready access to the best tradition of the early Church on this subject — affirms that the Gospel according to Luke was written for the sake of those Greeks who turned to the faith, and that it was also commended by Paul.[3]

Gregory Nazianzen, called also the Theologian, bishop of Constantinople in the fourth century, in his didactic and theological poems, affirms, for the edification of the Church, that "Luke, the companion of Paul, that great servant of Christ, wrote the wonderful works (in his Gospel) in Greece;" and also "for the Greeks." [4]

Jerome, in the prologue to his commentary on the Gospel of Matthew, in recording his view of the origin of the four Gospels, says: "The third is that of Luke, the physician, a native of Antioch, in Syria (whose praise is in the Gospel); who was also himself a disciple of the Apostle Paul; and who produced his work in the regions of Achaia and Bœotia, repeating some things more amply, and, as he confesses in his preface, describing what he had heard rather that what he had seen." According to another reading, the Gospel was produced "in the regions of Achaia and *Bithynia*." [5]

[1] *Against Heres.* iii. 14, 1.
[2] *Hist. Eccles.* vi. 25.
[3] Origen, as given by Euseb. *Hist. Eccles.* vi. 25.
[4] *Carmin.* lib. i. sect. i. 22, vers. 1; sect. i. 12, vers. 32.
[5] Hieron. *Comment. in Evang. Matth.* proleg. 3, 4.

Pertinent Facts. The chief facts touching the origin and design of the third Gospel, as presented by these witnesses, are, that Luke wrote the Gospel which bears his name; that it was substantially that which he and Paul had proclaimed to the Greek world; that it was produced and published among Greek peoples; and that while addressed formally to Theophilus, it was really written for the Greeks as representing the Gentile world, and suited to commend Jesus to them as their Saviour.

The main statements thus brought to light seem to have been received, almost without question, in the early centuries of the Church. The witnesses are substantially the same as those cited in Matthew and Mark, and are in general the writers on whom the Church depends largely for the settlement of the historical questions upon which our faith in the canon of the Scriptures ultimately rests. The considerations already presented, touching their character and competency, have equal weight in their application to the origin of the third Gospel.

In fine, it cannot be reasonably maintained that their statements are not in agreement with history, and that they did not arise out of history. Luke undoubtedly prepared his Gospel for the Greeks, for the purpose of commending to them Jesus as their Saviour.

SECTION II.

THE CHARACTER AND NEEDS OF THE GREEK.

If the third Gospel originated in the preaching of Paul as moulded by the agency of Luke, and was prepared for Theophilus as a representative Greek, and for Greek readers in general, then the character and needs of the Greek must furnish the key to this Gospel.

What manner of man, then, was the Greek? What were his spiritual needs? Correct answers to these questions will render luminous the Gospel prepared under the influence of the Holy Ghost for the Greek race.

I. *The Greeks.*

The Greeks are clearly distinguished from the other great historic races by certain marked characteristics. They were the representatives of reason and humanity in the ancient world. They looked upon themselves as having the mission of perfecting men. They were the cosmopolites of that age. They made their gods in the likeness of men, in their own likeness, and therefore joined to human culture utter worldliness and godlessness.

Out of these peculiar characteristics, as modified by the age and circumstances, arose those spiritual needs of the Greeks which were to be met by the Evangelist. Along the line thus marked out must be sought the adequate understanding of the Gospel prepared by Luke.

The Representative of Reason. The Greek was the representative of reason and humanity in the ancient world. Every great race shows some part of man's nature in unusual development. In the old Jewish race, the spirit, or that part of man which links him to God, was the predominant element. The Jew belonged to the race of Shem, which has never done what is considered the world's great intellectual work, but which has, nevertheless, made all the grandest ventures out into the domain of the infinite, and as a result has given mankind those three systems of theism, — Judaism, Christianity, and Mohammedanism, — which contain the highest expression of the human soul from its spiritual and heavenly side. In the old Roman race, the will, or that part of man which pushes to action, and enables him to control and mould nature and mankind, was the predominant element. His herculean tasks and his universal empire furnish the highest expressions of the human soul as the repository of the energy for shaping the world to law and order. In the old Greek race, the humanity, especially as embracing intellect, taste, and feeling, was the prominent feature. The Greek belonged to that family of Japheth which has done all of what is usually regarded the world's great intellectual work, has given it all those grand secular literatures which contain the highest expression of the soul from its human and earthly side.

The Perfecter of Man. The Greek looked upon himself as having the mission of perfecting man. Through all the ages, in literature and art, in statecraft and gymnastics, he was working toward his one great idea of the perfect man. In his ideal, intellect and taste held the supreme place. His aim was not the beautiful man in the lower sense merely, but thinking, reasoning man, with his intellect full-summed, farthest reaching, most gracefully working. He accordingly bequeathed to the world the grandest models of beauty and of thought that the unaided human mind has ever produced. Counting the great poets of all lands and ages on the fingers of the right hand, Homer is among the number. Plato and Aristotle have contended until the present day for the place of authority in philosophy. Demosthenes has never yet been placed second on the roll of eloquence.

The Worshiper of Man. The Greek made his gods in the likeness of man, of himself. In his view of the universe, man was exalted above all other beings, and the Greek man wore the crown of perfectness. His religion was the highest of the idolatries, the most attractive of the polytheisms. The Hindoos asked men to worship monstrous emblems of physical power; the Egyptians, life in all its forms down to the most repulsive; the Roman, Rome and the Emperor. The Greek was broader than all these, the Greek idea nobler. Humanity seemed most divine to him — diviner than all physical forces, than all physical life, than empires and emperors; man himself diviner than all his own works, and than all the world. The man on earth, with the grandest power of thought and beauty of speech and action, was the highest man for the Greek, and nearest the place which he thought the gods ought to occupy.

The Universal Man. These characteristics of the Greek brought him into sympathy with man as man, and made him in the ancient world the representative of universal humanity. The Jew and the Roman were by nature exclusive. The Jew could fraternize readily with him only who came from Abraham and received the prophets; the Roman with him only who wielded power in the empire, or was born to a place in the empire. The full-grown Jew was a Pharisee; the full-grown Roman a Cæsar; but the full-grown Greek was a world-man. Every man had something — and that among the chief things in his manhood — in common with the Greek. Man is a thinking, reasoning being. He was made to seek the true, to love the beautiful, to sympathize with human kind. All men could, therefore, meet the Greek as they could not the Jew or the Roman. The Greek could meet all the world on the common platform of humanity as the Jew and Roman could not.

The Worldly and Godless Man. It is evident that there were some fearful defects in that old Greek view of things.

His religious system provided for taking out all the virtue from the world. The Greek deified all of man, — what was base as well as what was truly noble and godlike. To him, the passions — even to the basest — were as godlike as the virtues; Venus and Bacchus and Pluto as much gods as Jupiter and Apollo and Minerva. It was the ever-recurring and always unsuccessful attempt of poor fallen man, unaided of Heaven, to make a god in his own image, that should satisfy the wants of his soul. His was a system that held, planted in its very heart, the seeds of moral decay and death, and which must, therefore, end in debasing man and in perishing of internal corruption.

It left no room for spirituality. In deifying man, it brought God down to the level of man and to the baseness of man. Man was made in the image of God, and there is a sense in which he must make his god for himself in his own image; but he must do it by an upward sweep of thought, reaching the true idea of God by removing the limitations, casting aside the defects, and exalting the excellences of his own nature. The Greek attempted it by making his gods just like himself. There was nothing heavenly and spiritual about them; they were "of the earth, earthy." His gods made his religion base and unspiritual as themselves. His "sweetness and light" became the bitterness and shadow of sin and death.

His religion had in it a kind of attractiveness, but it took all the grandeur out of the universe. Instead of seeing the supreme God and Father everywhere and in all things — shining in the beauty, dazzling in the glory, giving in the fruitfulness, speaking in the truth — he saw himself imaged there. It was man's universe, not Jehovah's. He humanized the clouds, the forests, the rivers, the seas; peopled them with deities and half deities, with satyrs and fauns, with muses and nymphs, each of which represented some side of man's nature. He set upon everything his own image and superscription. If there was any real and mighty God, any power irresistibly making for righteousness and yet overflowing with love, the Greek had pushed him afar off and out. At best there remained but a horrible dream of God in his conception of all-comprehending and relentless fate.

The altar "to the unknown god" became the only Greek altar which was in any sense an altar to the true God.

In short, the Greek theory blotted out the other and higher world, and left him utterly worldly, "having no hope and without God in the world." This world was his province, his home, his grave. He sought his happiness in it. His only wish was that it might last forever. "The more the Greek attached himself to this world," says F. W. Robertson, "the more the unseen became a dim world of shades. The earlier traditions of the deep-thinking Orientals, which his forefathers brought from Asia, died slowly away, and any one who reminded him of them was received as one would now be who were to speak of purgatory. The cultivated Athenians were, for the most part skeptics in the time of Christ. Accordingly, when Paul preached at Athens the resurrection of the dead, 'they mocked.' This bright world was all. Its revels, its dances, its theatrical exhibitions, its races, its battles, its academic groves where literary leisure luxuriated, these were blessedness, and the Greek's hell was death. Their poets speak pathetically of the misery of the wrench from all that is dear and bright. The dreadfulness of death is one of the most remarkable things that meet us in those ancient writings."[1]

II. *The Key to Luke's Gospel.*

In the character and condition of the Greek civilization in the apostolic age is to be found the key to the third Gospel.

The Greek thought and culture had been the common possession of mankind for four centuries, when Luke sent forth his Gospel from Antioch. It had done its best for

[1] *Sermons.* First Advent Lecture, "The Grecian."

the world in bringing the races together and preparing them for the grander Christian view of the brotherhood of humanity; but it had, nevertheless, utterly failed to help the Greek to attain to his ideal of the perfect manhood. The vices of the system had everywhere brought decay and corruption. The old faith in it was gone beyond possible recovery. Its beauties and graces remained in the memory of the race only as pleasant dreams or poetic fancies.

Its polytheism, as always, had brought dissipation of mind. When Paul entered Athens, he found that "all the Athenians and strangers which were there, spent their time in nothing else, but either to tell or to hear some new thing;" and were ready to think him a "babbler" who should have aught to say of God and immortality. A thirst for something new, equaled only by the despair of the old, had everywhere taken possession of the mind of the age.

The indiscriminate worship of humanity had ushered in the reign of materialism and sensuality, and the Greek had almost ceased to be more than a reasoning animal. The worship of the beautiful had ended, as always, in putting the accomplishments in the place of all manly and womanly virtues. In short, religion had become a mockery, and virtue had perished.

There was nothing left to the Greek worth living for, — no divine fatherhood to bear him comfort; no grand mission in this world to gird and train him to power, no golden age save in the distant past, no glorious immortality in the world beyond to open before him sublime reaches of progress and measureless heights of hope, — nothing but the earth and the present, with failure already crushing him, and death with its everlasting sleep remorselessly pursuing him. Utter restlessness and wretchedness had seized upon the greatest and purest minds, and the old, undefined longing for some divine man was everywhere verging toward despair, save as the Jew had quickened and made it more hopeful by spreading abroad his idea of the Messiah, as the coming deliverer of the world.

When the Gospel went forth from Antioch for the regeneration of the Greek, it found the world-language waiting to bear the world-religion to this longing and despairing but desperately corrupt race, and to all who had been moulded to its ways of thinking and living.

It is, therefore, evident that the Greek must be reached by a peculiar presentation of the Gospel, a presentation shaped by these characteristics in his nature and condition.

As the Messiah of the prophets, Jesus of Nazareth had an interest for the Jew; as the Son of God, the almighty worker and conqueror, he had an interest for the Roman; but in neither of these aspects would he interest the thinking Greek. A Gospel for the Greek must be shaped by the Greek idea; must present the character and career of Jesus of Nazareth from the Greek point of view, as answering to the conception of a perfect and divine humanity; must exhibit him as adapted, in his power and mercy, in his work and mission, to the wants of the Greek soul, and of humanity as represented in it. It must present Jesus as the perfect man, to meet the Greek ideal; as the divine man, to cure the wretchedness of the despairing Greek. It must bring God and the invisible world near, to meet the wants of the longing Greek soul, and elevate it above itself and into communion with God; must open the eyes of the blind Greek to see the sinfulness of sin and the beauty and desirableness of virtue and holiness. Reason and beauty, righteousness and truth, dignity and earnestness, must be exhibited as they meet in Jesus in their full splendor, and his divine tenderness and compassion must have universal sweep. It must open the way to a mission grand enough for man here, and must bring to light an immortality beyond. In short, the Gospel must meet the true and correct the false in the Greek ideal.

Wordsworth has well said: "The universality of man's apostasy from the primeval Law of God; the universality of the guilt of mankind; the universality of the misery in which the human race lay; the universality of their need of a Redeemer and a Saviour; the universality of the redemption accomplished by Christ dying upon the cross for the sins of the world; the universality of the Christian Church, constituted by him to be the dispenser to all nations of all the means of grace flowing from his sacrifice; and the preparatory and transitory character and function of the Levitical law and priesthood,—these were solemn topics on which all men needed to be instructed, particularly the Gentile world." [1]

To the Greek these are the credentials of Jesus, no less essential than prophecy to the Jew, or power to the Roman. Without them there could not even be a reasonable hope of arresting his attention, much less of leading him to submit to Jesus as his Saviour. The Greek soul of that age furnishes the true key to the third Gospel.

SECTION III.

THE AUTHORSHIP OF THE THIRD GOSPEL.

The authorship of the third Gospel accords with the historic facts concerning its origin and design. As Matthew was eminently fitted by his Jewish nature and culture to embody the Gospel for the Jewish race; Mark, by his character, wide knowledge of the empire, and intimate association with Peter, the man of action, to do

[1] Wordsworth, *Introduction to St. Luke's Gospel*, p. 161.

the same work for the Roman race; and John, by his rich and ripe spiritual experience and deep sympathy with his Lord, to do like work at a later day for the gathered Church; so it may be shown that Luke, in connection with Paul, was just the man to give literary shape to the Gospel for the Greek race.

I. *Luke.*

Four things made Luke the proper instrument for this work: that he was of Greek origin; that Antioch was doubtless the place of his birth and residence; that he was a physician by profession; and that he was the disciple and companion of Paul, the Apostle to the Gentile world.

Trustworthy tradition, as preserved by Eusebius and Jerome, has it that Luke was a native of Antioch in Syria, or at least had his usual residence there, and that he was a proselyte or follower of Paul. Paul places him among those of his fellow-workers who are not of the circumcision, or who, in other words, are of Gentile origin (Col. iv. 10–16). Both the Gospel which bears his name and the Acts of the Apostles abundantly show that his culture was Grecian. He belonged to a profession which was at that day almost exclusively in the hands of the Greeks. From the earliest times it has been the general opinion that he was probably a Greek proselyte, first to Judaism, and afterward to Christianity.

Epiphanius asserts that Luke was one of the seventy disciples sent out to preach to the Gentiles in Peræa (Luke x. 1). Theophylact declares that he was not only designated by some as one of the seventy, but that he was the one who, with Cleopas, met with the risen Saviour on the way to Emmaus. The fact that Luke alone describes the mission of the seventy and the journey to Emmaus tends to confirm this tradition. It is certain that he was possessed of that Greek nature which would bring him into sympathy with the Greek soul, and enable him to understand its wants.

That he was a physician appears from the tradition cited above, from the statement of Paul in the Epistle to the Colossians (iv. 14), and from abundant indications of his knowledge of the profession, found in his Gospel and in the Acts of the Apostles.[1] This was an important element in his preparation for the work of the Evangelist of the Gentiles. His profession required him to be a man of culture, gave him influence with the more refined classes of society, brought him into sympathy with suffering humanity, made possible such a companionship as that which existed with Paul, and made him at once a fit amanuensis of that Apostle, and a fit co-laborer with him in giving the Gospel to the Greek world.

It has been remarked that his Greek culture fitted him to prepare a Gospel, to which the objection, sometimes urged against the other Gospels, that they are the productions of ignorant and credulous men, cannot possibly apply. He was both able and disposed to apply to all the facts before him the scientific tests properly applicable to them, and he did actually apply those tests.

His birth or residence at Antioch had a still more im-

[1] Luke constantly looks upon things with the eye of a physician. For example the maladies that are mentioned in this Gospel are described with more detail, and partly indicated by their proper technical names. The fever of which Peter's wife's mother was sick is spoken of by Luke only (iv. 38) as a *strong*, a *great* fever, in accordance with a scientific distinction still found in Galen. Several similar illustrations occur in the Acts of the Apostles, as in the Greek terms used to describe the obscuration of vision in the sorcerer Elymas (Acts xiii. 11), the disease (*fever and dysentery*) of which Paul cured Publius at Malta (Acts xxviii. 8), and the ailment (*an eating by worms*) of which Herod Agrippa died (Acts xii. 23). It has often been remarked that Luke alone looks upon the sins and sufferings of men and the scenes on the cross with the eye of a physician. See Da Costa, *The Four Witnesses*, p. 146.

portant bearing upon his mission. It was there that the work of the Gospel among the Greek Gentiles was first begun by those who were scattered abroad by the persecution in which Stephen lost his life (Acts xi. 19, 20); there that the disciples were first called Christians (Acts xi. 26); there that Paul was trained for his life-work (Acts xi. 25) as the Apostle to the Gentiles, and sent forth to that work (Acts xiii. 1–3). Antioch was the metropolis of the Seleucid dynasty; in culture the rival of Corinth and Alexandria. It became the capital of Gentile Christendom, as Jerusalem was of Jewish Christendom. It was the city in which the great missionary impulse of that age was given, and in which the sympathy of Christianity with all the perishing world reached, under the fostering and moulding influence of Barnabas, Saul, and their co-laborers, its greatest breadth and depth. To live in Antioch in that age, and to come into sympathy with the Christian missionary spirit there, would give an essential part of the preparation necessary to fit Luke to be the Evangelist for the Gentile world.

Most important of all, in its bearing upon his work, was the association of Luke with Paul in the actual missionary work. When the call came from Macedonia, "Come over and help us," it came to Luke as well as Paul (Acts xvi. 10), and he was with the Apostle in that first entrance of the Gospel into Europe. All through the later missionary work of Paul, "the beloved physician" appears from time to time as a most cherished companion and fellow-laborer, accompanying him in his most perilous journeys,[1] and standing by him in the critical moments of the Apostle's final struggle for the faith when all others forsook him (2 Tim. iv. 11).

[1] This appears in the Acts, in the use of the plural of the pronoun of the first person, *we*, xvi. 9–17; xx. 5–38; and thence to the end of the book.

II. *Paul.*

Paul, who played so important a part in the preparation of the Gospel for the Gentile world, was preeminently fitted to furnish, with the aid of Luke, the complete instrument for that work. No more striking example of the fitness of the means devised for the accomplishment of divine ends can be found even in Sacred History.

His was the soul for the world-apostle.

There are a few men who in grandeur of soul tower above all others. It is easy to pick them out along the ages; in truth, the venerable names rise unbidden, — Moses, Plato, Aristotle, — any one can complete the list. Among these confessedly belongs the man Paul. The world may be challenged to find his superior in simple power of soul. Judged by the thought in his writings, he stands unsurpassed. There is nothing like them in iron logic, in profound insight, in comprehensive breadth, in all-embracing grandeur of view. There is nothing like them in their expression of a great human heart, in its compassion for man, in its love for God, in its devotion to Jesus Christ, — bearing the burden of the apostate and perishing Jew, reaching out after the dying Gentile, and in visions of the ineffable glory anticipating the ecstacy of heaven. Where in all the centuries has there ever appeared another such indomitable will? Those best fitted to judge have not hesitated to affirm that, estimated by his work, Paul's was the grandest, merely human spirit that ever walked embodied among men.

His was the culture for the world-apostle.

He was born and lived a Roman citizen, — a free-born citizen of the one universal Empire of all ages, and so a citizen of that great world to which he was to bear the Gospel.

His birthplace was Tarsus, which at that time, as we learn from Strabo, was the rival of Athens and Alexandria as a place of learning and philosophical research. The entire Greek civilization was thus opened to him in his very childhood and youth; and one of the greatest authorities, Dr. Bentley, does not hesitate to affirm, that "as Moses was learned in all the wisdom of the Egyptians, so it is manifest from the twenty-seventh chapter of Acts alone, if nothing else had been now extant, that St. Paul was a great master in all the learning of the Greeks." That was just the point where the culture of the heathen world was at its highest; and in the full blaze of that Greek civilization, which even now furnishes us with some of the great models of poetry and the grandest models of eloquence, Paul was born and spent his early life.

Born of Jewish parents, he went early to Jerusalem, the great centre of Judaism. He there became a disciple of Gamaliel (Acts xxii. 3), a distinguished teacher of the law, — doubtless the person of that name celebrated in the writings of the Jewish Talmudists as the first of the seven teachers to whom the title of "Rabban," *great master*, was given, and who was also known as "the glory of the law,"[1] — one of the seven preëminently wise teachers. Judaism, of his knowledge of which we have such evidence in his Epistle to the Hebrews, was unfolded to him, by this its greatest teacher, in its length and breadth and in its sublimest form. He himself affirms that he "profited more than all his equals in the Jew's religion" (Gal. i. 14).

One other thing is needed to complete the view, — his relation to Christianity. Such was his situation in Jerusalem, and such his connection with the Pharisee party, that he must have had extraordinary opportunities for

[1] See Smith's *Dictionary of the Bible*, article "Gamaliel."

knowing the character, work, and fate of Jesus Christ. He must have been thoroughly acquainted with the sect of the Nazarene to be so bitter a hater and persecutor of it.

In accordance with a law of Divine Providence often illustrated in history, the man who was to combat the errors of the world was born and educated as a world-man — Jew, Greek, and Roman at once — at the very point in time and space where the brightest rays of Greek and Roman paganism and of Judaism and Christianity all converged to a common focus.

His was just the human experience of salvation for the world-apostle, — the widest possible.

He writes to Timothy (1 Tim. i. 15, 16), "This is a faithful saying and worthy of all acceptation, that Christ Jesus came into the world to save sinners; of whom I am chief. Howbeit for this cause I obtained mercy, that in me first Jesus Christ might show forth all long suffering, for a pattern to them which should hereafter believe on him to life everlasting." This passage sums up his qualifications as a saved sinner to preach salvation to all the lost world.

He was the chief of sinners. His great soul and his great light together rendered it possible that he should be this. His obstinacy in unbelief, and rage in persecution confirm the fact that he was this. True, men have attempted to explain away his words by making them merely an expression of his *modesty;* but the attempt has been a vain one. If ever in all history there was a man who had no such modesty, that man was Paul. If in speaking or writing for his Master it became necessary to set forth his great work for Christ, he did not hesitate to declare, in the plainest and most forcible Greek at his command, that he had endured more suffering and labored more abundantly than all the other Apostles (1 Cor. xv.

10; 2 Cor. xi. 23). If it became necessary to defend his apostolic authority, he was neither slow nor weak in showing that he was not one whit behind even the chief of the Apostles. Moreover, there is no consistent meaning in the passage in which Paul's declaration, that he is the chief of sinners, occurs, if it be not taken at its plainest sense. The whole force of the illustration that follows depends upon so taking it. One who will think of his mighty soul, with its world of light, and then look on him in his work of persecution, — as he stands, the master spirit of the hour, with the garments of the righteous Stephen at his feet and consents to his death (Acts viii. 1); as he moves on his way to Damascus, with a soul "breathing out threatenings and slaughter" (Acts ix. 1) against the innocent Christians, — will not think it too much for him to say of himself by divine inspiration: "*Of whom I am chief.*"

He was saved by the greatest of miracles of grace. The story of his conversion is perhaps more familiar than almost any other in the Bible except the story of Calvary. All the features of the scene are familiar, — the company journeying toward Damascus; the sudden light from heaven at midday, surpassing the brightness of the sun; the voice of Jesus speaking with authority to his persecutor; the answering question and response; Saul struck to the ground, blinded, and overcome; the three days of suspense; the coming of Ananias as the messenger of the Lord, and Saul's baptism and mission, — every child can fill up the outline. Saul, the chief of sinners, was saved and brought back to God, to appear as Paul the saint, prepared to do his grand work for the Gentile world, and to go up at the last to wear his everlasting crown of righteousness. Amazing fact, that *he*, the chief of sinners, was saved by Jesus Christ! Jesus Christ showed forth *all* long-suffering in this man's salvation! Who does not see the marvelous patience of God with Paul, the persecutor and blasphemer, the Pharisee of the Pharisees, through those long years? Has there been anything else equal to it in all the past ages? And lest the fact should not be brought prominently enough before perishing men, this same story of Paul's conversion is written in three different places in the New Testament (Acts ix.; xxii.; xxvi.), that all the world may know it.

The greatest of sinners saved by the greatest of grace was just the man to illustrate and to preach the world-salvation to the universal man, and to push the work with resistless energy out toward the ends of the earth. Who could so preach Christ to all men, even the worst, as he? Unlike Peter, Paul from the beginning had all the essential requisites of the man of action. With him all thought was nearest possible to the powers of motion. With him the thought and motive were grand and the will indomitable even from the first; but when Jesus Christ took possession of his being, the grandest of all thoughts, feelings, and purposes filled his soul, and he went forth an intelligent and divinely-guided co-worker with God in his infinite plan for human redemption, — to weep and plead and labor for lost men, under the deepest possible sense of sin and salvation and under the greatest weight of gratitude that ever rested upon a human soul; to brave danger and death with a purpose that never faltered because he had a profound and abiding consciousness that the life which he lived was the life of Christ living in him.

Such was the great Apostle whose coadjutor Luke was. They went forth together to the conflict and conquest, the hearts of both throbbing with a sympathy and love that reached out beyond the Jew to all mankind.

It is the unvarying testimony of the early Church, that

Luke's Gospel originated in his companionship and work with Paul, and that it was moulded and inspired by that great Apostle, who combined the Jewish soul with the culture of the Greek, the world-citizenship of the Roman, and the undying devotion of the chief of sinners saved by grace. No other men could have been found at all equal to these two in their fitness for reaching and influencing the Greek world by the Gospel.

Such a nature, residence, culture, companionship, joined with inspiration, fitted Luke to trace the life of Jesus "in its wide comprehensiveness, as the Gospel of the nations, full of mercy and hope, assured to a whole world by the love of a suffering Saviour."[1] Matthew, Mark, John, could not have prepared a Gospel suited to the wants of the Greek nature, for that nature was not in them; the Holy Ghost chose and prepared Luke in conjunction with Paul for that special work.

CHAPTER II.

CRITICAL VIEW OF THE GREEK ADAPTATION OF THE THIRD GOSPEL.

The complete adaptation of the third Gospel to the needs of the Greek world of the apostolic age will be made clear by a careful examination of the Gospel itself in the light of its origin, design, and authorship, as thus historically ascertained.

SECTION I.

THE GREEK ADAPTATION IN THE GENERAL PLAN OF THE THIRD GOSPEL.

The suitableness to the Greek is to be seen in the general plan of the Gospel according to Luke. It may be

[1] See Westcott. *Introduction to the Study of the Gospels,* ch. iv. p. 241.

conveniently divided into three principal parts, — presenting the successive stages of the work of Jesus as the divine man for the redemption of all mankind, — with an appropriate introduction and conclusion.

In these divisions the character and career of Jesus are unfolded in their appropriate connection with the necessities of the world as seen in the representative world-man of the age. The historical personage, Jesus of Nazareth, is exhibited in the progress of his human development and of his work for mankind.

OUTLINE OF THE THIRD GOSPEL.

INTRODUCTION.

The Advent of the Divine Man. The Evangelist exhibits the origin, development, and preparation of Jesus as the Perfect Man, for his work of Saviour of mankind. i. 1–iv. 13.

Prologue. Statement of the literary aim. i. 1–4.

Section 1. Jesus, the perfect man, is presented in his origin, birth, and manifestation to men. i. 5–ii. 20.

A. In the previous announcement from heaven of his advent. i. 5–56.

a. The annunciation, to Zacharias, of the forerunner, the Baptist. 5–25.

b. The annunciation to Mary, the visit to Elizabeth, and the song of triumph. 26–56.

B. In the birth of his forerunner, and the poetic prophecy of Zacharias. 57–80.

C. In his own birth, and in his manifestation, through the angels, to the shepherds of Bethlehem. ii. 1–20.

Section 2. Jesus, the perfect man, is presented in the development of his human nature under law, divine and human. ii. 21–52.

A. In the circumcision and manifestation to the true

Israel represented in Simeon and Anna, in the temple. ii. 21–38.

B. In his visit to Jerusalem at twelve years of age, and in his later life of subjection and growth at Nazareth. ii. 39–52.

Section 3. Jesus, the perfect man, is presented in his special preparation for his work as Saviour of the world. iii. 1–iv. 13.

A. In the work of the forerunner, John the Baptist, till the baptism of Jesus. iii. 1–22.

B. In the descent, traced back to Adam and God. iii. 23–38.

C. In the temptation by the devil in the wilderness. iv. 1–13.

PART I.

The Work of the Divine Man for the Jewish World. The Evangelist exhibits Jesus as the fully developed Divine Man, in his work of divine power for Israel, and in his laying the foundations of the Kingdom of God. iv. 14–ix. 50.

Section 1. He presents the work of divine power in connection with the teaching in the synagogues of Galilee, resulting in rejection. iv. 14–vi. 11.

A. In Nazareth, where his gospel for the poor and suffering is rejected with violence. iv. 14–30.

B. In Capernaum and its neighborhood, where his works of power include the raising of the dead, the pardon of sin, and lordship over all the natural and spiritual world, — compelling the acknowledgment of his divinity, but leading the Jews to rage and plotting. iv. 31–vi. 11.

Section 2. He presents, in connection with the work of divine power and mercy, the teachings of Jesus concerning the constitution and development of the kingdom of God. vi. 12–ix. 50.

A. The kingdom of God and its constitution. vi. 12–viii. 3.

a. Originating in communion with heaven, by the call of the Twelve, and the proclamation of its constitution in the Sermon on the Plain. vi. 12–49.

b. Based on the faith of man (healing of the centurion's servant), and the compassion of Christ (raising of the widow's son). vii. 1–15.

c. Embracing all classes: the people at large; the Baptist and publicans and sinners, but not the Jewish rejecters of the forerunner; the penitent sinner (the woman), but not the proud Pharisee; the ministering women. vii. 16–viii. 3.

B. The development of the kingdom. viii. 4–56.

a. From the seed of the truth (the sower). viii. 4–18.

b. Through obedience to the word of God (the coming of the relatives). viii. 19–21.

c. By faith in the divine power of Jesus (the storm; the demoniac and the swine; the daughter of Jairus, and the woman with the issue of blood). viii. 22–56.

C. The pressing of the claims of the kingdom upon the Galilean Jews and disciples. ix. 1–50.

a. In the mission of the Twelve, and the resulting fame, withdrawal, and miracles. 1–17.

b. In the confession of Peter, the attendant prediction of death, and the subsequent transfiguration and miracles. 18–43.

c. In the second prediction of death, and the rebuke of ambition and exclusiveness. 43–50.

PART II.

The Work of the Divine Man for the Gentile World. The Evangelist exhibits Jesus as the Divine and Universal Man, in his gracious work for the Gentile world, chiefly in heathen Peræa and on his last journey to Jerusalem. ix. 51–xviii. 30.

Section 1. He records the beginning of the last journey and the sending out of the Gospel to the Gentiles. ix. 51–xi. 13.

A. The gracious messengers to Samaria and their rejection; the terms of discipleship laid down; and the sending out of the Seventy (under the law of evangelistic effort). ix. 51–x. 24.

B. Mankind but one family (the good Samaritan); but one thing needful (Mary and Martha); but one way of securing it, by prayer for the Holy Spirit (the disciples instructed). x. 25–xi. 13.

Section 2. He records the portrayal, judgment, and condemnation by Jesus of the religious world of that age. xi. 14–xiii. 21.

A. The malignant rejection of Jesus by the hypocritical Pharisees, in contrast with the required confession (the dumb demoniac healed, and the dinner eaten with unwashed hands). xi. 14–xii. 12.

B. The worldliness and covetousness of the Jew in contrast with the heavenly mind and the faithful stewardship (the rich fool). xii. 13–53.

C. The signs of the impending judgment of this world for sin and formality (the barren fig-tree), in contrast with the mercy of the kingdom of God (healing of woman with infirmity on the Sabbath), and its expansive and transforming growth (the mustard-seed and the leaven). xii. 54–xiii. 21.

Section 3. He records the teachings concerning the number of the saved, — showing that the grace of salvation is universal to sinners. xiii. 22–xv. 32.

A. The question, on the journey, and the answer, presenting the urgency of salvation (the shut door), and the bringing in of the Gentile and the apostasy of the Jews (the man with the dropsy, and the great supper). xiii. 22–xiv. 24.

B. The strict terms of salvation and the danger of losing it (self-renunciation and cross-bearing), in contrast with the free offer to all sinners and the desire of the Son (the shepherd and the lost sheep), the Holy Ghost in the church (the woman), and the Father (the father of the prodigal), for their salvation. xiv. 25–xv. 32.

Section 4. He records the teachings concerning the life in the kingdom of God. xvi. 1–xviii. 30.

A. It is a life of faithful stewardship in the things of this world, ending in the rewards of the heavenly world (the unjust steward and the rich man and Lazarus). xvi. 1–31.

B. It is a life of forgiveness (the law of offenses), humility (the master and servant), faith and gratitude (the Samaritan leper), and of waiting for the spiritual coming of "the Son of Man" in his glory. xvii. 1–37.

C. It is a life of prayer, believing and humble (the unjust judge, and the Pharisee and Publican), of child-like resting in God, and of obedience and self-denial (the rich young ruler), ending in present joy and everlasting salvation. xviii. 1–30.

PART III.

The Sacrifice of the Divine Man for all Mankind. The Evangelist exhibits Jesus, as the Divine Man, voluntarily suffering and dying for all the lost world. xviii. 31–xxiii. 49.

Section 1. He presents the preparation for the sacrifice. xviii. 31–xxii. 38.

A. In the prediction of his death, the approach to Jerusalem, and the public entry as Messiah. xviii. 31–xix. 46.

B. In teaching daily in the temple, and there vindicating his authority as Messiah before the plotting rulers and the rejoicing people. xix. 47–xxi. 4.

C. In predicting to his disciples his second coming, with the rejection of the Jews and the bringing in of the Gentiles. xxi. 5–36.

D. In the progress of the conspiracy, in connection with the teaching in the temple and the keeping of the Passover. xxi. 37–xxii. 38.

Section 2. He presents Jesus, the compassionate divine man, voluntarily yielding himself up to his enemies and to the sacrificial death on the cross. xxii. 39–xxiii. 49.

A. In the agony, betrayal, arrest, trial, unjust sentence, and delivery to his enemies to be crucified. xxii. 39–xxiii. 25.

B. In the crucifixion, — with the lamentations of the people, the compassionate prayer for the scoffing murderers, the saving of the dying thief, the supernatural darkness and rending of the veil of the temple, and the verdict of innocence by the centurion and the people. xxiii. 26–49.

CONCLUSION.

The Divine Man, Saviour of all Nations. The Evangelist exhibits Jesus in his triumph over death, as the Saviour of all nations. xxiii. 50–xxiv. 53.

Section 1. In his burial by a just man, and in his rest in the grave of humanity. xxiii. 50–56.

Section 2. In his resurrection, in fulfillment of his own prediction concerning himself as the Son of man. xxiv. 1–12.

Section 3. In his manifestation to his disciples, in teaching that his death is part of the one great plan of God, in sending them to preach repentance and remission of sins in his name among all nations beginning at Jerusalem, and in his parting blessing and ascension. xxiv. 13–53.

SECTION II.

THE GREEK ADAPTATION IN THE CENTRAL IDEA OF THE THIRD GOSPEL.

With the aid of the outline, which clearly bears the marks of the Greek aim, it may now be shown how the Gospel according to Luke, in its organic idea and general tenor, falls in with the testimony of history that it was produced and published especially for Greek readers.

I. *The Central Idea.*

It is a familiar fact in literature, that unity of plan and aim does not necessarily preclude the existence of a twofold idea in any production, an external and an internal, provided one be subordinate to the other. Hence some have viewed the Julius Cæsar of Shakespeare as a historical tragedy, others as a character tragedy. It is both at once, — for the poet evidently intended to give a view of the external movement of events in one of the greatest crises in all history, the one that hastened the preparation of the Roman world for the Advent; and at the same time to delineate the internal but deadly struggle of the ideas of the old Rome and the new, of the Republic and the Empire, as embodied in the noble and patriotic but weak Brutus and the mighty but ambitious Cæsar. The true unity is found in the subordination of the external to the internal.

The Gospel according to Luke may be regarded as having such a twofold idea, and as maintaining real unity in a similar way.

The External. The central idea of the third Gospel, in its outward aspect, is found in the opening verses of the first chapter. It is the presentation of an accurate history of Jesus of Nazareth. This may be called the literary aim of Luke.

As clearly as we recognize in the first Gospel a perpetual comparing of the person of Jesus Christ with the prophecies concerning the Messiah, for the Jew; and in the second Gospel, the exhibition of the mighty deeds of the conqueror of the world in compressed, graphic, and living form, for the Roman; so clearly do we recognize in the third Gospel the presence of the historian, preparing for the accurate and philosophic Greek. The author states at once the two main objects of the historical writer: to draw up a continuous narrative, derived from a careful scrutinizing of the testimonies of eye-witnesses and ministers of the word; and to commit it to writing in chronological order (Luke i. 1–4).

The historical structure is found in Luke, with the greatest definiteness in dates and events, the clearest and most accurate knowledge of Jewish and Gentile contemporaneous history, and with the widest and firmest grasp of the workings of the human soul and of the condition and wants of mankind. These features may readily be illustrated and verified from the Gospel itself.

The third Gospel manifestly takes the form of complete historical narrative. It does not, like that of Matthew, "content itself with a short notice of our Lord's conception and birth. It carries events farther back in their sublime continuity; it leads us to the first beginnings, and, as it were, to the very dawn of our Lord's coming in the flesh; it commences with various details relating to the annunciation, the conception, and the birth, not only of our Lord himself, but also of his forerunner, the Baptist (Luke i.). It opens with an expression (i. 5) which subsequently occurs above sixty times in the two compositions of St. Luke; *there was*, or *it happened that*."[1] The use of this expression is signifi-

[1] See Da Costa, *The Four Witnesses*, p. 150.

cant of the historic point of view maintained by the Evangelist throughout.

The attention to dates, so requisite to history, is found everywhere in Luke. From the very opening he carefully determines the dates of the great events which he narrates. It was in the days of Herod, the king of Judæa, that a certain priest named Zacharias, of the course of Abia, while officiating in the temple in the order of his course, received from the angel Gabriel pre-announcement of the birth of John Baptist (i. 5–20). It was in the sixth month after that the angel Gabriel was sent to Nazareth to make to Mary the pre-announcement of the birth of Messiah (i. 26). The date of the entrance of the Baptist upon his public ministry is given with even greater accuracy: "Now in the fifteenth year of the reign of Tiberius Cæsar, Pontius Pilate being governor of Judæa, and Herod being tetrarch of Galilee, and his brother Philip tetrarch of Ituræa and of the region of Trachonitis, and Lysanias the tetrarch of Abilene, Annas and Caiaphas being the high priests, the word of God came unto John the son of Zacharias in the wilderness" (iii. 1, 2). With respect to our Lord himself, it is also Luke alone who speaks of his being circumcised *on the eighth day* (ii. 21); of his being brought into the temple *after the days of the purification* were fulfilled (ii. 22, and following verses); of Jesus, at the age of *twelve years*, as sitting in the midst of the doctors in the temple (ii. 42, etc.). He is also the only Evangelist that informs us of Jesus' being of the age of *thirty years* when he received the rite of baptism at the hands of John, and from the Holy Spirit from heaven (iii. 23).[1]

No other Evangelist enters so deeply into the Jewish history of those times. He alone, for example, records our Lord's allusion to the massacre of the Galileans by

[1] See *The Four Witnesses*, p. 152.

Pontius Pilate at one of the festivals, and to the fall of the tower of Siloam which caused the death of eighteen persons (xiii. 1–4). Luke, in addition to what the other Evangelists relate of the connection of Herod Antipas with John the Baptist, connects him with Jesus himself. He alone tells us that there came certain of the Pharisees and said to him: "Get thee out, and depart hence, for Herod will kill thee;" and that Jesus answered them: "Go ye, and tell that fox, Behold I cast out devils, and I do cures to-day and to-morrow, and the third day I shall be perfected" (xiii. 31, 32). He alone records the fact that Jesus, when on trial, was sent to that same Herod, and that the murderer of the Baptist became a reviler of the Son of God, and at the same time one of the witnesses of his innocence (xxiii. 5–12; Acts iv. 27). It is from Luke, also, that we learn that among the godly women who ministered to the wants of Jesus with their substance, "there was Joanna, the wife of Chuza, Herod's steward" (viii. 3).

Probably no books of antiquity contain so many, varied, and wide-reaching references to the institutions, customs, geography, and history of their times, as do the two books written by Luke. They were written at a time when it would have been the more difficult for any one but a contemporary to maintain perfect accuracy and fidelity to the truth, along with such detail and definiteness of statement and allusion, in proportion as the period was marvelously "fertile in great events, in changes in governments and in the boundaries and names of countries and peoples." And yet the result of the most searching scrutiny of these writings, "sifted fact by fact, detail by detail, expression by expression, in the light of all that the most civilized and the most enlightened antiquity directly witnesses or incidentally suggests to our researches," has vindicated for them such a claim to the faith of the world as no secular histories of that or the succeeding ages can pretend to urge for themselves, — so that Luke is justly and preëminently called *the historian.*

The history is still better adapted, by the selection of the material, to suit the æsthetic Greek. It is not made up of dry, dead facts. Poetry and song flash out from its pages. The profound wisdom of the parable and the rapt inspiration of eloquent discourse combine to chain the attention. The beauty of this world in which the Greek delighted, and the glories of the heavenly world of which he had scarcely dreamed, unite to charm the soul. The revelations of new and sublime conceptions of the universe, of human duty and destiny, and of the Deity, expand and exhaust the powers of the most capacious imagination. In short, the Gospel combined in itself everything that could attract and absorb the true Greek soul.

The Internal. The central idea of the third Gospel, in its internal aspect, appears throughout. It is this: Jesus is the perfect, divine man, the Saviour of the world.

Luke takes the point of view of the Greek and maintains it to the end. The perfect manhood of Jesus with the consequent mercy and universality of his covenant, rather than the temporal relations or the eternal basis of Christianity, furnishes his central subject. "In the other Gospels we find our King, our Lord, our God; but in St. Luke we see the image of our great High Priest, made perfect through suffering, tempted in all points as we are, but without sin, — so that each trait of human feeling and natural love helps us to complete the outline and confirms its truthfulness." [1]

The Gospel seizes upon the humanity of Jesus as the idea most attractive to the mind of the Greek. Jesus

[1] Westcott, *Introduction to the Study of the Gospels,* p. 371.

is preëminently man, *the man.* He is neither Roman, Greek, nor Jew. He rises above the conditions of time and place. What the Greek blindly strove to reach, what Paul in some measure approximated, that Jesus illustrated in its perfection, — the universal man, the pattern and brother of all the race. This *man*, Luke exhibits in the various stages of his human development; in his intellectual grasp of things earthly and heavenly; in his marvelous sympathy with all of human kind; in his matchless work as the one who was to give light to them that sit in darkness and in the shadow of death; in his consummate genius, his lofty enthusiasm, his divine inspiration.

Especially does the third Gospel present the universal grace of God. A very large portion of it is taken up with what is now quite generally acknowledged to be Christ's ministry in Peræa, or across Jordan, and on his last journey to Jerusalem (ix. 51–xviii. 30), — a ministry to a Gentile race, and therefore peculiarly suited to the Greek and to all the world represented by him. The grace of God for all men, foreshadowed in the song of the angels of the annunciation (ii. 10–14), is made luminous in the teachings, especially in the parables, of this *heart* of the third Gospel.

At the same time, as will subsequently appear more fully, the Evangelist intelligently aims to correct the false Greek notions. He shows him man as he really is. He reveals his true position and destiny. By contrast with the truth he exhibits the shallowness and absurdity of the Greek theogony and theology. He unveils the invisible and future worlds to him. He shows him God as he really is, not in relentless Fate, but in the person of Jesus, the God-man, as the infinitely compassionate and gracious One.

The external form and historical aim of the Gospel,

so far from being out of harmony with this its internal idea, furnish rather the perfect vehicle for its presentation. The Evangelist prepares for the Greek — as he announces his purpose to do — an accurate and systematic exhibition of the facts of the career of Jesus; but this is only the more perfect frame-work for the exquisite portraiture of the perfect man, who is himself the pledge of the blessedness of faith and the exaltation of the lowly, and who appears in the world to give light to them that sit in darkness and in the shadow of death.

II. *The General Drift.*

The influence of this central Greek idea, in its two-fold form, is made apparent by a general movement and drift peculiar to the third Gospel.

No one can mistake the presence and moulding power of the æsthetic and philosophic spirit, in the choice of materials and in their embodiment in literary form. The entire plan, the parts, even the sentences and the words show it. This will appear in every phase of the present investigation.

The human and universal aim will also be everywhere manifest to the careful reader. It is brought out clearly in the general drift of the Gospel, as seen by the help of the outline view.

In the Introduction, after the Evangelist has stated the literary aim of his work, he presents Jesus the perfect man, first, in his origin, birth, and manifestation to men; secondly, in the development of his human nature under law, human and divine; and, thirdly, in his special preparation for the work of the Saviour of the world. This is the true unfolding of the manhood of Jesus in its relations to all mankind, and is just the view adapted to the Greek mind.

In Part First, the Evangelist proceeds to exhibit that

first work of Jesus, as the fully developed divine man, in which the world at large was interested, — the work of divine power for Israel, in laying the foundations of the kingdom of God. This work is illustrated, in its beginnings, by the manifestation of Christ's power and wisdom in Nazareth, his native city, where his Gospel for the poor and suffering is rejected with violence; and in Capernaum and its neighborhood, where he raises the dead, pardons sin, and exercises lordship over all the natural and spiritual world, thereby compelling the acknowledgment of his divinity, but driving the Jews to rage and conspiracy. In its later stage, it is illustrated by continued works of divine power and mercy, connected with the teachings of Jesus concerning the constitution and development of the kingdom of God. That kingdom, originating in communion with heaven, constituted by the call of the Twelve, based on the faith of man and the compassion of Christ, and embracing all classes, is to be developed from the seed of the truth, and by faith in the divine power of Jesus; and the pressing of its claims upon the Galilean Jews and disciples, together with the results, is delineated.

In Part Second, the Evangelist presents the second of the stages in Christ's public work in which all the world is interested, — the gracious work of the divine and universal man, chiefly in heathen Peræa and on his last journey to Jerusalem, for the Gentile world. In the course of this presentation he records, first, the beginning of the last journey, and the sending out of the Gospel by messengers to the Samaritans, and by the Seventy to the Gentiles at large; and the teaching in the parable of the good Samaritan that there is but one family of mankind. He gives, secondly, the portrayal and judgment, by Jesus, of the religious world of that age, dwelling upon the malignity and hypocrisy, the worldliness and covetousness, of the Jew, in contrast with the true spirit of the children of God, and upon the signs of impending destruction. He unfolds, thirdly, the wonderful teachings of Jesus which show that the grace of salvation is offered to sinners universally. He depicts, fourthly, from the teachings of Jesus, the life in the kingdom of God, in the fidelity of its stewardship, in the breadth of its charity, and in its pervading spirit of prayerfulness, faith, and devotion. These are the great central facts and truths of the public work of Christ that were best fitted to commend him to the Greek race.

In Part Third, the Evangelist unfolds the voluntary suffering and death of Jesus the divine man for all the lost world, — showing how everything is colored by the human perfection and compassionate tenderness, and by the divine compassion and saving power, exhibited to all classes of men.

The Conclusion sets forth the experience of the divine man in his triumph over death, and as the Saviour of the world, showing the place of his career in the plan of God and sending out his followers with salvation to all nations.

This was just what was needed to commend Jesus as a Saviour to the man of Greek soul. It was at the same time a true view of the Prophet of Nazareth, whose many-sided character embraced not only the Messiah, the ideal Jew, and the almighty worker and victor, the ideal Roman, but also the divine and universal man, the ideal Greek. This Jesus, the inheritor of all the real perfection and manhood, of all the natural reason and culture found in the Greek nature, and adding to all these a divine perfection and manhood and a supernatural reason and beauty, is the Jesus represented by Luke.

SECTION III.

THE GREEK ADAPTATION IN THE OMISSIONS AND ADDITIONS OF THE THIRD GOSPEL.

I. *The Omissions of the Third Gospel.*

It will appear in the light of a careful examination, that Luke omits so much of the facts and teachings given by the other Evangelists as does not suit his special aim of commending Jesus as the Saviour of the world to the Greek mind.

The distinctively Jewish, Roman, and Christian portions of the general mass of Gospel material are passed over as being of comparatively little value for his purposes. The comparison of the historic Jesus with the prophetic Messiah, which was the one thing for the Jew in whom the hope of the coming deliverer foretold in the prophets had been growing in power and definiteness for ages, could have only a minor and subordinate interest for the man of reason who had scarcely heard of prophecy. The picture of the wonderful and universal conflict and conquest of the Son of God, which was just the thing to command the attention of the Roman, in whom the wildest dream of universal dominion had been realizing itself for ages, could have little weight with the man of reason whose devotion to philosophy and art, which had enabled him to shape the thought and culture of the world, had made him despise the pomp and circumstance of outward sovereignty. The supernatural and divine, in their higher spiritual aspects, which were just what the Christian, the man regenerated, transformed, and lifted into sympathy with heaven, delighted in, were as yet almost meaningless to the man who had dwelt for ages only in the natural and human, and who was to be transformed from the godless man into the godly.

From Matthew. Luke omits the distinctively Jewish narratives and teachings given in the first Gospel.

This is illustrated by a comparative view of the introductions to the first and third Gospels. To the careless reader they might seem to cover the same ground and to embrace the same material. The truth is, however, that so far is this from being the case, that, while the first Gospel presents the origin and preparation of the Messiah, the third gives the human origin and development of the perfect man. But what is more remarkable is, that the material used by the two is almost totally different, since Luke omits the most of what Matthew gives. By following the narratives it will be seen that he passes over the royal lineage by Solomon and Joseph; the prophetic divine origin; the coming of the Magi; the massacre of the innocents; the flight into Egypt and the return to Nazareth; while he retains the mission of the Baptist and the temptation. The portions omitted have exclusive reference to prophecy and to Jewish wants.

Passing on to the public ministry of Jesus, it will be observed that Luke does not record the opening of the ministry in Galilee (Matt. iv.), in which prophecy is fulfilled and all Syria roused; it was a Gospel for the Jew only, and therefore of subordinate interest to the Greek. So the Sermon on the Mount (Matt. v.–vii.) finds no place in the third Gospel; it was on its very face a proclamation of the constitution and character of the kingdom of heaven for the Jewish hearers. The portion of Luke's Gospel that has sometimes been confounded with the Sermon on the Mount (Luke vi. 17–49) is entirely without the marked Jewish references found in that production as given by Matthew.

Still more noteworthy is the absence from the third Gospel of all those discourses recorded by Matthew, which are especially condemnatory of the Jews, and which in so many instances exalt the Gentiles above the Jews. These were absolutely essential in a Gospel designed to open the eyes of the descendants of Abraham and lead them to a deep sense of their need, and to a cordial spiritual reception of God's Messiah. But they would undoubtedly have been a source of evil to the Gentile readers of Luke, and that for a twofold reason,— that they did not at all reveal their own besetting sins, and that the preaching against other men's sins would have led — as it always leads — to spiritual pride rather than spiritual profit. So Luke passes over the upbraiding of the cities of Galilee (Matt. xi. 20–30) which had been the centre of Christ's mighty works, together with the comparison with the Gentile cities of Tyre and Sidon and Sodom, and the gracious invitation to salvation. He likewise passes over the discourses connected with the Pharisees' charge against Jesus of collusion with Beelzebub in casting out demons, and with the demand of the Scribes and Pharisees for a sign (Matt. xii. 22–45); and the discourse on the treatment of the little ones and the law of forgiveness in the kingdom of heaven (Matt. xviii. 10–35), aimed at Jewish implacability and Jewish longing for a temporal kingdom. He gives barely a sentence (Luke xx. 45–47) of that most terrible discourse ever uttered in the ears of men, which Matthew (xxiii. 1–39) records fully, — the final woes pronounced upon the Scribes and Pharisees and upon Jerusalem itself.

Turning from discourses to parables, it will be found that the third Evangelist deals in like manner with the parables aimed directly at the Jew. Of the parables of the kingdom (Matt. xiii.), three out of the seven are retained, — the sower (Luke viii. 4–15) as illustrating productiveness in the kingdom; and the mustard-seed and the leaven (xiii. 18–21), as portraying the outward growth and the inward change of the kingdom; while four are left out, — the tares and the drag-net, as illustrating the mixed condition of things in the Jewish world and the Church; and the hid treasure and pearl of great price, as setting forth the search and sacrifice required of Messiah in order to secure the true kingdom, which the apostate Jews vainly supposed themselves to constitute. Of the later parables of Matthew, Luke drops those of the laborers (Matt. xx. 1–16), of the two sons (xxi. 28–32), and of the marriage of the king's son (xxii. 1–14), as presenting the exaltation of the Gentiles over the Jews in such a light as to develop the pride and self-righteousness of the former rather than conduce to their salvation. He also leaves out those closing parables, of the ten virgins and of the talents, and the judgment scene (Matt. xxv.), which were all-important to the Jew who had almost lost out of his ideas of life all true fidelity in watching, all sense of need of the inward grace of God, all feeling of responsibility for well-directed, productive effort to the extent of his powers for God, and all sense of a judgment strictly in accordance with human conduct toward humanity and Christ in humanity; but which might have been of no real profit to the Gentile, who already overestimated works and therefore needed first to learn the lessons of prayer and faith.

This investigation might be extended to the smaller and less prominent parts of the first Gospel omitted by Luke, — such as the healing of the blind man (Matt. ix. 27–34), Peter's confession (xvi. 17–20), the temple tax (xvii. 24–27), and others,— but the student of the Scriptures can examine them for himself. However extended the examination, the same evidences of a Gentile, as distinguished from a Jewish, aim will be readily detected in Luke's omissions from Matthew's Gospel.

From Mark. Luke omits the distinctively Roman features found in the second Gospel.

The historic and philosophic spirit, in which the third Gospel was written, almost precluded the presence of those vivid details and scenic representations which are the distinguishing feature of Mark's production. The absence of this feature may be illustrated by comparing almost any of the narratives common to the two. This peculiarity of Mark has already been brought out in connection with the two mites of the poor widow (p. 196). Luke gives it as a simple narrative, stripped of all the picturesque features: "And he looked up, and saw *the rich* men casting their gifts into the treasury. And he saw also a certain poor widow casting in thither two mites. And he said, Of a truth I say unto you, that this poor widow hath cast in more than they all; for all these have of their abundance cast in unto *the offerings of God;* but she of her penury hath cast in all the living that she had" (xxi. 1–4). It will be observed at once, that Luke, as a historian, "has recorded the matter more concisely, rather avoiding anything like scenic effect; but *his* narrative compensates for this by the touching expression, applied from the nature of its contents to the treasury: *the offerings of God.*"

A cursory examination will make it clear that Luke's omission of the teachings peculiar to Mark is in harmony with his Greek aim. The parable of the seed-corn (Mark iv. 26–34), the healing of the blind man of Bethsaida (viii. 22–26) and of the deaf man of Decapolis (vii. 31–37), and the form of the last commission (xvi. 15–18), all are marked, as has already been seen, by those striking features that suited them to the man of action and of universal dominion.

From John. No less striking is Luke's omission of the distinctively spiritual and Christian portions of Gospel teaching found in John's Gospel.

With the rare exception of an incidental statement, such as that concerning the work of Christ in Galilee (Luke iv. 14, 15; John iv. 43–46), Luke omits everything that John records, up to the last passover week. From that point onward he passes over all that spiritual instruction which John preserves from the last hours of the Saviour's intercourse with his disciples. The unspiritual Greek was not yet prepared for such lessons when Luke gave the Gospel permanent form for him.

Of the events of that last week Luke has nothing in common with John, save the record of some of the facts common to all the Evangelists, as centring in the sacrifice of Christ, — such as the entry into Jerusalem (Luke xix. 29–44), — with perhaps the single exception of a very brief statement of Peter's first visit to the sepulchre (Luke xxiv. 12; John. xx. 3–10). Then, as now, the man who deified reason and gloried in a merely human culture was the least in sympathy with the true Christian spirit. John's Gospel, if given to the Greek before Luke's, would have been in the profoundest sense foolishness to him (1 Cor. i. 23).

II. *Additions of the Third Gospel.*

The Greek bearing of the extensive additions of the third Gospel is still more manifest.

A mechanical analysis has shown that the portion of the entire Gospel material peculiar to the third Gospel is much larger than that peculiar to either the first or second, in fact, much larger than that of both these combined. If this Gospel be regarded as made up of 100 parts, 59 of these are peculiar to itself, and only 41 common to it with one or more of the other Gospels. The important point, however, in this connection, is, that all the 59 parts peculiar to Luke may be shown to be especially appropriate to the Greek soul and its needs.

The additions resulting from the historic and philosophic aim with which Luke prepared his Gospel, and appearing mainly in the literary form, have already been noted. So important are they, that even if the Evangelist had used precisely the same facts and teachings with the other Evangelists, his Gospel would have been a very different one from theirs. Luke's view given of Jesus of Nazareth, while in real harmony with that of Matthew or Mark, would yet have differed from them as greatly as Plato's delineation of Socrates differed from that of Xenophon. But such additions, arising from the spirit and aim of a writer, cannot be clearly expressed in words; they must be intuitively discerned by the soul of the appreciative reader, if they are to be known at all.

But the fifty-nine parts peculiar to Luke are tangible additions and may be examined in detail. The scope of the present discussion leaves space for only a cursory examination. This, however, is all that is needed for the present purpose.

To any one familiar with this Gospel, it will at once occur that there are two very extensive portions of it almost entirely its own: the Introduction, and Part Second.

The wonderful apparent likeness, with the equally wonderful real difference, of the Introductions of the first and third Gospels, has been remarked in considering the omissions of Luke, from the common Gospel material. There is not even the appearance of likeness between the opening chapters of Luke and those of Mark and John.

Luke's introduction is exactly suited to the Greek. It starts out with a clear and concise statement of the literary aim. It is chiefly occupied with the presentation of every stage in the development of the veritable humanity of our Lord, beginning from the counsels of God and ending with the completed manhood of the Son of God, the

Saviour of the world. Luke alone records those revelations from heaven, concerning the forerunner and the Messiah, which preceded their birth, and indicate the special and intense interest of the invisible and spiritual world in the coming Son of man, — including the poetic outpouring of the souls of Mary and Zacharias, and the song of the angels at the Advent. Luke alone gives the Gospel of the infancy and youth of Jesus, — including the wonderful events, natural and supernatural, accompanying the birth and cradling in the manger; the strange recognition attending the circumcision and the first presentation of the child in the Temple; the unique experiences marking the subsequent visit of the child at twelve years of age to his Father's house; and the law of progress in his human development, in the family at Nazareth, toward the perfect manhood. The perfecting of the man Luke then represents as completed in the baptism of John, which introduces him as the Jehovah of prophecy, the teacher of the world, and the beloved Son of God; in the genealogy, which traces his descent from Adam and God; and in the temptation, which is his conquest over the great foe of humanity. Every line will be seen to bear the Greek mark.

The second of the extended portions peculiar to Luke (ix. 51-xviii. 30), known as the record of Christ's gracious work for the Gentile world, chiefly across the Jordan, in heathen Peræa, and on his last journey to Jerusalem, is no less characteristic. The fact that it is the record of a work for Gentiles demonstrates its fitness for the representative of the Gentile world. Leaving out of view the aim of the third Gospel, it would most certainly be a marvelous thing, in short, perfectly inexplicable, that all the other Evangelists should have wholly passed by this period of Christ's work; while Luke draws almost half of his entire Gospel — two thirds of the heart of it

—from its unique work and doctrine. But the Greek design of the third Gospel once admitted, this choice of its main material at once commends itself as in agreement both with the human reason and the divine guidance which entered into the preparation of the Gospels. The rejected messengers of mercy to the Samaritans and the mission of the Seventy to the Gentiles; the picture of the sinfulness of the apostate religious world of that age in contrast with the true faith in the kingdom of God; the universal reach of the offer of God's salvation; and the portrayal of the spiritual life in the kingdom; all these things, as brought out clearly and fully in this record of the Peræan ministry, were precisely adapted to the wants of the Greek world.

But besides these extended portions of Luke's Gospel, which contain most of its peculiar teachings, there are other and briefer sections, given by this Evangelist alone, that equally bear the marks of his Greek aim. These are found either in connection with the Galilean ministry of Jesus, or with those final events of his career which find their centre in the cross.

Of the former additions, the bearing may readily be seen. Luke alone gives an account of the early rejection of Jesus at Nazareth (iv. 16–30), which led him to change his abode to Capernaum. He tells us that Jesus, after reading Isaiah's prophecy (lxi. 1, 2), concerning the anointing of the Messiah to preach a gospel of grace to the poor and needy, declared that the prophet referred to him, and was thereupon rejected by the Nazarenes, because he was one of themselves. The Evangelist adds, that Jesus then enraged them by showing that, even in the times of Elijah and Elisha, the Gentiles were sometimes preferred before Israel in the dispensation of God's blessings. Luke alone records the teaching from the ship on Gennesaret, when, by the miraculous draught of fishes, so deep an impression was made upon Simon Peter of his own sinfulness, and he was called to become a fisher of men, and when he and James and John forsook all and followed Jesus (Luke v. 1-11). He alone gives the Sermon on the Plain (vi. 17–49), in which are unfolded the great principles that should govern men as men in the kingdom of God, and in following which they shall ultimately attain to complete salvation. He alone preserves the account of the raising of the widow's only son at Nain (vii. 11–17), and the manifestation of the tender compassion of Jesus toward the poor widow, in the presence of the disciples and all the people. Luke alone records the anointing of Jesus by the penitent woman, in the house of Simon (vii. 36–50), and the application of the parable of the two debtors called out by that event, and teaching the boundless love of Christ to great sinners and their boundless gratitude in return for his forgiveness, as illustrated in that one sinner. All these passages bear the marks of the tenderness and humanity of Jesus, and contain hints of his later revelations of himself as the Saviour of the whole world.

The later additions give evidence of a like spirit and aim. This is manifest in the story of Zaccheus the publican, and the parable of the pounds (xix. 1–27), showing how freely Jesus received publicans and sinners; in the account of the strife among the disciples at the last supper (xxii. 24–30), probably over the washing of each other's feet (John xiii. 1–20), teaching the lesson that true greatness in the kingdom is to be attained by humble service for humanity; in the account of the trial before Herod (xxiii. 6–12), depicting the treatment of Jesus by the representatives of the Jewish and Gentile worlds; and in the narrative of the walk of Jesus with the two disciples toward Emmaus (xxiv. 13–35), portraying the intense sympathy with God and man of him who could so scan the farthest-reaching purposes of the former, and so set on fire the inmost hearts of the latter. All these gospel teachings are found in Luke alone, and they are all in perfect harmony with his Greek spirit and aim.

The more carefully both the omissions and the additions of the third Evangelist are examined, the more clearly will it appear that they were eminently suited to commend Jesus to the Greek world of that age.

SECTION IV.

THE GREEK ADAPTATION IN THE INCIDENTAL VARIATIONS OF THE THIRD GOSPEL.

A careful examination of the incidental variations and peculiarities of the third Gospel will make still clearer its Greek adaptation. The Greek spirit and purpose will be found to pervade the entire production, shaping both its teaching and its forms of expression.

I. *Incidental Variations.*

It has been shown that Luke was preëminently the historian and man of culture among the Evangelists, and at the same time the one most fully in sympathy with Paul the world-apostle. His production bears the marks of all these characteristics, throughout the entire extent of its variations from the other Gospels. The influence of the historic and philosophic spirit have already been sufficiently illustrated, so that there is necessity for only a brief consideration of this branch of the subject.

Narrative Changes. Almost every passage in which Luke records something in common with one or more of the other Evangelists will illustrate with equal clearness and force his distinctive peculiarities.

He gives, in common with Matthew and Mark, the

account of the ministry of the Baptist. By comparing the three narratives, it will appear that a large part of Luke's is made up of materials not given by the others. He alone names the exact date of the opening of John's ministry, "*in the fifteenth year of the reign of Tiberius Cæsar;*" and makes it still clearer by naming all the contemporary rulers, Jewish and Galilean, civil and ecclesiastical (iii. 1, 2). He alone continues the quotation from the prophet (iii. 4–6) till it includes the capital sentence for the Gentile world: "*And all flesh shall see the salvation of God.*" He also adds that passage, — of so much wider than Jewish application, — unfolding the duties of the people, and especially of publicans and soldiers, in preparation for the coming of the kingdom: "*And the people asked him, saying, What shall we do then? He answereth and saith unto them, He that hath two coats, let him impart to him that hath none; and he that hath meat, let him do likewise. Then came also publicans to be baptized, and said unto him, Master, what shall we do? And he said unto them, Exact no more than that which is appointed you. And the soldiers likewise demanded of him, saying, And what shall we do? And he said unto them, Do violence to no man, neither accuse any falsely; and be content with your wages*" (iii. 10–14). So Luke alone tells us that it was "*as the people were in expectation, and all mused in their hearts of John*" (iii. 15), that the Baptist uttered the clear and decisive declaration concerning the coming of the mightier one, the Messiah; and he alone adds to what is common to the first three Evangelists, as if to complete the historic form: "*And many other things in his exhortation preached he unto the people*" (iii. 18). At the same time he passes over the prophetic credentials of the forerunner (Matt. iii. 4), and transforms what in Mark is a vivid picture into a sober historic account.

The account of our Lord's experience in Gethsemane is also given by the first three Evangelists. While Matthew maintains his habit of careful grouping of events, and Mark his of intense and vivid expression, and both record the fact that Jesus went thrice from his disciples and repeated the prayer to his Father; Luke represents the whole as a season of prayer, connected with a great crisis in the spiritual experience of Jesus, in which the agony increased in power until it reached the intensest pitch; and he alone adds: "*And there appeared an angel unto him from heaven, strengthening him. And being in an agony, he prayed more earnestly; and his sweat was as it were great drops of blood falling down to the ground*" (xxii. 43, 44). So only Luke tells us, with a touch of human tenderness, that Jesus found the disciples "*sleeping for sorrow.*"

These examples might be extended to cover all the narratives of events common to Luke with some other Evangelist; and, however far extended, would always bear the marks of special adaptation to the Greek, the man of universal human sympathies.

Slighter Additions. The same characteristics appear in the slighter incidental additions found throughout the third Gospel.

There are indications here and there of Luke's sympathy with Paul in his well-known predilection for the number *three*, as the symbol of perfection, which often influenced that Apostle even in the construction of his sentences, and which manifests itself in his Epistles "in his constantly tracing back all doctrine to the most Holy Trinity of God, Jesus Christ, and the Holy Ghost; and, in the practice of the Christian life, to the trinity of Faith, Hope, and Charity."[1] Where Matthew (vii. 9, 10) gives two similitudes intended to animate to be-

[1] Da Costa, *The Four Witnesses*, p. 176.

lieving prayer, Luke (xi. 11, 12) at the same time that he emphasizes the *father*, adds a third similitude: "If a son shall ask bread of any of you *that is a father*, will he give him a stone? or if he ask a fish, will he for a fish give him a serpent? *or if he shall ask an egg, will he offer him a scorpion?*" Where Matthew (xxiv. 40, 41) gives two examples of the difference that the great day of his coming would make in the condition of persons most resembling each other externally, Luke (xvii. 34–36) adds a third: "*I tell you, in that night there shall be two men in one bed; the one shall be taken and the other left.* Two women shall be grinding together; the one shall be taken, and the other left. Two men shall be in the field; the one shall be taken, and the other left." So it has been observed, that whereas Matthew (xviii. 12–14) illustrates the restoration of the wandering sinner to favor by the parable of the lost sheep, Luke (xv.) adds the still more striking ones of *the lost piece of silver* and *the prodigal son;* and where Matthew (viii. 19–22) records two examples of what is required in following Jesus, Luke (ix. 57–62) adds a third.

There are likewise remarkable evidences of the tenderness toward the chosen people Israel, which Paul exhibits so strikingly in his Epistle to the Romans (ix. 4, 5; xi. 18, 28), and which was so becoming to one who, like Luke, had the breadth of the Greek soul while he owed all his hope of salvation to the Jews. The Evangelist delights to record the recognition by Jesus of the *sons* and *daughters of Abraham* whom he had benefited. He alone gives an account of the conversion of Zaccheus, adding his nationality: "This day is salvation come to this house, forasmuch as he also is *a son of Abraham*" (xix. 9). It is Luke (xiii. 16) who gives our Lord's defense of the woman who was bowed together, addressed to the hypocritical ruler of the synagogue: "Ought not this woman *being a daughter of Abraham*, whom Satan hath bound, lo, these eighteen years, be loosed from this bond on the Sabbath-day?"

While Luke is distinctively the Evangelist of the Greek world, he shows the spirit of the universal man, in his appreciation of the relation of salvation to the Jews. It is he that writes, in giving the announcement of the angel concerning the Baptist (i. 16): "And *many of the children of Israel* shall be turned to the Lord their God;" and in the announcement concerning Jesus (i. 32, 33): "The Lord God shall give unto him *the throne of his father David*, and he shall reign over *the house of Jacob* forever." It is true also that Luke alone records all three of Christ's lamentations over the doomed Jerusalem (xiii. 34, 35; xix. 41–44; xxiii. 27–31). "Finally, it is Luke who, in addition to the detailed prophecy of the destruction of Jerusalem, given by all the three synoptical Evangelists, records the hint that was given of the restoration that she might one day expect. In his Gospel alone, we read, in the prediction uttered by Jesus on the mount of Olives, these significant words (xxi. 24): 'And they shall fall by the edge of the sword, and shall be led away captive into all nations: and Jerusalem shall be trodden down of the Gentiles, *until the times of the Gentiles be fulfilled.*'" [1]

Word Changes. The Grecian drift of the third Evangelist may also be traced throughout his Gospel, in his departure from the usage of the other Evangelists in the employment of words.

The prominence given by Luke to the word *sinner* in its various forms will be alluded to elsewhere. His use of the word *people* will still better illustrate the point under consideration. He uses it oftener than all the other Evangelists. A single example will suffice. In relating the healing of the blind man of Jericho, Matthew

1 *The Four Witnesses*, p. 183

(xx. 29) says that "a great *multitude* (*crowd*) followed him," and rebuked the blind men when they cried for mercy (31); Mark, that "he went out of Jericho with his *disciples* and a *great number of people*" (x. 46), and, that when the blind man cried out, "*many* charged him that he should hold his peace" (48); Luke, that "*they which went before*" rebuked the blind man (xviii. 39), and that *all the people* when they saw it gave praise unto God (43). That definite and, so to speak, organized body, *the people*, thus takes the place of the indefinite *crowd*, *many*, and *great number*.

The examination might be extended to the entire Gospel with like results. The moulding presence of the Greek aim and spirit would be everywhere manifest, and that in proportion to the thoroughness of the investigation.

II. *Other Peculiarities.*

The survey, thus far taken, of the third Gospel, has prepared for the more definite presentation of some of those incidental features, in assumption or expression, which demonstrate most clearly its Greek adaptation. These features may be brought out in connection with the character of Jesus as the perfect man, and with the revelation of God and the invisible world.

Jesus the Universal Man. It has already appeared that Jesus bears in the third Gospel the character of the perfect, divine man, the Saviour of the world. This may be more fully demonstrated by tracing the progress of his human development, and bringing out the elements of complete manhood and the distinctive features of his work as the Saviour of the world, as these things are presented in the Gospel according to Luke.

The Evangelist records the early human development of Jesus.

In this Gospel alone do we read of the salutation of Elizabeth, "Blessed art thou among women, and blessed is the fruit of thy womb" (i. 42); that the babe "was wrapped in swaddling clothes" (ii. 7); that the child was "circumcised on the eighth day" (ii. 21); that he "was presented to the Lord in the Temple" (ii. 27); that "the child," or lad, "grew and waxed strong in spirit" (ii. 40); that "the grace of God was upon him" (ii. 40); that when he was twelve years old his parents took him with them, after the custom of the Jews, to Jerusalem, to the feast of the Passover (ii. 41, 42); that after his interview with the doctors he gave to his mother that wonderful answer, indicative of the dawning consciousness in the child's soul of his mission (ii. 49); that then he "went down" again with his parents, and "came to Nazareth and was subject to them" (ii. 51); that he "increased in wisdom and stature, and in favor with God and man" (ii. 52); that when he was baptized by John he "began to be about thirty years of age" (iii. 23).

But besides giving so minutely his early human development, Luke, throughout his whole Gospel, is constantly tracing and dwelling upon the peculiar marks of our Lord's humanity to the end of his career. In Luke alone do we read of "the paps which he had sucked" (xi. 27); of his "rejoicing in spirit" (x. 21); of his weeping over the city (xix. 41); of his kneeling down in prayer (xxii. 41); of the appearance of an angel from heaven in Gethsemane strengthening him (xxii. 43); that being in an agony he prayed more earnestly, and his sweat was, as it were, great drops of blood falling down to the ground (xxii. 44); that like "a righteous man," which the centurion is here said to have called him, he cried with his latest breath, "Father, into thy hands I commend my spirit" (xxiii. 46); that after his resurrection, he verified his resurrection-body to his disciples by sitting at meat with them, by taking a piece of broiled fish and of a honey-comb and eating it before them, and by bidding them to handle him and see that it was himself; that he said, "It is I myself; for a spirit hath not flesh and bones as ye see me have" (xxiv. 39); that he made the hearts of those two disciples burn within them by the power of his human sympathy, as he walked and talked with them on their way to Emmaus (xxiv. 32). These features, brought out in this Gospel alone, are enough to tell the complete and connected story of the development of the veritable man Jesus. They are but surface indications on the great current of his life, as presented by the Gentile Evangelist for the Greek.

It is no less remarkable that all the elements of a complete manhood are brought out in the third Gospel with wonderful distinctness.

Keenly incisive as were the thoughts of Jesus of Nazareth, he was no "clear, cold, logic engine." The reality of his human sympathies and affections is exhibited in an almost exhaustless variety of interesting details, while he is shown to be possessed of a depth and breadth and intensity of human feeling before unknown to the world. This element in his character is seen to the best advantage in the relations which Luke represents him as holding to those classes of humanity for which the age cared the least: to children; to woman; to the outcasts from society.

The other Evangelists tell us of our Lord's blessing children, but Luke commonly adds something that brings out the tenderness of his regard for them. He alone tells us that they were *infants* that were brought to Jesus when he so graciously and winningly presented himself as the children's Saviour: "And they brought unto him also infants that he would touch them" (xxiii. 15); that the daughter of Jairus was only a child: "one only daughter about twelve years of age" (viii. 42); that the demoniac healed at the foot of the Mount of Transfiguration was a child: "Master, I beseech thee, look upon my son, for he is mine only child" (ix. 38). Taking such incidents in connection with Luke's remarkable presentation of the childhood of the Baptist and of Jesus in the opening chapters of the Gospel, it is easy to understand why this should have been called the children's Gospel.

The affectionate regard of our Lord for woman is an equally marked feature of this Gospel. Luke tells us of "certain women which had been healed of evil spirits and infirmities, Mary, called Magdelene, out of whom went seven devils, and Joanna, the wife of Chuza, Herod's steward, and Susanna, and many others which ministered unto him of their substance" (viii. 3); of the penitent woman who anointed him at the feast in the house of Simon the Pharisee (vii. 46); of certain women who lifted up their voices and blessed him (xi. 27); of his address to the women of Jerusalem who followed him to the cross weeping (vii. 38); of the restoration of the son of the widow of Nain (vii. 11–16). It is Luke who first introduces us to those typical women of all ages, Martha and Mary, the one cumbered with much serving, and the other sitting at the feet of Jesus, while he teaches both herself and the sister who rebukes her, the true mission of woman, and her real glory in devotion to him (x. 38–42). Such incidents as these, in connection with the tender regard so often exhibited for the widowed and bereaved, and, more than all, in connection with those wonderful events in the lives of Elizabeth and Mary, unfolded only here, by bringing Jesus into closest sympathy with true womanhood, and by exalting the glory of true motherhood through her who was "blessed among women (i. 28, 42)," entitle this Gospel to be called in a peculiar sense, the Gospel of woman, for whom that old Greek world had no Gospel.

More wonderful still was the affectionate sympathy of our Lord, depicted in this Gospel, with the poor, despised, suffering, outcast classes of society. While he constantly rebuked and warned the hypocrite, the self-sufficient, the self-righteous, the rich, the luxurious, the frivolous, and the thoughtless, — as in the case of the ruler of the synagogue who found fault with him for loosing the woman, on the Sabbath, from the spirit of infirmity which had bowed her together for eighteen years (xiii. 11) ; in the case of those who complacently told him of the Galileans whose blood Pilate had mingled with their sacrifices (xiii. 1) ; in the case of the Pharisees who derided his teaching concerning man's stewardship, and whose character and destiny he unfolded in the parable of the rich man and Lazarus (xvi. 19–31) ; and in the case of the rich man who had much goods laid up for many years (xii. 19), — he is yet everywhere presented as the friend of the poor and the needy. In Luke's Gospel alone the beatitudes all become blessings to the poor and suffering (vi. 20–22) ; the most precious of the parables, — as the great supper, the marriage feast, Lazarus and the rich man, the good Samaritan, and the prodigal, — all mark this Gospel as preëminently for the poor. The experience of our Lord himself is presented as that of one of the poor, since he became poor, was laid in a manger, and his parents were obliged to offer at his presentation in the Temple the offering of the poor, "a pair of turtle doves or two young pigeons" (ii. 24).

But Luke makes the sympathy of Jesus with the absolute outcasts to stand out still more clearly. It appears in the friendly recognition of publicans ; in the parable of him who went up to the Temple to pray, and standing afar off with downcast eyes smote his breast and prayed, "God be merciful to me, a sinner" (xviii. 13); in the story of Zaccheus (xix. 1–10); in the treatment of the sinful but penitent woman who anointed him (vii.); in the parables of the lost piece of money and the lost sheep (xvi. 11); in that wonderful "Gospel within the Gospel," — the parable of the prodigal (xv.); in the memoir of the penitent malefactor on the cross (xxiii. 42, 43). It is no marvel, then, that this Gospel, more than all the others, may be said to have given birth and inspiration to all the great reformatory movements, — the care for the poor, the deaf, the dumb, the insane, the maimed, the widowed and orphaned, the aged, even the criminal, — which distinguish modern Christendom. The third Gospel is in a peculiar sense the Gospel of those for whom in all ages this world has had no Gospel.

But the expressions of this limitless tenderness and compassion, on the part of Jesus, reach their height in his treatment of the apostate and doomed Jews. Luke alone twice records Christ's weeping over Jerusalem (xiii. 34, 35; xix. 41–44), bringing out with graphic power those sadder features of the coming ruin which Matthew does not present (Matt. xxiii. 37–39). Luke alone records the compassionate address of Jesus to the women of Jerusalem, who made lamentation over him as he went forth to Calvary with his cross (xxiii. 27–31), with its equally graphic picture of the impending ruin of the doomed city. He alone records the prayer for the forgiveness of his defiant and scoffing and cruel murderers (xxiii. 34). He who died upon that cross could weep over the remediless ruin of the worst of apostate and doomed races, and could pray for the forgiveness of the most cruel and guilty murderers of all ages.

This man of such matchless sympathies, so tireless in his beneficent activities, so boundless in his self-sacrifice for others, Luke exhibits as combining perfect moral purity with an unapproached and inapproachable faith, piety, and devotion toward God.

This, most of all, was needed to correct the Greek idea of manhood. Not all in man is divine, nor even, in the noblest sense, manly. From that hour when Luke sent forth his Gospel, the character of Jesus of Nazareth became the perpetual condemnation of the appetite and passion, and the earthliness and godlessness, of the Greek world. In Jesus appeared a conscious and constant dependence on God, expressing itself in prayer, which is found linked with all the great events of his career, from the descent of the Holy Ghost at his baptism, to that last act by which he yielded up his spirit to God on the cross ; a perfect devotion to God, which never faltered in all that weary way from the manger to the grave ; and that perfect, conscious freedom from taint of sin, in which he stands alone in all the ages, and by which he realized that ideal of perfect manhood of which the highest Greek thought, the profoundest Greek philosophy, and the noblest Greek art, were at the best but anxious and troubled dreams. All the elements of a true and complete manhood thus unite in the Jesus of the third Gospel, to attract to him the Greek soul wherever it is found.

This true and perfect man is also presented as the universal man, the one "Son of Man," whose human interest and sympathy and affection and mission are bounded only by the race.

That Luke wrote his Gospel for universal humanity, and not for Jew, Roman, or Christian, appears abundantly in what has already been said ; but it likewise appears everywhere in the Gospel, from the announcement that he shall be "a light to lighten the Gentiles" (Luke ii. 32), and that he shall "bring peace on earth" and "good will to men" (Luke ii. 14), until that last declaration to the disciples, that "repentance and remission of sins shall be preached in his name among all nations, beginning at Jerusalem" (Luke xxiv. 47). The genealogy here given (Luke iii. 23–38) is not that of his legal, royal, and covenant descent, as Messiah by Joseph from David and Abraham, which was needed for the Jew; but his actual, natural descent from Mary, traced all the way up to the one father of the great human brotherhood, to Adam, "which was the son of God" (iii. 38); and which would show the Greek that man was not *autochthonous*, or sprung from the earth, as he vainly supposed, but of divine origin. Here, in the latter half of this Gospel, are gathered together all those gracious parables found nowhere else, which present the freeness and fullness of God's love to all the suffering and sorrowing world, and which have always been esteemed the choicest treasure of the nations: the good Samaritan, the great supper, the lost sheep, the lost piece of money, and the prodigal. Here alone do we find the sending out of the Seventy, and the work of our Lord himself among that heathen people in Peræa, which were the precursors and promises of like work for all mankind, and the events and teachings of which furnish nearly all of the second ten chapters of this Gospel. Here alone the last great struggle, in which Jesus is borne to the cross, is fully represented as being, what it was in fact, not simply a struggle between Jesus and the Jewish people, but also a struggle between the leading classes at Jerusalem, who envied and hated Jesus, and the people who followed him, heard him gladly, rejoiced in him, and went back from the crucifixion beating their breasts for grief at his death (xxiii. 48), — a struggle in which the leaders succeeded in accomplishing their bloody purpose, only by making a compact with one of the followers of Jesus (xxii. 4), by taking advantage of the darkness and by calling in the

Roman power to aid them (xxiv. 1, 7). Thus, from beginning to end, does this Gospel everywhere prove itself to be in very truth the Gospel of universal humanity.

This universal man, brother of human kind, is presented in Luke's Gospel as being at once both God and man, the divine man.

It has been shown by a modern writer how difficult a thing it is to dramatize, and to represent in action, a character embracing the human and divine, in an imperfect world. There never has been a successful attempt to do it except in the Gospel history of Jesus of Nazareth. Each of the Evangelists achieves the difficult task; but in the Gospel according to Luke it is achieved in the face of greater difficulties than in the other Gospels, for the reason that he brings out the humanity of our Lord most fully. While he makes the humanity so prominent, he makes the Divinity scarcely less prominent. Jesus is brought forward as Jehovah, in the angelic message to Zacharias (i. 11–21), in the poetic prophecy of Zacharias (i. 67–80), in the annunciation by the angels to the shepherds (ii. 13), and in the preaching of the forerunner (iii. 3–17). He appears as the "Son of the Highest," and as the "Son of God," in the message of the angel to the Virgin Mary (i. 26–38), and is acknowledged to be the "Son of God" by the Father at the baptism (iii. 22), and by the world of evil spirits (iv. 41; viii. 28). He is represented as claiming to be God by assuming the prerogative and exercising the power of the almighty Moral Governor in forgiving sin, and then as establishing his right and power to do it by healing the palsied man (v. 18–26). He is exhibited as going through life, performing works of power that are possible to God only. God was everywhere in the perfect man, Jesus. Here, certainly, was just the Saviour the Greek needed. He wanted some living image of God in some truly perfect man. He had striven after this in his poor blind way; but the end was only godlessness, or the altar to "the unknown God." He had longed for humanity in its perfection and glory, for a God who should be a son of man. Jesus was that. So Luke portrays him. Jesus was Deity taking human form. Through that deep heart and matchless intellect and marvelous sense of the beautiful God himself shone. In that spotless character and that active life of love, God himself lived and wrought. Jesus was most human, the great and perfect brother, and yet most divine, the great and perfect God.

The Revelation of God and the Invisible World. The third Gospel is equally unique in the fullness and vividness of its revelation of God and the spiritual world, both in themselves and in their relations to man and this present world.

In Luke's portrayal of the divine man, that God, whom the Greek had put far off to the utmost bounds of the universe, and whom he regarded as taking no interest in the affairs of men, is brought very near, and shown to have the deepest interest in human affairs, and the closest sympathy with man in his joys and sorrows, in his life and death.

In truth, this Gospel swept away all the gods of Greece. "There is but one God," was the voice of the word. It swept away nymphs, satyrs, and fauns, furies, fates, and muses, — everything with which the Greek imagination had peopled mountain and forest, land and sea, the depths of the earth and the expanse of the sky. It took the life out of much of Grecian art, made mere airy fancies of the finest works of Phidias and Praxiteles, of Homer and Æschylus, of even Plato and Aristotle; but it revealed an invisible world, with its hosts of heavenly beings far more pure and beautiful than any creation of man's art or thought, and engaged as messengers of God in ministries of love to men. God himself is interested in the sorrow of Zacharias and Elizabeth, and the heavens open and Gabriel descends with the promise of blessing; He would make the virgin "blessed among women," and the heavens open again and the angel comes down to crown her with perpetual honor and joy; He would give glad tidings to the sorrowing earth, and his glory bursts the barriers of the skies and shines upon the lowly shepherds, and the angel of the annunciation proclaims to them the tidings of great joy, while the angelic host becomes visible joining the first "glory in the highest" with peace and good will to men. The nearness and tenderness of God are made evident in all the compassionate work of Jesus, his incarnate Son; in the teachings of all the great distinctive parables of this Gospel; in short, in its whole matter and manner.

But this revelation of the powers of the unseen world is represented to the Greeks as having a great and beneficent design.

Luke exhibits, with a distinctness and fullness not approached by the other Gospels, the ruined and miserable condition of human nature as sinful and corrupt; the twofold possible destiny of man; and the design of God to lift him out of his condition of evil, and bring him into union and communion with himself.

The Greek required especially to be taught the true condition of human nature. The idea and nature of sin needed to be made familiar to him, and a sense of his own sinfulness to be aroused in him. He had been accustomed to find the cause of his failure to become the perfect man, and the cause of the weakness and the suffering in the world, in human limitation or misfortune; before he could be saved he must be taught to find it in human sin. Luke, therefore, unfolds, in a manner equally striking and peculiar to himself, the sinfulness of man. He uses the word *sinner* oftener than all the other Evangelists combined. Any one who will carefully examine this Gospel for himself with this point in view, will be astonished to see how the ideas of righteousness and unrighteousness, sin and holiness, repentance and remission, color all its teachings, from the opening scene, where it is declared that Zacharias and Elizabeth "were both righteous before God, walking in all the commandments and ordinances of the Lord blameless" (i. 6); all through the vivid presentations and clear condemnations of the prevalent forms of sin, — such as hypocrisy, formality, and covetousness, — which abound in the body of the Gospel; to the conclusion, where the work to which the disciples are sent is to preach "repentance and remission of sins" (xxiv. 47) among all nations.

In harmony with all this is the portrayal of the sad state of man, in those inimitable pictures, the parables of the prodigal and the good Samaritan. In the latter parable, "the wretched condition of human nature, straying from God's presence, and swerving from obedience to his law, is displayed in the person of the traveler going forth from Jerusalem, the holy city, to Jericho, the city of the world. In its way it falls among thieves. Human nature was encountered by the arch-thief, Satan, and was stripped of its original righteousness, and was left half dead. The priesthood came by, and the law came by, and cast a transitory glance upon it; but they only showed its misery and evinced their own inability to heal it, by leaving it where it was and passing by it on the other side. But at last the Samaritan came. He had compassion on it, and bound up its wounds, pouring in the oil and wine which he had with him, and laid it on his own beast, and brought it to the inn and took care of it. Christ, the good Samaritan, came from heaven on a blessed journey, and saw mankind lying helpless in the road of this world, stripped and naked, full of bruises and putrefying sores. He bound up its wounds, and poured in the oil and wine of his own cleansing and sanctifying blood, and lifted it up from the ground and put it on his own beast. He himself bore our griefs and carried our sorrows. He himself bore our sins in his own body on the tree. He brought us to the inn and has given us to the keeping of the host, with a charge to take care of us; and at his departure he provided for us, and he has promised to come again and demand an account of our treatment."[1] Equally pertinent and graphic, as might readily be shown, is the parable of the prodigal. And throughout this Gospel that wondrous love and grace of God, which Luke delights to trace, and the aim of which is to deliver humanity from its sad condition, bring out more strikingly by force of contrast this heavy background of sin and misery.

The Greek required that the future destiny of man should be made clear to him. "The state of the disembodied soul was a question on which the mind of the Greek world had indulged in many inquisitive speculations, and on which it needed instruction. The terrors of Tartarus and the joys of Elysium, which had been displayed in the writings of their poets, exercised a dominant influence on the imagination and practice of heathendom; and, in the apostolic age, they had a strong hold on the popular mind, and alarmed it with superstitious fears, or mocked it with illusory hopes. Men, indeed, of a more philosophical temper, looked on with skeptical indifference, and treated these representations as legendary fables, and denied the resurrection of the body and the doctrine of future retribution. Therefore, the healing art of the beloved physician, St. Luke, might well be

[1] Wordsworth, *Introduction to St. Luke's Gospel*, p. 161.

employed in providing a remedy for this spiritual malady. Accordingly, we see that he has taken care to record two sayings of our blessed Lord, which reflect the clearest light on this mysterious subject, — the state of the soul immediately after death, and during the interval of its dissolution and the day of resurrection and of judgment. He has done this in his recital of the history of the rich man and Lazarus, and in the speech of our Lord to the penitent thief on the cross, 'To-day thou shalt be with me in Paradise.' He also, alone of the Evangelists, in his recital of the miracle of the raising of the daughter of Jairus, has taken care to specify the fact that her spirit came back to her again (viii. 55). He thus corrected the erroneous notions of popular belief and philosophical incredulity, and revealed to the Greeks the great doctrinal and practical truth, that the human soul, on its separation from the body by death, passes immediately into a place of joy or of sorrow; and that it remains there until the last day, when it will be reunited to the body, and be admitted to the full fruition of heavenly bliss, or be consigned to the bitter pains of everlasting woe."[1]

The Greek needed to have the way opened for him to God and heaven. Luke, therefore, taught him how communication is to be had with God and the world of invisible realities, and how man is to reach up after the perfect manhood here, and the immortal manhood of glory hereafter. The prayer of faith is the great agency. The Greeks must be taught to fall down on their knees and pray, and so to reach out after the invisible but living Father. "Their temples were not houses of prayer. Their worship consisted mainly in sacrifices, or in religious pomps and processions, or in theatric shows. But no ritual or liturgy of heathenism has been preserved to

[1] Wordsworth, *Introduction to St. Luke's Gospel*, p. 159.

us." In a word, the Greek mind was to be schooled in the duties of devotion. Hence, Christ appears as the great example of prayer and its power over the unseen world. He prays at his baptism and the Holy Ghost descends upon him (iii. 21). He withdraws into the wilderness and prays before he heals the palsied man and forgives his sins, and engages in the conflict with the Scribes and Pharisees (v. 16). He prays all night and then chooses his disciples (vi. 12). He prays on the Mount of Transfiguration and the glory of heaven comes down upon him (ix. 29). He prays alone in his retirement from his public work and the disciples, with Peter in the lead, make their first full confession of his Messiahship (ix. 18). He prays in the garden before he goes to the cross; and, being in an agony, he prays still more earnestly and an angel comes down to strengthen him (xxii. 41–45). Even on the cross he prays for his murderers (xxiii. 34), and in his last words commits his spirit into the hands of his Father (xxiii. 46).

And in harmony with this wonderful example is the not less wonderful teaching, given in this Gospel only. Twice is he represented as saying, "Men ought always to pray." The effects of urgent prayer by man are here exhibited, not only by the promise, "Ask, and it shall be given you," and that peculiar promise of the Holy Spirit for the asking (xi. 1, 3); but also in the two parables, of the friend coming for bread at midnight (xi. 5–8), and the widow before the unjust judge (xviii. 1–8). He teaches how to pray in that form everywhere known as the Lord's Prayer (xi. 1–4), given only here and in Matthew; and by that inimitable incident of the two men who went up to the Temple to pray (xviii. 9–14), which has, perhaps, had a more powerful influence in directing man to the true prayer than any other teaching of the Bible.

But the Greek needed to be taught that prayer is more than the power which brings heaven down to men; that it is also the power by which man's soul is to go out in gratitude toward heaven, and by which it is to mount up toward heaven. "The duty and blessedness of thanksgiving to God for benefits received from him, supplied another subject on which the Gentile world needed instruction. They '*glorified him not*,' neither were they '*thankful*,' is the sentence pronounced upon them by St. Paul. A beautiful picture of gratitude, and of its reward, is displayed by St. Luke, and by St. Luke alone, in the record of our Lord's miracle of mercy wrought upon the ten lepers who stood afar off (xvii. 12). The blessing pronounced upon the one who returned, and with a loud voice *glorified God*, and fell down at his feet, giving him *thanks*, is made more striking and emphatic by its juxtaposition with the divine command, 'Go show yourselves to the priests'; and brings out more prominently the paramount obligation and exceeding felicity of the moral act of thanksgiving, because it is put in contrast with an express command to discharge a ritual duty of the Levitical law. *That*, also, was to be done; but the *first* thing to be done was to *glorify God*." [1]

Da Costa has suggested that, if it be true that the distinctive character of the facts and doctrines collected by Luke is, that they, in the most marked and profoundly interesting manner, place over against the depths of man's sinfulness, wretchedness, weakness, and poverty, in strong relief, mercy, compassion, charity, salvation, prayer and answers to prayer, faith, grace, and joy, — then there is no word better fitted to convey an impression of all this, than *unction*.

"The Gospel of the beloved physician and Evangelist, the fellow-laborer of Paul, is emphatically a Gospel full

[1] Wordsworth, *Introduction to St. Luke's Gospel*, p. 160.

of unction. But that very word involves a new suggestion with respect to the harmonies to be found among these writings. Unction, according to the writers of the Old Testament, but still more according to those of the New, proceeds from the *Holy Ghost*." [1]

As compared with the first Gospel, or the second, it will be found that the third gives peculiar prominence to the Holy Ghost, and his gifts, operations, and divine personality. The very opening of the Gospel, in the promise made to Zacharias and Elizabeth, declares of the Baptist: "He shall be great in the sight of the Lord, and shall drink neither wine nor strong drink; and he shall be *filled with the Holy Ghost*, even from his mother's womb" (i. 15). The literal accomplishment of this prediction is recorded in the same chapter (i. 41–44). The miraculous conception of Jesus by the power of the Holy Ghost is recorded with peculiar fullness by Luke (i. 35); Elizabeth, Mary, and Zacharias, being *filled with the Holy Ghost*, spoke and sang as inspired by him (i. 41, 46, 67). The Holy Ghost was upon the aged Simeon, and revealed to him that he should not see death until he had seen the Lord's Christ, and moved him to go into the Temple just as the child Jesus was brought in for his presentation according to the law (ii. 25–27). Luke emphasizes the descent of *the Holy Ghost in a bodily shape*, at the baptism of Jesus (iii. 22), and the fact that Jesus, when he went to the temptation, was *full of the Holy Ghost* (iv. 1). So Luke alone, in the encouragement which Jesus gives to prayer, defines the *good things* which Matthew (vii. 11) declares that the heavenly Father is so ready to give for the asking, as being *the Holy Ghost* (Luke xi. 13).

If sinners of the Greek world were to be lifted up into union with God and the things invisible, the unction from this Holy One was a prime necessity. For ages they

[1] *The Four Witnesses*, p. 198.

had enjoyed the inspiration of genius, and it had made them learned, and wise, and eloquent, and cultivated, and beautiful, according to the standards of this world, but it had brought only moral wreck, and wretchedness, and deformity, and death. In the Holy Ghost Luke reveals to them the agent who shall assist them to attain to the heavenly wisdom, and beauty, and perfection, and life.

In fine, this whole Gospel is throughout a delineation of the way for the sinner of the Gentile world to the perfect, holy, blessed, and immortal manhood, which was to be reached by the grace of God alone, which grace could be secured by the prayer of faith alone, and which alone could satisfy the Greek soul. Walking in the way of the returning prodigal, wrestling with God like the poor widow and the humble publican, resting in the Saviour like the penitent thief upon the cross, treading in the footsteps of the good Samaritan the divine man of Nazareth, aided by the Holy Ghost, even the chief of Gentile sinners might hope to reach the perfection of manhood on earth, and to be lifted with Lazarus to Abraham's bosom, or rapt with Jesus himself into the paradise of God.

SUMMARY.

Taking into account all the various facts brought to light in the survey of the third Gospel, and giving to them their due weight, its peculiar fitness for the Greek mind of that age cannot reasonably be denied.

It has been shown to be a fact of history, that Luke, a Greek in birth, character, and culture, prepared this Gospel, with the aid of Paul, for Greek readers, the men who were the representatives of the race at large. This is the historical basis of the theory.

The adaptation to the Greek soul and its needs has been shown to furnish the satisfactory explanation of the various peculiarities of this Gospel, — in its general plan, in its central idea and general movement, in its omissions and additions, and in its incidental variations.

In fine, it is not too much to affirm that the third Gospel is so suited to the wants of the Greek soul as to prove that it must in reality have been prepared, as tradition testifies, for the Greek as the representative of universal humanity. In distinction from Matthew, the Gospel for the Jew, the man of prophecy; from Mark, the Gospel for the Roman, the man of power; and from John, the Gospel for the Christian, the man of faith; Luke is the Gospel for the Greek, the world-man.

PART V.

JOHN, THE GOSPEL FOR THE CHURCH.

"Deep strike thy roots, O heavenly Vine,
Within our earthly sod,
Most human and yet most divine,
The flower of man and God!

. . . .

"We faintly hear, we dimly see,
In differing phrase we pray;
But, dim or clear, we own in thee
The Light, the Truth, the Way!"

JOHN GREENLEAF WHITTIER.

"But as many as received him, to them gave he power to become the sons of God, even to them that believe on his name: which were born, not of blood, nor of the will of the flesh, nor of the will of man, but of God."

JOHN i. 12, 13.

"And many other signs truly did Jesus in the presence of his disciples, which are not written in this book: but these are written, that ye might believe that Jesus is the Christ, the Son of God; and that believing ye might have life through his name." John xx. 30, 31.

"Ultimus Joannes apostolus et evangelista, quem Jesu amavit plurimum, qui supra pectus Domini recumbens (Joann. xiii. et xxi.), purissima doctrinarum fluenta potavit, et qui solus de cruce meruit audire: *Ecce mater tua* (Joann. xix. 27). Is cum esset in Asia, et jam tunc hæreticorum semina pullularent, Cerinthi, Ebionis, et cæterorum qui negant Christum in carne venisse (quos et ipse in epistola sua antichristos vocat, 1 Joann. ii. 18), et apostolus Paulus frequenter percutit (Rom. iii.; 2 Cor. v.), coactus est ab omnibus pene tunc Asiæ episcopis, et multarum Ecclesiarum legationibus, de divinitate Salvatoris altius scribere, et ad ipsum (ut ita dicam) Dei Verbum, non tam andaci, quam felici temeritate prorumpere."

JEROME.

CHAPTER I.

HISTORICAL VIEW OF THE CHRISTIAN ADAPTATION OF THE FOURTH GOSPEL.

SECTION I.

ORIGIN AND DESIGN OF THE FOURTH GOSPEL.

WHAT was the actual origin of the Gospel according to John? For what class of readers was it originally designed? It is clearly a fact of history that the fourth Gospel was prepared and given to the Church long after the other three had been completed, and with a different purpose.

Witnesses. Until recently no testimony of Papias concerning the origin of the fourth Gospel was supposed to be extant, as none has been preserved by Eusebius. But during the visit of Professor Tischendorf to Rome, in 1866, an extract from the work of Papias was found in a Latin manuscript of the Gospels in the Vatican Library. In this manuscript, in a prologue to the Gospel of John, it is said that the "Gospel of John was proclaimed and given to the Church while he was yet living, — as Papias of Hierapolis, the beloved disciple of John, declared at the close of the fifth book of his exposition of the oracles of our Lord."[1]

Of almost equal antiquity is the evidence furnished by the fragment of the Canon of Muratori, or the list of canonical books of the Scriptures which Muratori found in an old manuscript in the library of Milan. "That priceless document of the second century," as Van Oosterzee styles it, declares that "John wrote in answer to

[1] See Tischendorf, *The Origin of the Gospels*, p. 199; also Lange's *Com. on John*, p. 26

the express application of his fellow disciples and bishops."[1]

Irenæus makes a similar statement concerning the origin of the Gospel in the preaching of John. In accordance with the polemic purpose of his work, he adds that one object of the Gospel was "to remove that error which by Cerinthus had been disseminated among men, and a long time previously by those termed Nicolaitans, who are an offshoot of that 'knowledge' falsely so-called," and "to put an end to all such doctrines, and to establish the rule of truth in the Church." He says, "John excels in the depth of divine mysteries. For sixty years after the Ascension he preached orally, till the end of Domitian's reign; and after the death of Domitian, having returned to Ephesus, he was induced to write (his Gospel) concerning the divinity of Christ, co-eternal with the Father; in which he refutes those heretics, Cerinthus and the Nicolaitans."[2]

Clement of Alexandria gives still more explicitly the origin of the fourth Gospel, in the celebrated passage quoted by Eusebius. He used to say that, "last of all, John, observing that in the other Gospels those things were related that concerned the body (of Christ) and being persuaded by his friends and also moved by the Spirit of God, wrote a spiritual Gospel."[3]

Eusebius, the historian, besides adopting the statements of many of those who wrote before his time, and in measure summing up the past testimony, makes additions of his own. Among other things he gives the origin of John's Gospel substantially as follows: "While Matthew prepared his Gospel for the Hebrews, and Mark and Luke published their Gospels, they say that John in

[1] Van Oosterzee, *St. John's Gospel*, p. 104.

[2] Irenæus, *Against Heresies*, iii. 11.

[3] Euseb. *Hist. Eccles.* vi. 14.

all that time preached without writing. When the books of the three Evangelists were spread throughout the world, and came into his hands, he approved them and acknowledged them a true testimony; but wished that the declaration of those things which were done at the first preaching of Christ had been made in their books."[1] He therefore wrote his Gospel recording the ministry in Judæa and the early miracles.

Jerome, in the same passage in which he declares the origin of the first three Gospels, testifies no less explicitly of the fourth. "The last is John, the Apostle and Evangelist, whom Jesus loved the most, who, reclining upon the bosom of our Lord (John xiii. and xxi.), drank the purest streams of doctrine flowing forth from it, and who alone was worthy to hear from the cross: 'Behold thy mother' (John xix. 27). When he was in Asia, and the seeds of the heretics, Cerinthus, Ebion, and others, who denied that Christ has come in the flesh, had already sprung up, he was compelled by all the contemporary bishops of Asia, and by messages from many churches, to write more fully concerning the Divinity of the Saviour, and, with a presumption not so bold as happy to reach, so to speak, in his presentation of the Gospel, the very 'Word of God.'"[2]

Gregory Nazianzen teaches that "Matthew wrote the wonderful works of Christ for the Jews; Mark for the Romans; Luke for the Greeks; John, a herald who reaches the very heavens, for all."[3]

The great Augustine writes: "The three former Evangelists had narrated our Lord's temporal acts and the sayings that were of most avail for regulating the conduct of this present life, and which specially concerned

[1] Euseb. *Hist. Eccles.* iii. 21.

[2] Hieron. *Comment. in Evang. Matth. Proœm.*

[3] Greg. Naz. *Carmin.* lib. i. sect. i. 12, vers. 31–33.

the inculcation of active duties. St. John relates fewer acts of Christ, but is more full and minute in recording his sayings, particularly concerning the unity of the ever blessed Trinity and the felicity of life everlasting, and applies himself to the commendation of contemplative virtue. Hence the three other living creatures, by which the three other Evangelists are symbolized in the book of Ezekiel and in the Apocalypse, the lion, the man, and the calf, walk on the earth, because the three other Evangelists were principally occupied in relating those things which Christ wrought in the flesh, and the practical precepts which he delivered to those who are in the flesh; but St. John soars, like the eagle, above the clouds of human infirmity, and contemplates the light of never-waning truth with the keen and steadfast eye of faith; he gazes at the Divinity of Christ, by which he is equal to the Father, and endeavors to present it in his Gospel."[1]

Pertinent Facts. Such testimonies might be multiplied indefinitely, but those already given are sufficient for present purposes. They justify the belief in the following facts: that the Apostle John wrote the fourth Gospel at the close of the first century; that it was substantially the embodiment of his preaching to the early Church, of those spiritual doctrines and experiences which had come from his most intimate communion with Jesus, and which, in an important sense, supplemented the other Gospels; that it was written, not for the Jew, Greek, or Roman, as such, but for the Church; and that it was fitted to commend Jesus to Christians in the Church, as the divine Son of God, the light and life of the world.

Some of these facts have been disputed by modern writers, who have introduced their own crude hypotheses in their places. Especially has this been the case with the

[1] August. *de consens. Evang.*

facts concerning the date of the origin of the Gospel and concerning its design.

The facts themselves may be better understood and the false hypotheses more fully appreciated in the light of the historic changes of the times. It was almost half a century after the Gospel according to Luke, the last of the missionary Gospels, was given to the Greek Gentile world, that John wrote the Gospel which bears his name. In this interval of time the Apostles had preached the Gospel throughout the world, and they had all fallen asleep except John. Jerusalem had been taken by the Romans and the Jewish system overthrown. The Temple had been destroyed and its sacrifices and ritual had been abolished. The great telegraphic system which had been constituted by the Temple and the synagogues had passed away. The Christian religion as embodied in the Church of Christ had taken the place of the Jewish and was extending itself into all lands.

The first great missionary work had therefore been done, and John in writing his Gospel addressed a generation that had been taught the historical truths recorded by the other Evangelists and the doctrines of the Epistles and the Apocalypse. In fact they had in their hands all the books of the Old and New Testaments except the fourth Gospel, and were thoroughly acquainted with the doctrines, the sacraments, and the worship of the Christian system.

The last Evangelist, therefore, wrote for a generation of Christians. The earlier Gospels, intended for men unacquainted with Christian truth, intentionally presented to their readers only the simpler ideas concerning God and Christ and redemption; but John, writing for the Christian Church as a whole and for the world at large, could take for granted their familiarity with the earlier truths, and present the profounder aspects of the Gospel for which their previous training had filled the entire Christian Church with an intense longing.

Design. In the light of this unique history and experience of the age and the Church the design of the fourth Evangelist may best be made clear. Various aims have been attributed to him, most of which find some show of justification in the statements of the early writers.

It has been held by some that the original design of this Gospel was polemic or controversial. Various heresies arose in the early Church even before the death of the last of the Apostles. Prominent among these was Gnosticism, which taught that all natures, intelligent and material, are derived by successive emanations from the Deity. Against these, we are told, John was commissioned to write. In fact, Irenæus expressly says that it was John's purpose to confute the Gnostic Cerinthus.

Now it is obvious that in any full development and presentation of the truth it must come into necessary antagonism with error in all its forms, so that in John's Gospel we cannot fail to find an express opposition to all the theological and christological heresies of that age and of later ages. It is certainly true, in a very intelligible sense, that this Gospel was designed to meet these heresies. It may even be admitted that one object before the mind of the Evangelist was to meet the particular heresy of Cerinthus. But, as Tholuck has well remarked, there is certainly no pervading controversial aim. Still more to our point is it that John distinctly declares his chief aim to be a different one (xx. 30, 31). The controversial aim must, therefore, have been a subordinate one.

It has been held by others that the main object of the Evangelist was to supplement what had been already written. He undertook to supply the facts passed over in the other Gospels.

That John assumes that his readers are familiar with the ordinary traditional circle of Gospel truth is clear from many passages that presuppose the accounts of events as given in the other Gospels. It is evident, for example, that his declaration: "For John was not yet cast into prison" (iii. 24), assumes the knowledge, on the part of his readers, of the account of the imprisonment of the Baptist given by Matthew (xi.), Mark (vi. 14–29), and Luke (iii. 20).[1]

But that the historical completion of the three synoptical Gospels cannot be admitted to have been the specific aim of John may be made equally clear. The unity of the Gospel proves it impossible. "This Gospel," says Hase, "is no mere patchwork to fill up a vacant space." "Not even as a distinct subordinate purpose," says Tholuck, "kept in view by the Evangelist throughout, can we perceive a design of filling out what had been omitted by the others. It is in conflict with such a view, in fact, that so much has been embraced in the fourth Gospel which is also found in the first three; that not a few of at least apparent contradictions to them occur, which might have been harmonized; that, on the other hand, the apparent contradictions between the synoptical Gospels are not cleared up; that, at the point where he declares his purpose (xx. 30) some statement of this aim might justly be looked for; and, finally, that to embrace this view strictly would force us to think of a literary assiduity of a comparatively modern stamp." The fact is that John adds but very little of purely historical matter, except the chronological outline which has been seen to be of such great value. But besides this there must be noted

[1] Compare also John xi. 2 with Matt. xxvi. 6–13, and Mark xiv. 3–9; John i. 32 with Matt. iii. 13–17, Mark i. 9–11, and Luke iii. 21, 22; John xviii. 2, 3 with Matt. xxvi. 14, 15, Mark xiv. 10, 11, Luke xxii. 3–6; John xxi. 15 and xiii. 36–38 with Matt. xxvi. 33, and Mark xiv. 29, for further illustrations of such assumptions.

an entire absence of any express allusion to the other Evangelists, which is simply unaccountable on the hypothesis that John was a historical supplementer.

These hypotheses take into account only the very fewest of the facts, in short, scarcely more than a single fact each. The true theory must be broad enough to account for all the peculiar facts of the Gospel. The view drawn from history meets these demands. The fourth Gospel was written by John in response to an appeal from the Church — already possessing the other Gospels — for a spiritual Gospel, and written with the view of furthering the spiritual life of the Church.

This accounts for the fact that the Gospel actually meets the theological and christological heresies of that and after ages, — since a full development of Christian truth could not fail to do this. It explains the diverse and supplementary nature of the Gospel, — since there was no need for the reiteration of the facts already recorded by the other Evangelists, and none for the merely missionary aspects of Gospel truth; while there was a demand for a Christian theology from the lips of Christ himself.

Accordingly the Church in all ages has regarded this as distinctively the spiritual Gospel, the special Gospel treasure for the Christian. This view, impressed by the Gospel itself, has been embodied by leading writers in the different ages.

Says Origen: "We may presume then to say that the Gospels are the first-fruits of all the Scriptures, and the first-fruits of the Gospels is that of John, into whose meaning no man can enter, unless he has reclined upon the bosom of Jesus, ... and, as it were, become a second John."

Says Augustine: "In the four Gospels, or rather in the four books of the one Gospel, the Apostle St. John, not undeservedly with reference to his spiritual understanding compared to an eagle, has lifted higher, and far more sublimely than the other three, his proclamation, and in lifting it up he has wished our hearts also to be lifted. For the other three Evangelists walked, so to speak, on earth with our Lord as man — of his divinity they said but few things; but John, as if it oppressed him to walk on earth, has opened his words as it were with a burst of thunder, has lifted himself not only above earth and every sphere of sky and heaven, but even above every host of angels, and every order of invisible powers, and reaches to him by whom all things were made, as he says: 'In the beginning was the Word,' etc. He proclaims other things in keeping with this great sublimity with which he begins, and speaks of the divinity of our Lord as no other person has spoken. He pours forth that into which he had drunk. For not without a reason is it mentioned in his own Gospel, that at the feast he reclined upon the bosom of his Lord. From that bosom he had in secrecy drunk in the stream, but what he drank in secret he poured forth openly."

In short no Christian can read the Gospel according to John without being impressed with its preëminently spiritual character. Accordingly, in all ages the Church has regarded it as her chief Gospel treasure.

Nor can it be reasonably denied that this view is more in harmony with the testimony which has been brought from the early Christian writers. It will subsequently be seen to be more in accordance with the structure and spirit of the fourth Gospel itself.

Date. Nor is there any good reason for doubting that John's Gospel was written at the close of the first century. The testimony of the Fathers is clear on this point. The progress made by the Christian Church rendered the Gospel necessary at that time. The argument for a later date, drawn from the character of the doctrine embodied in it, is utterly baseless. An able writer has shown that the doctrinal system of John is precisely that of the Epistles, while it is utterly unlike the teachings of the writers of the second century![1]

To the candid historical critic the main facts have, therefore, the very firmest foundation. It will at once appear that the witnesses cited are substantially the same as those on whom we depend for our knowledge of the origin of the first three Gospels, and on whom the Church depends chiefly for the establishment of the canon of the Scriptures. Their statements were received without question in the early Church. There is no sufficient reason for doubting them, since the witnesses were of the highest character, had both the ability and opportunity to ascertain the facts, and had no motive for perpetrating or perpetuating such a fraud as would be implied by the falsity of their statements.

It cannot be maintained with even a show of reason that their statements are not in accordance with history, and that they did not arise out of history. John, undoubtedly, prepared his Gospel for the Church, for the purpose of presenting more fully to the Christian heart the character, work, and doctrine of Jesus as the light and life.

SECTION II.

THE CHARACTER AND NEEDS OF THE CHRISTIAN.

If, as has been seen, the fourth Gospel had its origin in the preaching of John, after the missionary Gospels had been preached and the Church established throughout the world, then the character and needs of the Christian must furnish the key to this Gospel.

[1] See *The Doctrinal System of St. John, considered as Evidence for the Date of his Gospel,* by the Rev. J. J. Lias, M. A.

What manner of man was the Christian? What were his spiritual needs? The answer to these questions will cast light upon the Gospel prepared under the influence of the Holy Ghost for the Church.

I. *The Christian.*

The Christian is readily distinguished by marked characteristics from the natural man, whether Jew, Roman, or Greek. The Christian is the man who has heard the great facts of the Gospel, and who has accepted Jesus Christ as his Saviour. He has attained, through faith in Christ, to a new life which is different in its origin, motives, and aims, from the earthly life. This life, originating in divine power, leads him to complete submission to Christ and to entire devotion to him in the cause of the Gospel. He lives this spiritual life of faith and obedience by fixing his eyes upon the central fact of the cross, and through guidance and help given in the Scriptures or by the Holy Ghost directly from above, which guidance and help he ever longs to receive in increased measure. He is reaching out toward that everlasting life of glory with Christ, of which this new life is the beginning.

Out of these peculiar characteristics arose those spiritual needs of the Christian Church which were to be met by the Evangelist. By the aid of them must be sought the full understanding of the Gospel prepared by John.

The Man of Faith. The starting point in the Christian life is found in the personal acceptance of Jesus Christ as the Saviour from sin. This act involves the knowledge of God and the relation of man as a sinner to God, and of the incarnation, work, death, and resurrection of Jesus; the belief in his divine character and mission; and the practical resting of the soul on him for salvation. To this act the preaching of the Apostles and the promulgation of the first three Gospels brought that portion of the ancient world which at the close of the first century was found fully prepared for God's deliverer. By the grace of God the true Israelite accepted Jesus as his Saviour, because he found in him the Messiah, the fulfiller of the Law and the Prophets, the Emmanuel who was promised for his salvation; the true Roman, because he found in him the Son of God, the almighty and universal conqueror, who was able to save him; the true Greek, because he met the Greek idea of the perfect and divine man, who longed for the salvation of the race, and who had the power to save it. Thus the true men of all the races found in him the satisfaction of their spiritual wants; and in the very act of accepting him they were transformed in character and life.

The Man of the New Life. The transformation, resulting from the acceptance of Christ, introduced the Christian of whatsoever national extraction to a new life, different in its origin and motives from the mere worldly life. The latter has its source in the natural birth; the former in the birth from heaven by the Holy Spirit. And when this new life in Christ is once begun, its motive forces are found in things heavenly rather than in things earthly. The Jew lost his narrow Jewish ideas, and turned from the prophecies of Christ and the forms and ceremonies to Christ himself; the Roman ceased to care for the temporal king in finding the spiritual king and deliverer. The Greek parted with his low, humanitarian ideas of perfection, in having his eyes opened to see the divine and universal man. They were all brought into one brotherhood, all alike recognizing in Jesus the elder brother, the spring and moving power of their new life, and being all alike linked in living union with him through faith.

The Man of Christ. The Christian is the man who

finds the aim of his life in Christ, and who can say with Paul "to me to live is Christ." If by his natural birth a Jew, he yet sees that the Jewish life of form and ceremony is no longer worthy of his soul, since in Christ's own example is the true ritual; if a Roman, he sees that the Roman life of earthly industry and conquest and supremacy is no longer worthy of him, since in Christ's gracious work, in his victory over sin, and in his kingdom are to be found the true work and conquest and empire; if a Greek, he sees that the Greek life of perfection sought through philosophy and art is no longer worthy of him, since through faith in Christ, whose reason is divine, and whose beauty is divine moral excellence, is to be realized the perfection of humanity. Whatever his earthly nativity he follows Christ, obeys him, aims to become like him, and devotes himself to him in the work of advancing the kingdom of God in the conquest of sinners. He finds the centre of his system of faith and life, and the centre of his Christ too, in the cross. The incarnate Son of God, crucified and raised from the dead, is the ground of all his hopes. He receives the remission of sin through the blood of Christ. By faith he eats of the broken body of Christ, and drinks of his shed blood, partakes of the boundless grace of God to sinners, and especially is made the recipient of the Holy Ghost who is given to enlighten, renew, and sanctify the children of God.

The Man of Endless Divine Life. The Christian is the man who expects an everlasting life with Christ beyond this present life on earth. In Christ life and immortality are brought to light. As by faith in him the life is begun, so by continual faith in him it is sustained and nourished on earth, and by faith in him as the resurrection and the life it is completed in the life of immortality. Even while waiting for the revelation of the glory, he is evermore found living for the invisible, spiritual, and eternal, evermore reaching out after communion with Christ his risen, ascended, and glorified Lord.

II. *The Key to John's Gospel.*

If the character of the Christian is such as it has been represented, it will furnish the key to the Gospel intended for him. That Gospel must be suited to meet his wants.

It was an age of great intellectual activity in which John wrote his Gospel. Reason was asserting its power and speculation was rife, and men who professed the faith in Christ were called to combat the errors of philosophy. It was an age of equally great worldliness, when there was need of asserting and vindicating the spirituality of Christianity against the prevailing earthliness.

The Gospel for the Christian must present Jesus as the revelation of God, — the word, the truth, the light, which the Christian needs in the new life. It must make plain all the great essential matters concerning the Christian course, so that in its light he may see clearly to avoid the danger, error, and death. It is obvious that the missionary Gospels do not deal largely with these subjects, — do not deal with them at all, except as they have to do with leading men to the first acceptance of Christ and the beginning of the divine life in him. They leave the wants of this higher and peculiarly spiritual sphere for some later hand to supply. The fourth Gospel must in this sense be the supplement of the first three.

Most assuredly, if the Christian is to be in any high degree intelligent, he especially needs light concerning the divine life which, by the grace of God, he has undertaken to live, — concerning its nature; its relations to God and Christ; its origin and beginnings; the modes of sustaining it to its full vigor; its mission in this world and its issues, after the death of the body, in the regions of immortality. These spiritual needs become the great ones with the Christian.

To the Christian these are the credentials of Jesus, no less essential than prophecy to the Jew, or power to the Roman, or the perfection of manhood to the Greek. Without them his most pressing needs would be left unsupplied. There could, therefore, be no Gospel for him in any production which should omit or pass slightly over these grand themes of the divine and immortal life of faith. The Christian soul of that age — essentially the same as in all other ages — furnishes the key to the fourth Gospel.

SECTION III.

THE AUTHORSHIP OF THE FOURTH GOSPEL.

The author of the fourth Gospel was peculiarly fitted to prepare the truth of the Gospel for the Christian. There is no valid reason for doubting that the Church from the beginning received it as the production of the Apostle John.

Modern Doubts. It is only of late years that attempts have been made to destroy the faith in its genuineness. Individual skeptics, at the close of the last century, denied that it was the work of John; but their attack merited and received but little attention. Bretschneider, by his "Probabilia," published in 1820 with the special "view of anew exciting and extending inquiry into the genuineness of the Johannine writings," first made the serious discussion of the question necessary.

The assault has since been renewed by the Tübingen school of critics with Baur at their head, and has lately given rise to a more earnest and exciting controversy. Assuming "the radical difference and hostility between the Jewish and Gentile types of Christianity," — between the party of Peter and the other disciples, and that of Paul, — these assailants represent John's Gospel as having been written about the middle of the second century by some Gentile Christian, who aimed to bring about peace between the two hostile parties, and forged the name of John to his writing in order to give it the weight of that Apostle's character. Hence John's Gospel so-called is to be rejected. The difference between it and the first three Gospels is made an additional argument for its rejection.

This is not the place to enter at length into the consideration of the genuineness of the fourth Gospel. Those who wish to read a thorough discussion of the questions involved may best gratify their desire by consulting some one or more of the able and popular works devoted to the subject.

It is sufficient to note that the arguments adduced should have little weight with Christian men of average common sense. They have no basis of fact to rest upon. The clear testimony of all Christian antiquity is against them. John's Gospel can be traced back to the close of the first century. It exactly accords with his character. The theological quarrel between the Petrine and Pauline parties in the early Church is a myth. Moreover the historic view, which it is the object of the present work to set forth and vindicate, fully explains the characteristic differences of John's Gospel from the others, and shows these differences to have been a necessity if the practical wants of the Church, in that age, and in all subsequent ages, were to be met by the Gospel. So manifold and conclusive are the evidences of the authorship, that it would be as easy, perhaps easier, to prove that Shakespeare did not write "Hamlet," or even that Milton did not write "Paradise Lost," or that Bacon did not write the "Novum Organum," as to prove that the Apostle John did not write the fourth Gospel.

Character and Career. That John was just the man to give shape to the Gospel for the Christian Church may readily be shown. His birth and early history; his character as transformed and exalted by the power of the Gospel; his intimate union with his Master and his intense sympathy with him; his long and profound Christian experience and his wide acquaintance with the needs of the Church, combined to make him the fit instrument for the work to which he was divinely called.

The history of John, so far as it has been recorded, is too familiar to require extended rehearsal. He appears to have been born in Bethsaida of Galilee. His father, Zebedee, was a respectable and well-to-do fisherman on the Sea of Galilee able to possess his own boats and to have hired servants. His mother, Salome, was one of those women who ministered to Jesus of their wealth, and who followed him to the cross. She went with the Marys on the morning of the resurrection to the sepulchre to embalm the body of Jesus. Born of such a mother, it is not surprising that John early became one of the disciples of the Baptist, nor that when the Baptist introduced him to Jesus he at once followed him as the Messiah.

Perhaps the character of no scriptural personage has been more misunderstood than that of "the beloved disciple." The idea formed of him is that he was a "soft, tender, almost femininely affectionate spirit." So the painters have manifestly conceived him, and so the Church has too generally regarded him. Nothing could be farther from the truth. Such a character would be poorly as possible fitted to prepare a Gospel for the Church. It has only the elements that win from strong and earnest souls a mild contempt. John was in fact the very best evidence, to the men of his day, of the power of the Gospel to harmonize the most different and apparently contradictory elements of character.

Says a late writer: "The character of John is composed of two vastly differing elements, rarely found in such combination except under the transforming power of the Christian spirit, but found there in its perfection and consummation. These two elements are, very great masculine strength, joined with affections so overflowing and tender, that the strength is concealed under their profusion, except when occasions and emergencies bring it to the test. The granite is hidden under the tendrils that overhang it with flowers. It is only by assuming that these two elements are inconsistent with each other that the critics have raised their objections against the congruity of the canonical Johannean writings, whereas to blend them together is the great achievement of Christianity in human nature, and the blending is most perfect when the disciple leans most intimately on the bosom of his Lord. The combination does not impair the masculine intrepidity, but preserves and tones it, though concealing it sometimes under the mildest of womanly gentleness."[1]

That this is the true view may readily be verified. The rugged nature of John — sometimes verging almost upon savageness — was embodied in the name, "Boanerges," sons of thunder, given to him with his brother (Mark iii. 17); and was clearly manifested in the zeal which prompted him to call down fire from heaven on the Samaritan city that refused them its hospitality (Luke ix. 54). It appeared in the ambition which led him, with his brother, to seek, through their mother, the chief places in the magnificent temporal kingdom which the disciples expected (Matt. xx. 21; Mark x. 37); in the fact that when, at the arrest of Jesus in Gethsemane, the other disciples fled for their lives, the youthful John kept close to his master, and followed on to the judgment

[1] Sears, *The Fourth Gospel the Heart of Christ*, p. 65.

scene (John xviii. 15); in the fact that at the cross, amid the raging of the multitudes, John alone was standing close by, ready to receive the dying message from his Lord (John xix. 26). Later, it is John who, in his Epistles, hurls the most terrible anathemas at the false teachers of his day; and who, in the Apocalypse, pens the visions of the melting universe, of the assembling judgment, and of lost souls.

To all this terrible power, which, unsanctified might have made almost a demon, his writings and history show that he joined a depth of tenderness equally marvelous, — the tenderness of no sentimentalist or weakling but that of one of the very strongest natures.

Special Fitness. Such a nature, under the sanctifying power of that divine grace which softened the ruggedness and exalted the tenderness, was just the nature needed in the man who was to prepare and present the Gospel truth that should lead the Christian in making the greatest attainments in the divine life. He was able to understand the heights and depths of human temptations and trials, of human wants along the line of Christian struggle and endeavor, and to treasure up from his Master's lips and appreciate the divine doctrines and motives needed to sustain and cheer the Christian onward and upward toward the heavenly goal.

It might almost be said that no other man appears in the original college of Apostles who could possibly have accomplished this great task for the Church without a radical change of nature. Most certainly Matthew had too exclusive a regard to prophecy to do such a work, and Peter and Mark were too exclusively active. John alone had that combination of intuition and reason that was needed, and that fitted him for the work provided he could secure the other special requisites for it, — such as close union with Christ and sympathy with him, and large acquaintance with the needs of the Church.

It is a well known fact that he had the requisite union and sympathy with Christ.

He belonged to that inner circle, consisting of himself, Peter, and James, to the members of which alone Jesus permitted a near view of the great crises in his life and work on earth, — such as the transfiguration and the agony. Among the three he was the beloved disciple, the disciple who leaned on Jesus' breast at the table at the last supper. He was one of the first to follow Jesus, and he was the one to cling most closely to him to the end. To him was intrusted the mother, with whom in his earthly career Jesus had been so closely bound, and from the affecting hour on the cross to the death of her whose heart had been pierced with many sorrows, Mary and John were as mother and son.

But more important still was the intense sympathy of the beloved disciple with his divine Master in his highest spiritual moods, views, aspirations, and purposes.

His peculiar nature, softened and elevated by grace, fitted him to understand and bring forth something of the secret of the spiritual life of Jesus, — to give to men what Ernesti has called "the heart of Christ."

It is well known that when men, differing in temperament, culture, or experience, look upon the same landscape, each takes into his mind and carries away different features. One sees in it the hills and valleys, lakes and water-courses, that remind him of some other and perhaps more familiar scene. Another fixes upon the grander features of forest and mountain, of gorge and cataract, which awaken in him a sense of power. A third takes note of the various products of art and civilization, the signs of the presence of man with the moulding forces of his reason. A fourth grasps the higher harmonies of nature and art, of earth and sky, in which a voice speaks to men declaring the presence and glory of Him who is of all Creator and Lord. Like these were the four Evangelists in what they saw in the grand and varied life of Jesus of Nazareth. John was the last. He saw for all the Church what the other three saw not at all, or saw chiefly for themselves. He heard for every Christian through the ages the higher truths which the others heard not at all, or heard chiefly for their own edification. For this he was fitted by his nature; to this he was called; for this he was inspired.

Were it not for the so-called Johannean passages in the other Gospels, there might almost have been a doubt cast upon the existence of such a world of truth as John presents.[1] But these glimpses of the same truth prevent the doubt. In their missionary work the other Apostles had little occasion to use these higher spiritual truths, even if they knew and understood them.

Still another peculiar element of fitness in John, as the instrument for preparing the Gospel of the Christian life, was his long, varied, and profound Christian experience.

In this he was alone among the Apostles. If, as is generally agreed, his Gospel was not written until almost the close of the first century, he was ripened for it by an experience of nearly seventy years. In him appears the contemplative spirit of the early Church. For half a century he seems to have been comparatively silent concerning the higher truths of the Christian life, although doubtless brooding over them, until God's hour came. During three quarters of a century he lived upon the words of his Master, the eternal Word, — in filial intercourse with Mary, in spiritual communion with the Church, in living union with the ascended Christ, — until those words became the very thought of his thought

[1] See Matt. xi. 25–27; Luke x. 21, 22, etc.

and the very life of his life, and he could give them a reality in the utterance such as no other man could ever give them. Hence it is that to-day men cling to the Gospel of John as the very voice of the innermost soul of the divine Redeemer.

His long and wide acquaintance with the needs of the Church completed his fitting for his work. His knowledge of the temptations and trials, of the sufferings and persecutions, of the rising errors in faith and practice, in that age which had infolded in it the germs of all the ages, brought him to the clearest apprehension and fullest appreciation of the needs of the Christian Church, and enabled him to speak as directly to the innermost soul of the Christian as he spoke from the innermost soul of Christ. For the regenerated man, whether Jew, Roman, or Greek, he could embody in its highest form the doctrine concerning Jesus Christ as the light and life.

The impulse which led the Christian Church to ask for the permanent record of John's Gospel, and that which led the Evangelist to comply with the request, were both from the Holy Ghost, the Spirit of light and life. Out of all the men, of that age, connected with the apostolic body, the Holy Ghost chose the man best fitted in Christian character and experience to prepare and write the Gospel for the Christian world.

CHAPTER II.

CRITICAL VIEW OF THE CHRISTIAN ADAPTATION OF THE FOURTH GOSPEL.

The fitness of the fourth Gospel for the Christian Church of the apostolic age will appear from an examination of the Gospel itself in the light of its origin, design, and authorship.

SECTION I.

THE CHRISTIAN ADAPTATION IN THE GENERAL PLAN OF THE FOURTH GOSPEL.

The Gospel according to John, may be divided into three parts, — presenting the successive stages in the revelation of Jesus, the incarnate Word, as the light and life, to the faith of men, — together with an appropriate introduction and conclusion.

In these divisions the character and doctrine of Jesus are exhibited in their connection with the necessities of the Church, which had been gathered out of the world by the proclamation of the earlier forms of the Gospel. The eternal Word, as incarnate in Jesus of Nazareth, is set forth in the progress of his highest spiritual work for believers throughout the world.

OUTLINE OF THE FOURTH GOSPEL.

INTRODUCTION.

The Advent and Incarnation of the Word. The Evangelist opens his Gospel by exhibiting Christ the Eternal Word, in his Divine Origin and in his manifestation to men in the Incarnation. i. 1–13.

A. His eternal, divine origin, and his pre-historic work and manifestation. i. 1–5.

B. His manifestation to men in time. i. 6–13.

a. As heralded by the Baptist and commended to the faith of the world. 6–8.

b. As the true light, but rejected by the world and by his own. 9–11.

c. As giving to those who received him power to become the children of God through faith on his name. 12, 13.

PART I.

The Incarnate Word, the only Life of the World. The Evangelist presents the spiritual revelations of the Word during the public ministry in Judæa.

Jesus appears as the Incarnate Son of God, full of grace and truth, the only Life of the World. The true Israelites believe; but the false reject him, and prevent the continuance of his work in Judæa. i. 14–vi. 71.

Section 1. John records the testimony to the grace and truth of the incarnate Word, — given before the first Passover of the public ministry. i. 14–ii. 12.

A. By John the Baptist. i. 15–36.

B. By Jesus himself, — in personal intercourse and by the miracle at Cana. i. 37–ii. 12.

Section 2. John records the manifestations of the spiritual truth and power at the foundation of the kingdom of God, — and the rising faith between the first and second Passovers of the public ministry. ii. 13–iv. 54.

A. In the special revelations of Jesus, as the Messiah, the life and light, to the Jews, as the chosen people. ii. 13–iii. 36.

a. To the masses and rulers, — in cleansing the Temple, teaching its spiritual design and presenting himself as the true temple and passover. ii. 13–22.

b. To Nicodemus, a representative of the awakened faith among the Jews, — in teaching the doctrine of the new birth through the death and mediation of the Son of God. iii. 1–21.

c. To the disciples of the Baptist, — in the Baptist's public testimony to Christ as the Son of God, and made by the Father, through faith, the only way of everlasting life. iii. 22–36.

B. In the special revelation of Jesus, as the Messiah, the living water and the only Saviour of the world, to the Samaritans, — to the woman at the well, and to the men of Sychar. iv. 1–42.

C. In the special revelation of Jesus, as the author of life, to the Galileans, — in the healing of the nobleman's son. iv. 43–54.

Section 3. John records the greater subsequent manifestation of Jesus in connection with two successive Passovers, in which he proclaims himself the only bread of eternal life, and in consequence of which many of his disciples forsake him and the Jews seek to kill him. v. 1–vi. 71.

A. To the Jews, — in Jerusalem at the second Passover of his public ministry, — as the life of the world. v. 1–47.

a. In healing the impotent man on the Sabbath. 1–15.

b. In the vindication of himself, — at the subsequent judicial arraignment for Sabbath-breaking, — on the ground of his being one with the Father and the true Messiah of the Scriptures. 16–47.

B. To the multitudes, — by the Sea of Galilee, at the time of the third Passover, — as the only bread of eternal life. vi. 1–71.

a. In the miraculous feeding of the five thousand and the stilling of the storm. 1–21.

b. In the discourse of the following day, teaching the doctrine of eternal life through faith in his flesh and blood as the true bread of life from heaven, — leading to the desertion of many disciples, to the confession of the Twelve, and to his withdrawal from the open public work in Judæa. 22–71.

PART II.

The Incarnate Word, the Life and Light, in Conflict with the Spiritual Darkness. The Evangelist presents some of the spiritual revelations of Jesus to the unbelieving Jews, during the period of occasional and private visits to Jerusalem.

Jesus appears on various extraordinary occasions, presses his claims as the Son of God, the only life and light of the world, and rouses his enemies to successive attempts to destroy him. vii. 1–xi. 54.

Section 1. John records the private visit of Jesus to Jerusalem, at the Feast of Tabernacles (six months before the last Passover), — when he presents himself as the water of life, the light of the world, and the only Saviour from the bondage of sin. vii. 1–viii. 59.

A. His first appearance in the Temple, — the only life of the world. vii. 1–viii. 1.

a. Renewing his old claim to have come from the Father and to be the water of life for the thirsting world.

b. Thereby raising a conflict of opinions concerning himself and leading the Sanhedrim to send officers to take him.

B. His second appearance in the temple, — the only light and deliverer. viii. 2–59.

a. Showing to the people, by the case of the adulterous woman, the darkness and sin of the Scribes and Pharisees, and contrasting himself, as the Son of God, the only Saviour of the world from the darkness and sin. 2–30.

b. Declaring to those who believed him to be the Messiah, that he, the Son of God ever-abiding with the Father, alone can free them through the truth, from their bondage to sin and Satan, — thereby rousing their hatred and leading them to attempt to stone him. 31–59.

Section 2. John records certain subsequent visits of Jesus to Jerusalem, when he presents himself as the only Healer of spiritual blindness, and the only Saviour of men through his sacrificial death, — resulting in unbelief and rage. ix. 1–x. 21.

A. The restoring of sight to the man born blind, and the revelation of Jesus to the blinded Jews as the one Sent of God to heal their spiritual blindness through faith in himself. ix. 1–41.

B. The claim of Jesus to be the Son of God, the Good Shepherd, through the laying down of whose life the sheep can alone find life. x. 1–21.

C. Still later, at the feast of Dedication, the claim of Jesus — when urged to declare himself — that he and the Father are one. x. 22–42.

a. The appeal to the works done in his Father's name as proof of his claims, and the reiteration of his oneness with the Father. 22–30.

b. Thereby leading to another attempt to stone him, and to his escape across the Jordan to the Gentiles. 31–42.

Section 3. John records the raising of Lazarus, when Jesus presents himself as the Resurrection and the Life, — thereby bringing the rage of his enemies to a crisis and hastening his own death. xi. 1–54.

A. The death of Lazarus and the interposition of Jesus as the resurrection and the life. xi. 1–44.

B. The results, — faith on the part of the people, and the settled purpose to destroy him on the part of the Sanhedrim. xi. 45–54.

PART III.

The Incarnate Word securing the Life of the World through his Sacrificial Death. The Evangelist presents the bold public return of Jesus to Jerusalem, and the clearer spiritual revelations connected with the close of his career.

Jesus, claiming to be the Messiah, voluntarily sacrifices himself on the cross, as the Passover of the world. xi. 55–xix. 42.

Section 1. John records the public return and claim of Jesus, together with the events which preceded and brought about his sacrificial death. xi. 55–xiii. 30.

A. The crisis with the chief conspirators occurs when Judas and the Sanhedrim are roused to enmity, by the anointing for the burial at Bethany, and by the public entry as Messiah into Jerusalem. xi. 55–xii. 19.

B. The crisis with the world at large is heralded by the coming of certain Greeks, — calling forth a renewed declaration of the claims of Jesus. xii. 20–50.

a. The public announcement to the people by Jesus, that the hour of his glorification by the Father, and of his lifting up to draw all men to him, has arrived. 20–33.

b. His final appeal to the people, as the only light of the world, the only representative of his Father, and the only way of everlasting life, — resulting in unbelief and rejection. 34–50.

C. The crisis with the disciples is reached at the feet-washing, at the Passover supper, when Jesus in his boundless love teaches the lesson of humble service, and singles out and sends away Judas the betrayer. xiii. 1–30.

Section 2. John records the last private teaching of Jesus, during the evening of his betrayal, to his own true disciples, containing the complete unfolding of the Christian life. xiii. 31–xvii. 26.

A. The discourse in the room, after the Passover supper, containing the announcement of immediate departure and glorification, and the consolations administered. xiii. 31–xiv. 31.

B. The discourse on the way to Gethsemane, concerning the new life of reconciliation with the Father. xv. 1–xvi. 33.

a. Its features, starting from the vine and branches, —

the living union of believers with Christ by faith; the loving union of believers with one another; the accompanying hatred by the world. xv. 1–25.

b. Its development through the mission of the Holy Ghost, the Comforter (Helper). xv. 26–xvi. 15.

c. The necessary preparation for it, in the departure of Jesus by the cross, thus at once winning the boundless favor of God the Father and overcoming the world for those who believe on him. xvi. 16–33.

C. The intercessory prayer in which Jesus links the everlasting life with the Father and concludes his special spiritual revelation to his disciples. xvii. 1–26.

Section 3. John records the voluntary surrender and sacrifice of Jesus, with the attendant evidences of his being the Messiah, the light and life of the world. xviii. 1–xix. 42.

A. Jesus voluntarily surrenders himself into the hands of his enemies the unbelieving Jews. xviii. 1–xix. 16.

a. The betrayal and apprehension, — in which he shows his power over his enemies and his omnipotence, and declares his purpose to drink "the cup of his Father." xviii. 1–11.

b. The trial before the Jewish authorities, in the presence of John, the faithless Peter, and others, — in which he solemnly reïterates his claims made before the people in his teachings. xviii. 12–27.

c. The trial before the Gentile ruler, Pilate, — to whom he is revealed as Messiah, the King of the Jews, by the power of truth, and as the Son of God possessing all power; by whom he is repeatedly declared innocent and yet is delivered up to the Jews to be crucified. xviii. 28–xix. 16.

B. Jesus voluntarily yields himself up to his executioners and is crucified as "Jesus of Nazareth the King of the Jews," fulfilling the prophecies concerning Messiah in his experience in finishing the sacrificial work. xix. 17–30.

C. Jesus yields himself to death and the grave as Messiah. xix. 31–42.

CONCLUSION.

The Incarnate Word, Crucified and Risen, the Saviour and Lord of all Believers. The Evangelist presents the manifestations of the risen Saviour to the faith of his followers, — establishing his identity, and the reality of his presence of sympathy and power with his Church in all ages. xx. 1–xxi. 25.

Section 1. John records certain appearances of Jesus to the disciples, after his resurrection, designed to comfort them and to lead to faith in him and to life through his name. xx. 1–31.

A. To Mary Magdalene, before his (first) ascension to his Father, — to comfort her in her sorrow. xx. 1–18.

B. To the disciples, with Thomas absent, in secret gathering in the upper chamber in Jerusalem, — to give peace in their trouble and to assure them of the gift of the Holy Ghost. xx. 19–23.

C. To the eleven disciples, in the same place, on the next Lord's day, — to relieve the difficulties of the doubting Thomas. xx. 24–29.

D. To the disciples, with many other signs, not recorded, but intended to work faith in Christ as the Son of God, and to lead to life through his name. xx. 30–31.

Section 2. John records the most extraordinary of Christ's manifestations, — that by the Sea of Tiberias, — completely establishing his identity and Messiahship, and preparing for the future work of his Church. xxi. 1–25.

A. The miracle of the draught of fishes, revealing Jesus to the faith of his disciples, who under the lead of Peter, had returned to their old occupation. xxi. 1–14.

B. The restoration of the backslidden Peter, and the delineation of his future work and destiny. xxi. 15–19.

C. The career of John marked out, and his final testimony to the truth of his Gospel. xxi. 20–25.

SECTION II.

THE CHRISTIAN ADAPTATION IN THE CENTRAL IDEA OF THE FOURTH GOSPEL.

The outline of the gospel according to John, with its marks of the Christian aim of the Evangelist, will assist in making it apparent that this Gospel agrees, in its central idea and general drift, with the testimony of history that it was produced and published especially for Christian readers.

I. *The Central Idea.*

Starting out with this view of the aim of the fourth Gospel, it is easy to trace the governing idea throughout its extent and in all the prominent features.

The central idea of the Gospel, as stated by the Evangelist himself, is found in the divine life which has its origin in faith in Jesus as the Christ, the incarnate Son of God. He distinctly states that his selection of material was made with this end in view: "And many other signs truly did Jesus in the presence of his disciples, which are not written in this book, but these are written, that ye might believe that Jesus is the Christ, the Son of God; and that believing, ye might have life through his name" (xx. 30, 31).

It is evident from the needs of the Christian as already presented, that the Evangelist who would lead him to a higher and fuller life must present Jesus in his relations to the life of faith. John accordingly presents his character, not as the fulfillment of Messianic prophecy, nor as the personal embodiment of the Son of God, the almighty worker and conqueror, nor as the perfect and universal man, but as the eternal, divine Word, incarnate, crucified, and risen from the dead, the object of faith and the source of life.

The contrast is doubtless sometimes too sharply drawn between John, as *the Gospel of the Son of God*, and the other Gospels; for while in the former Jesus more expressly and frequently declares himself the Son of God, the latter always assume his Deity, often demonstrate it, and are utterly unintelligible except upon its admission. Nevertheless the ground of the contrast is real. The Christian consciousness affirms that the same thing is true of the contrast in spirituality between John's Gospel and the others, — it may be too sharply drawn, but every chapter and verse shows it to be real. In short, the fourth Gospel is everywhere the manifestation of Christ as the spiritual light for the building up of the spiritual life of believers. Ernesti might have said that *it is the heart of Christ in its most direct appeal to the faith of the Christian heart*, for every part of it bears the marks of its Christian aim.

That this is the Gospel of the incarnate Son in his relation to the divine life in man is made manifest everywhere. Its teachings would have been unintelligible to the men of that age without the more external and elementary teachings of the first three Evangelists. It presupposes the previous practical acceptance of Christ as the Saviour by those to whom it was addressed. It is the Gospel of faith, of life, of love.

This is the Gospel which gives the Christian the requisite instruction concerning the secret springs and laws of the life of faith and obedience to God, and concerning the mission of the Holy Ghost as man's divine helper in that life. It is obvious that these teachings are given nowhere else in the Gospels with such fullness, clearness, and directness. In short, all the great moving and controlling principles of the Christian life are here alone given in the form needed to prepare the way for an intelligent Christian career.

This is peculiarly the Gospel of everlasting life. It regards the divine life begun in the Christian soul as the germ of an endless life of purity and blessedness. It most clearly reveals in Christ the resurrection and the life, and the lifting up of even man's body from the grave to immortality. It alone, therefore, meets the longing of the renewed soul for the endless life in the heavenly mansions in perfect union and communion with God.

This is the Gospel of the risen and living Christ. It is to be remarked that in John's Gospel the perpetual ministrations of the risen and living Christ are brought out in the closing chapters as nowhere else in the Gospels. These chapters are accordingly among the most precious treasures of the Word of God.

These varied relations of Christ to the Christian appear throughout the fourth Gospel, as will be seen more clearly in its further consideration.

II. *General Drift.*

The presence of this central Christian idea manifests itself everywhere in the general movement of the fourth Gospel. It may be seen in the entire plan and in all the parts.

The Introduction exhibits our Lord, not as in Matthew, the Son of David, not as in Mark, the mighty conqueror, not as in Luke, the Son of man, but as the Son of God incarnate. As such, he is the Word, the Life, the Light, the Only Begotten of the Father, full of grace and truth. He is the Only Begotten which is in the bosom of the

Father; in short, he is God. The Word is made flesh and is rejected by many, but received by some who become in consequence the sons of God.

In these aspects he is presented throughout the Gospel.

In Part First, the Evangelist unfolds the spiritual manifestations of Jesus in the public ministry in Judæa. He appears during this period, especially to the faithful in the world, as the incarnate Son, the only life of the world, revealing the glory of God and a supernatural fullness of grace and truth, and meeting with rising faith and unbelief. The faithful ones who were waiting for his coming are found in the Baptist and his disciples, in such believing Jews as Nicodemus, in the woman of Samaria and her Samaritan neighbors, and in the Galilean nobleman; the enemies who meet him with persecution are found in the Jews at Jerusalem and in Galilee, who by seeking his life occasion his withdrawal from public work in Judæa.

In Part Second, the Evangelist exhibits some of the teachings of Jesus to the unbelieving Jews, during the period in which he visits Jerusalem only occasionally and privately. In these instructions Jesus presses upon them, with ever-increasing plainness and energy, his claim to be the Son of God, coequal with the Father, and through his sacrificial death the only source of light and freedom and life to men in their darkness and slavery and death, the only hope of a lost world. These teachings enrage the Jews beyond measure, and prepare them for his murder.

In Part Third, the Evangelist gives those last and clearest manifestations of Jesus as the light and life, made in connection with the close of his career. Jesus, as he voluntarily moves toward the cross, presents his claims in the fullest manner before all classes in Jerusalem, and reveals to his disciples on the evening of the betrayal the great doctrines of the Christian system and life. He then completes his sacrifice by yielding himself up to his enemies, to the cross, and to the power of death and the grave, — declaring with his closing breath that the work of redemption is "finished."

The Conclusion furnishes a fit completion of what the other portions have thus far carried forward. It manifests the risen Saviour to the faith of his followers, — establishing his bodily identity and the reality of his divine and human sympathy and power with his Church in all ages. These last two chapters of John, in presenting the risen Christ as the comforter of the weeping Magdalene, the peace-giver to the troubled band of disciples, the helper of the doubting Thomas, the provider for the fasting fishermen, the restorer of the backslidden Peter, and the rewarder of the faithful John, have ministered abundantly of like help to the faith of the people of God in all ages, and made the Church certain that it trusts not in a dead but in a living Saviour.

This Jesus, — who is not only the finisher of Judaism and the inheritor of all Jewish perfections, not only the satisfaction of the Roman idea in surpassing the best and mightiest of the Cæsars, not only the more than realization of the Greek ideal of manhood in being the perfect, divine man, but also the Incarnate Word, the perfect Revealer of God and eternal Life to a lost world, — this Jesus is the one whom John represents in his Gospel.

SECTION III.

THE CHRISTIAN ADAPTATION IN THE OMISSIONS AND ADDITIONS OF THE FOURTH GOSPEL.

I. *The Omissions of the Fourth Gospel.*

The Christian aim of the fourth Gospel appears especially in its omissions of facts and truths made prominent in the other Gospels.

As John contemplated the wants of the Church, in which there was properly no longer a distinction between Jew, Roman, and Greek, he had no need for the material presented in the missionary Gospels, and especially designed to commend Jesus to sinners in the representative races of the age. Even upon the assumption — at most but partially warranted — that the Jewish, Roman, and Greek Christians were still chiefly familiar with the Gospel prepared for each of them respectively, it is still true that the facts of the other and unfamiliar Gospels were not absolutely necessary for those to whom they had not been given. The peculiar facts of Mark and Luke would have added little toward producing conviction in the mind of the Jew who had Matthew's Gospel. The same is true of the facts of Matthew and Luke with reference to the Roman who had Mark's Gospel; and of those of Matthew and Mark with reference to the Greek who had Luke's Gospel.

Accordingly we have almost a clear sweep of omission, — none of the leading events detailed by the other Gospels, with a single exception, being recorded by John until he reaches the history of the Passion and the Resurrection, without which no Gospel could be written. That exception, in which John coincides with the synoptic Gospels, is the feeding of the five thousand (vi. 1–

24), retained in order to prepare for the discourse to which it gave rise, and in which Christ presented himself as the bread of life given to the world from heaven by the Father. Besides this the mere fact of the coming of Jesus to Bethany is retained (xii. 1), to explain the treachery of Judas connected with it, and for the instructive lessons conveyed in the anointing at that place.

This almost entire omission of the material found in the other Gospels is what would naturally be expected in a later and spiritual Gospel. *Quite another Gospel*, as Da Costa has said, must that one be which omits the human genealogy and divine origin of Jesus as Messiah, his early experience and preparation for his Messianic work, the Sermon on the Mount, the series of miracles and parables, and all the other treasures embodied for the Jew by Matthew in the first Gospel; the rapid and vivid progress of the Captain of our salvation in his work of conquering the world, as embodied by Mark for the Roman; the coming down of heaven to earth at the birth of John and Jesus, the marvelous exhibitions of the human tenderness of the divine man, the matchless system of parables unfolding the love of God to universal humanity, and all the other treasures embodied by Luke for the Greek, — *quite another Gospel*, and yet a Gospel with an aim just as marked and vastly higher. It passes by these facts, which appeal to the senses of the unspiritual man, to unfold that word of life which speaks to the soul of the spiritual man.

II. *The Additions of the Fourth Gospel.*

Still more clearly does the Christian aim of John's Gospel appear from the additions which he makes to the material furnished by the other Evangelists. These additions may be looked upon as made up of narratives of works of power and words of instruction, or as the embodiment of the doctrines of the Christian theology.

Works of Power. The fourth Gospel is only subordinately a record of outward events. Only six of our Lord's miracles are recorded in it; but these are all of the most remarkable kind, and surpass all the rest in depth, in specialty of application, and in fullness of instruction. Of these six, only one is found in the other three Gospels, — the feeding of the five thousand (vi. 1–15). The reason for John's recording it appears in another connection.

The peculiarities of the other five are very striking. They furnish a higher display of power over the ordinary laws and course of nature, than do the miracles of the other Gospels. John alone records the first of all the miracles that Jesus wrought, the changing of water into wine at Cana (ii. 1–11), in which without even the utterance of a word he *transforms the very nature of the substance* with which he deals. He records that of the nobleman's son (iv. 48–54), cured by Jesus *at a distance* from Cana. Out of the many cures of the lame and the palsied by the word of Jesus, he selects that of the man who had suffered from an infirmity *thirty and eight years* (v.), a case of the most utter friendlessness and of the most abject weakness, helplessness, and hopelessness. Out of the innumerable cures of the blind he chooses the case of the person *who had been born blind* (ix.), which was such a case as men had never known to be cured (ix. 32). He gives "the restoration of Lazarus to life, not from a deathbed, like the daughter of Jairus; not from a bier for the dead, like the young man of Nain, *but from the grave*, when, having lain buried there for four days, he had already begun to sink into corruption (xi.). Lastly, from among the signs and wonders which Jesus did while still upon the earth after his resurrection, and which are nowhere else recorded by the Evangelists, we have one example, in the miraculous draught of fishes on the sea of Tiberias (xxi.), when the disciples, at the command of their risen Lord, had thrown out the net on the right side of the ship, and Simon Peter *went up, and drew the net to land full of great fishes, an hundred and fifty and three; and for all there were so many, yet was not the net broken*."[1]

Still, John does not record these works simply because they are so wonderful; but because their extraordinary character made them so much the *better signs of the marvelous things of God*, and led Jesus to connect with them his profoundest spiritual reasonings, discourses, and conversations, alike with friends and foes, with his disciples and with the multitude.

The miracle at the wedding in Cana furnished the occasion for Jesus to define his relation, in his divine mission, to Mary, his earthly mother, and to exercise his creative energy in sanctioning the marriage relation and the home; while showing forth his own glory, and confirming the faith of his early followers. The healing of the man at the pool of Bethesda, occurring on the Sabbath-day, leads, not (as repeatedly happens in the case of the other Evangelists) to a single saying, but to a whole series of statements and instructions from the Saviour, respecting himself and his relation to the Father. The account of the opening of the eyes of the man born blind furnishes the vehicle for all the eminently spiritual teachings contained in the conversations between Jesus and the man whom he had healed, between the latter and the Pharisees, and between the Jews and the man's parents. With the narrative of the raising of Lazarus from the dead, the Evangelist has linked the clear and sublime teachings it occasioned concerning the doctrine of the resurrection, the account of the effect of the miracle upon the Jewish au-

[1] *The Four Witnesses*, p. 238.

thorities, and the story of the supper at Bethany when Mary anointed him for his burial and Judas and the chief priests determined upon his destruction. In short, one half of that portion of the Gospel of John which precedes the triumphal entry into Jerusalem is directly connected with the first five of these extraordinary miracles. The sixth and last, on the sea of Tiberias, prepares for the introduction of that wonderful conference of Christ with his disciples, in which he restores the fallen Peter, and makes his last revelation concerning the future of the Church.

Words of Instruction. The statements brought out in connection with the miracles of John's Gospel show it to be more properly a narrative of spiritual instruction than a record of historical events.

It will appear on examination that, with the exception of the miraculous events already noticed and those centring in the crucifixion, the Gospel is made up of conversations and discourses of Jesus, and summations of truth by the Evangelist himself. The latter may be illustrated by the testimonies to the divine character of Jesus which John gathers up from the Baptist and the early disciples (i., iii.); and by the account of the intercourse with Jesus after the resurrection (xx., xxi.). The former comprise the conversations with Nicodemus (iii.), with the Samaritan woman (iv.), with the Jews in the Temple at the feast of Tabernacles (vii., viii.), with the Jews in the Temple in Solomon's Porch at the feast of Dedication (x.); and the discourses concerning the shepherd and the sheep (x.), and the great series connected with the last Passover (xii.–xvii.).

But notwithstanding the predominance of instruction, it will be apparent to the careful observer that the personal and conversational element enters almost everywhere even into the discourses. Nowhere in the Gospels does the intense personality of Jesus so impress itself upon everything as in the last. He himself appears everywhere, in the events and the teachings, as the way, the truth, the life, the ever-present incarnate Son of God. In short, though so preëminently spiritual, no production of any age has ever been found more marked by a thorough and all-pervasive realism.

It might readily be shown that the great spiritual truths, which have been seen to be central to John, light up everything in his Gospel and decide and give color to every verse and sentence.

The Christian Doctrines. But preëminently is the fourth Gospel to be regarded as the embodiment of the theology of the Christian Church. This aspect of it may best be brought out by a systematic view of the truth in connection with the work of redemption and the Christian life.

The great doctrines are those concerning God, Christ, the condition of man, the redemption provided in the incarnation and propitiation, the mission of the Holy Spirit, and the resurrection and final judgment. On all these points the fourth Gospel is greatly in advance of the other three, although in entire agreement with the teaching of the Epistles and the Apocalypse.

God. John teaches, from the lips of Jesus himself, that "God is spirit" (not *a* spirit, for the article is neither expressed nor implied in the original), meaning by this, that He is the divine life-principle in itself (iv. 24).[1] He is beyond the range of the mortal senses: "No man hath seen God at any time" (i. 18; vi. 46). "Ye have neither heard his voice, nor seen his shape" (v. 37). It needed the revelation of the only-begotten Son, who ex-

[1] See Lias, *The Doctrinal System of St. John*, p. 17. The Greek word for *spirit* (πνεῦμα) "means either (1) a life-principle of whatever kind; (2) the Divine life-principle in itself; (3) the Divine life-principle in man." John uses it here in the second sense.

isted in his bosom from all eternity, to make him clearly known to the world (i. 18). His worship is not, therefore, to be confined to one place, Mount Zion or Mount Gerizim, but He is to be worshiped in spirit (or *by spirit* and not by mere form) and in truth, and his real temple henceforth is to be, not at Jerusalem, but wherever true worshipers are to be found in the whole world (iv. 21–24).

But God is not a mere abstract principle, underlying the world; He is a person, a Father, capable of love, care, tenderness (iii. 16). He is the source of all being whether uncreated or created. From him the eternal Son derives his being (v. 26). From him the Spirit of truth is sent (xiv. 16). From him, through the instrumentality of the Son, all things have derived their being (i. 3). As the Father he is the fountain of redemption: "God (*the Father*, as the sense requires) so loved the world that he gave his only-begotten Son" (iii. 16). He sends the Son (v. 37), commits his prerogatives into his hands (v. 22), bears witness to him (viii. 18). The Son came into the world to do his will (vi. 38), his pleasure (viii. 29), his work (xvii. 4). The Father and the Son are one (x. 30), not in a unity of personal existence, but in the possession of a common being and life (xvii. 11, 21, 22). The Father is the source of all life, "the living Father" (vi. 57). He has imparted this life to his Son, and through him it is communicated to all creatures (v. 26; i. 4, 18). The children of God are born of his will (i. 14). He is light, the power which illuminates the whole being of man.

So God the Father is the end of all being no less than its source. The life flowing from him enfolds in the end not only the Trinity itself, but all who are bound together by the indwelling of God. "The ultimate result of Christ's work, as declared by himself in the fourth Gospel, would seem to be a merging all the redeemed into the being of God, not in a pantheistic annihilation of all personality, but by bringing each personal soul, while in full and glad realization of its own separate consciousness, into a complete union, not only of will and affections, hopes and desires, but of being also with the Infinite Author of all" (xvii.).

The Person of Christ. Jesus is the Word (the Logos), the Revealer of God (i. 1). The word is the revelation of the thought, its incarnation, as it were, in order to convey it to the mind of another. The word in the Greek is also the reason of anything, "the unfolding of its true nature and meaning to him who knows it not." Jesus Christ claimed to be the Revealer of the Father (xiv. 9; Matt. xi. 27; Luke x. 22), and this is best expressed by his title, the Word.

His relation to the Father is absolutely unique. He came forth from the Father (xvi. 28), he ever turns his face toward Him (πρὸς τὸν Θεόν),[1] and he is himself very God (i. 1). In the bosom of the Father from all eternity, he is yet personally distinct from him (i. 1, 18; viii. 58; xvii. 5, 24), the only-begotten Son (i. 14, 18; iii. 16, 18). In his work he is subordinate to the Father (xiv. 28), he is sent by the Father (iv. 34; v. 23, 24, 30, 37, 38; vi. 39, 44, etc.), receives his name, the symbol of his power and greatness, from the Father (xvii. 11),[2] ascribes his power to the Father (v. 26, 19, 20, 22, 27; xvii. 22). Yet he declares himself one with the

[1] Liddon, *Bampton Lectures*, Lect. v. p. 342. The Greek is not, "*the* Word was *with God*," but "*toward God*," — "expressing the more significant fact of perpetual intercommunion. The Face of the Everlasting Word, if we may dare so to express ourselves, was ever *directed towards* the Face of the Everlasting Father."

[2] *The Doctrinal System of St. John*, p. 41. According to the best supported reading in John xvii. 11, the prayer of Christ is: "Holy Father, keep them *by thine own name which thou hast given me.*"

Father and equal with him (v. 17, 18; x. 30, 33). The Father is in him and he in the Father (x. 38; xiv. 9, 10, 20; xvii. 21, 23). Though on earth he is in heaven (iii. 13). Though from the Father he is yet self-existent (v. 26).

His relation to man evinces his unity with the Father. The life for lost man was in him (i. 4), and communicated by him (iii.). He is full of grace and truth (i. 14), he preaches the truth (viii. 40, 45), and he is the truth itself (xiv. 6). Whosoever has seen him has seen the Father also (vi. 46; x. 15; xiv. 9). Through his union with the Father, all power is given him (iii. 35; xiii. 3; ii. 2), he gives life to whom he will (v. 22, 25), he presents himself as an example for men to copy (xiii. 11), and he challenges the Jews to find a single blemish in his character (viii. 46).

On the other hand he is represented as a human being, and subject to the ordinary weaknesses and wants of men. When he fasted he was hungry and ate (ii. 1; xiii. 2; xxi. 12). When he traveled he was thirsty and weary (iv. 6). Being grieved he wept (xi. 35), and being crucified he died. He had a peculiarly human friendship and affection for the beloved disciple (xix. 26) and for the household in Bethany (vi. 5). He remembered the claims of filial duty even in that hour of supreme solemnity on the cross (xix. 26, 27). "'Woman, behold thy son,' is an exclamation which, uttered at such a moment, places beyond a doubt that the Gospel which sets forth most strongly the Divinity of Christ was also penetrated with the most clear apprehension of his humanity."

The Condition of Man. Before the grace of God bestowed upon him the enabling power of the light of life, man was in darkness, unprepared to appreciate or receive the blessings Christ came to give (i. 5, 10, 11). Many even preferred darkness to light (iii. 19, 21), and were moved to opposition to Christ's teaching and to persecution of his followers, by his works of divine power (xii. 37, 40), and by the elevation of himself and his followers above the world (xv. 19; xvii. 14, 16). The state of mind which leads to such results "John denotes by the word *flesh* (σάρξ, iii. 6; viii. 15, etc.), and it is placed in the sharpest antagonism to that possession of an inner life, breathed into the heart by divine influence, which is denominated by the word *spirit* (πνεῦμα, i. 13; iii. 5, etc.). From this condition of alienation from God, man cannot deliver himself; he needs an intervention from above to rescue him from the empire of darkness."[1]

Doctrine of the Incarnation. Christ came to enlighten this darkness, and to deliver man from this living death which it involved. "In him was life, and the life was the light of men" (i. 4). "The true light, which lighteth every man, was now coming into the world" (i. 9). Such are the announcements with which the Gospel opens. He came that men might have life, and "that they might have it more abundantly" (x. 10). He gives life to whom he will (v. 21). He is himself the life (xi. 25; xiv. 6). He is the light of the world (viii. 12; ix. 5; xii. 35, 36, 46). Such are the statements with which the Gospel is filled.

In transforming *the flesh* into *the spirit*, Jesus Christ imparts a breath from God to man to give him a new life (xv. 26). In entering into the kingdom of God man is born anew by the Holy Spirit (iii. 5), and his entire nature and relation to God are changed (iii. 6, 7, 8). In connection with this new birth, even the words of

[1] See *The Doctrinal System of St. John,* p. 67. The work of Professor Lias contains an admirable summary of the doctrines of the fourth Gospel.

Christ, being in a sense the breath of God, are endued, though in an inferior degree, with a kind of divine vitality (vi. 63).

The foundations of this new life are laid in the flesh and blood of Christ, that is, in his incarnation and in his sacrifice on the cross (vi. 51–58).

It is by virtue of his incarnation, or his partaking of human nature, that he becomes the source of life to the world. He is the vine and his disciples are the branches (xv.). A constant stream of life flows from him through them, a life which is governed by the same laws as man's natural life. It reaches its maturity by means of growth through nourishment. Its food is Christ, the living bread which came down from heaven (vi. 51), who is a source of permanent life to the world (vi. 58). The operating principle of this divine life is faith in Christ (iii. 18, 36; vi. 29, 47; xx. 31). This faith leads to good works. By union with Christ, the vine, alone, a union effected by faith, can the branches become fruitful (xv. 4), and by abiding in him alone can they increase in fruitfulness (xv. 5, etc.). The new life of faith leads to purity and truth (xiii. 10; xv. 3; xvii. 19), and to mutual love (xiii. 35; xvii. 26). It makes men again the children of God, and gives them a claim upon his love (xvi. 26, 27), and access to him in prayer (xiv. 13; xv. 7, 16; xvi. 23–27). It makes them the channels of blessing to others (vii. 37), the representatives of Christ in a mission for the saving of mankind (xiii. 20; xx. 21).

The kingdom of God, in John's view of it, assumes a new and more spiritual form. Jesus no longer confines himself to language which expresses only external relations. He does indeed speak of himself as a shepherd and his disciples as sheep (x.), and of the gathering of many flocks into one fold (x. 16); but he prefers to describe his kingdom as an organic whole, and he constantly recognizes "a deep interior unity, the result of the possession by its members of a life which they all enjoy in common, and which they all derive from him" (xv.). In the intercessory prayer (xvii.), he traces that union to its highest source, in the unity of the Godhead itself. He prays "that they all may be one; as thou, Father, art in me, and I in thee, that they also may be one in us" (xvii. 21). Herein in reality are to be found the communion of saints and the kingdom of God, in the living union of believers through Christ with the Father.

But back of the doctrine of the restoration of man through the implanting of a divine life by the incarnation of Christ, there lies throughout John's Gospel the doctrine of propitiation by the sacrifice of Christ. Sin is regarded not simply as a disease, from which the infusion of a new life could save, but rather as deliberate and willful disobedience to the righteous and everlasting Ruler of the universe. Without shedding of blood there is no remission of sin (Lev. xvii. 11; Heb. ix. 22). Hence it is that John introduces Jesus to the reader in the words of the Baptist: "Behold the Lamb of God that taketh away the sin of the world" (i. 29). There was an absolute *necessity* that the Son should be "lifted up" (iii. 14, 15) if he should "draw all men unto him" (xii. 32). He lays down his life for the sheep (x. 11, 15). He is identified with the Paschal Lamb (xix. 36), by the sprinkling of whose blood upon the door posts the Israelites could alone be saved from destruction (Exod. xii. 13). He is the propitiatory sacrifice for the sins of the world, so that by partaking of his flesh and blood the world may be saved.

The Doctrine of the Holy Spirit. It has been seen that Luke's teaching concerning the Holy Ghost is greatly in advance of that of Matthew and Mark; but it nowhere approaches the definiteness of John's. With the latter he is the applier of the redemption wrought by Christ. He is sent by Christ from the Father (xv. 26; xvi. 7, 8). By John alone is he named the Paraclete, or the Comforter, as our version has it, or the *Helper*, as the word would, perhaps, be better rendered (xiv. 16, 26; xv. 26; xvi. 7). He is a Person, associated with the Father and the Son, sent into the world to convince men of sin, of righteousness, and of judgment (xvi. 8). He is the Spirit of truth who is to lead the disciples of Christ into all truth (xiv. 17; xvi. 13). He is to give life to all who enter into the kingdom of God (iii. 5). From the time of Christ's ascension he was to be the present source of power with Christ's followers (vii. 39; xvi. 7; xx. 22, 23). He was to be the living water which should spring up unto everlasting life in their souls (iv. 14; vii. 38). The mightier works which the disciples were to do, after Christ's departure (xiv. 12), were to be done by the power of the Holy Ghost. He was the divine Person whom Christ went away to the Father to send, and without whose coming the work of redemption could not have been carried out (xvi. 7).

The Resurrection and Judgment. John teaches most clearly both the fact and the cause of the resurrection. "Verily, verily, I say unto you, the hour is coming and now is, when the dead shall hear the voice of the Son of God and they that hear shall live" (v. 25). This is the teaching throughout the Gospel (v. 28, 29; vi. 39, 40, 44, 54, etc.). "I am the resurrection and the life: he that believeth on me though he were dead, yet shall he live: and whosoever liveth and believeth in me shall never die" (xi. 25, 26). That Christ is the cause of the resurrection from the dead is the uniform doctrine of John (x. 18; xii. 24; xiv. 6, etc.).

The fourth Gospel is equally clear on the doctrine of the judgment and of the future life. "Marvel not at this: for the hour is coming in the which all that are in the graves shall hear his voice and shall come forth; they that have done good unto the resurrection of life; and they that have done evil unto the resurrection of damnation" (v. 28, 29). To come forth from the grave is, therefore, to come forth to judgment, and there are but two future estates. Those estates have their beginning in this present life, the one in faith in Christ, and the other in the rejection of him: "He that believeth on him is not condemned; but he that believeth not is condemned already, because he hath not believed on the name of the only-begotten Son of God" (iii. 18). For those who believe on him are the words of Christ: "In my Father's house are many mansions. If it were not so I would have told you. I go and prepare a place for you. And if I go and prepare a place for you, I will come again and receive you unto myself; that where I am, there ye may be also (xiv. 2, 3).

Such, in brief outline, is the doctrinal system of John's Gospel. It is the profoundest of Christian theology,—its truths ranging, in the revelations of the incarnate Word, from the lowest depths of the dark and carnal condition of humanity to the loftiest heights of Divinity, compassing, in the preëxistent Word and the everlasting life, the two eternities, and sweeping the whole horizon of Christian faith, purpose, endeavor, achievement, and hope. It is the essential element in just the Gospel for the Christian, the man of faith in Christ.

Both the omissions and additions of this Gospel are thus seen to furnish evidence of the Christian aim of the Evangelist.

SECTION IV.

THE CHRISTIAN ADAPTATION IN THE INCIDENTAL VARIATIONS OF THE FOURTH GOSPEL.

The adaptation of John's Gospel to the Christian needs appears also in the manifold minor variations and peculiarities.

I. *Incidental Variations.*

Narrative Changes. The Christian aim may be traced in the narratives given by John in common with the other Evangelists.

There is but one such narrative before the record of the triumphal entry into the Holy City, — the miraculous multiplication of the loaves and fishes (Matt. xiv. 13–32; Mark vi. 32–51; Luke ix. 10–17; John vi. 1–15). A careful comparison of the four forms of this narrative will bring out the distinctive touches of each of the Evangelists. In that given by John it will be observed in particular, that certain explanatory clauses are introduced for the benefit of the non-Jewish readers. He tells us that Jesus "went over the sea of Galilee, *which is the sea of Tiberias*" (vi. 1); that he "went up *into a mountain*" (3); that "*the Passover, a feast of the Jews, was nigh*" (4); that "*there was much grass in the place*" (10), etc. Here and there by the way his pen touches the spiritual and divine in Jesus and his mission. He alone tells us of the solemn *lifting up of the eyes* of the great Teacher (5); that even when Jesus asked Philip about buying bread for the multitude, he was omniscient and did not need an answer: "*And this he said to prove him; for he himself knew what he would do*" (6); that "*those men, when they had seen the miracle that Jesus did, said, This is of a truth that prophet that should come into the world. When Jesus therefore perceived that they would come and take him by force, to make him a king, he departed again into a mountain himself alone*" (14, 15), etc.

But most characteristic of all is the fact, already adverted to, that John, instead of pausing with the account of the storm on the lake, as the rest of the Evangelists do, proceeds to give — in double the space he devotes to the event — that practical and spiritual application of the miracle (vi. 25–59), so much more important than the mere event, the sum of which is found in the words of Jesus: "*I am the bread of life. Whoso eateth my flesh and drinketh my blood hath eternal life.*"

It has also been observed that the fourth Evangelist has his own way of avoiding the parables and similitudes in narrative form, which abound in the other Gospels; while by means of the more vivid metaphor he brings out with the greatest clearness the spiritual truths involved. In the other Gospels he compares himself to a shepherd who seeks after and brings back the stray sheep (Matt. xviii. 12, 13; Luke xv. 3–7); in John he says, *I am the good shepherd.* The good shepherd giveth his life for the sheep (xii.). In the other Gospels he compares the kingdom of heaven to a vineyard and to a marriage feast (Matt. xxi. 28–44; Mark xii. 1–11; Luke xx. 9–18); but in John Jesus is himself the *vine* and *his Father the husbandman* (xv. 1); he is himself *the bridegroom* (iii. 29).

These Christian features may be traced throughout all those portions of the fourth Gospel that have anything in common with the productions of the other Evangelists.

Slighter Additions. There are also to be found in John's Gospel, in single sentences and minute touches, the most remarkable elucidations and incidental confirmations of what is contained in the other three.

This may be illustrated by the false testimony mentioned by Matthew (xxvi. 61) and Mark (xiv. 57, 58). John alone tells us that, in the first cleansing of the Temple, after the opening of his ministry, when the Jews asked Jesus for a sign of his authority, he "answered and said unto them, *Destroy this temple, and in three days I will raise it up*" (ii. 19). That saying, uttered prophetically by Jesus, the false witnesses had interpreted as referring to the Temple at Jerusalem: "We heard him say, I will destroy this temple that is made with hands, and within three days I will build another made without hands" (Mark xiv. 58).

So John alone tells us that the real cause of the flocking together of the people and of their acclamations on the entry into Jerusalem — facts recorded by Matthew (xxi. 10, 11), Mark (xi. 8–10), and Luke (xix. 37) — was the resurrection of Lazarus from the dead: "*The people therefore that was with him when he called Lazarus out of his grave, and raised him from the dead, bare record. For this cause the people also met him, for that they heard that he had done this miracle*" (xii. 17, 18).

It may be remarked incidentally that the other Evangelists could not give this cause. They did not record this most notable of miracles, perhaps partly for the reason that, if they had done so, the Sanhedrim which had "consulted that they might put Lazarus also to death, because that by reason of him many of the Jews went away and believed on Jesus" (John xii. 10, 11), would have carried out their bloody purpose; and partly for the reason that the teachings concerning the resurrection were not suited to their unspiritual readers. When John wrote, Jerusalem had been long since destroyed and the danger to the family of Lazarus was past; while his Gospel would have been essentially incomplete without the sublime instruction given on that occasion.

Only the fourth Evangelist tells us that, when Mary

anointed Jesus, "*the house was filled with the odor of the ointment*" (xii. 3); that it was "*one of his disciples, Judas Iscariot, Simon's son*" that said, "Why was not this ointment sold for three hundred pence and given to the poor" (xii. 4). He alone makes it appear fully that it was avarice that moved the traitor's heart: "*This he said, not that he cared for the poor; but because he was a thief, and had the bag, and bare* (that is, *stole out*) *what was put therein*" (xii. 6). Only he brings out the real tenderness of the anointing by Mary and reveals her faith, as surpassing that of the Twelve, by declaring that she had kept the precious ointment for this occasion: "Against *the day of my burying hath she kept this*" ointment (xii. 7).

These are but specimens of the Christian touches by which the beloved disciple adds to the fullness and beauty and spiritual power of all the Gospel material which he has in common with the other Evangelists.

Word Changes. But in a Gospel embracing so much that is different in matter and in spirit from the contents of the other Gospels, the greatest variations must evidently be found in the vocabulary as marking out the range of new ideas. This is in part manifest from the Johannean system of Christian doctrine already given; but it may be made clearer by an examination of some of the characteristic words and expressions. John's is an eminently Christian vocabulary.

Common Words. The comparative infrequency of those words of theology and experience which properly have special reference to the earlier contact of the soul with Christ may first be noted. Matthew uses the word *sinner* five times; Mark, six times; Luke, seventeen times; John, four times. Matthew uses the words *repent* and *repentance* five and three times respectively; Mark, twice each; Luke, nine and five times; John, not at all.

Matthew uses *righteous* nineteen times; Mark, twice; Luke, eleven times; John, three times. Matthew uses *justify* twice; Luke, five times; Mark and John do not use it. The fair inference from these and like examples is that John does not deal largely with the ideas expressed by these words, and that the ideas belong rather to that earlier stage of the Gospel represented by the other Evangelists. In other words John's is not the Gospel that deals with the fundamental conceptions of sin, repentance, etc., in their simpler forms.

The frequent recurrence in John of the words which belong to the later or higher phases of Gospel experience is still more marked. It is a fact that the whole cycle of words connected with the Christian life is used with remarkable frequency by John.

Judged by its vocabulary John's is preëminently the Gospel of *faith*. It is a favorite idea with certain skeptical writers, that the foundation of Paul's system is faith, while that of John's is love. "We hear, on high authority," says a writer already referred to, "that the influence of St. Paul on Christian theology is destined henceforth to decline, and that the Christianity of the future will be colored principally by the teaching of the Apostle of love."[1] The truth is that, in the facts of the New Testament, there is not the slightest foundation for such a distinction. Matthew uses the word *believe* eleven times; Mark, fifteen times; Luke, nine times; John, in his Gospel alone, one hundred times, or almost as many times as all the other New Testament writers — Paul included — taken together. In fact, if such a distinction is to be made — which we deny, on the ground of the essential harmony of the two — John ought rather to be called the Apostle of faith and Paul the Apostle of love;

[1] *The Doctrinal System of St. John*, p. 76. The authority referred to is Matthew Arnold, "St. Paul and Protestantism."

for, while the word *love* (ἀγάπη) occurs only seven times in John's Gospel and seventeen times in his first Epistle, it is found seventy-three times (often translated *charity*) in Paul's writings. It remains indisputable that John makes faith far more prominent than any other writer in the Bible, so that if this one word were blotted out of his Gospel, its harmony would be gone, and there would be left little more than an unintelligible jargon.

It is nevertheless true that, as compared with the other Gospels, the fourth is the Gospel of spiritual *love*. This is another side of the many-sided truth, — its divine rather than its human aspect. Matthew uses the verb expressing reverential *love* five times ; Mark, once ; Luke, twice ; John, thirteen times. Matthew makes use of *love*, as expressing personal attachment, eight times ; Mark, five times ; Luke, thirteen times ; John, thirty-seven times. From this point of view everything may be said to be comprehended in love. The Father loves the Son (John v. 20). The Son loves his own ; he loves them to the end (xiii. 1). The Father, in like manner, loves them, and hath loved them (xvii. 23). Jesus loves them with a special personal love, each by name. He loved Lazarus, and Mary, and Martha, and the disciple who lay in his bosom at the paschal table (xi. 5 ; xiii. 23). Upon the one word *love*, in its two senses and its many relations, the restoration of Peter, at the Sea of Tiberias, turned (xxi. 15–17). It is in harmony with this feature that John's is the Gospel of the *Fatherhood of God.* The word *Father*, in its application to God, occurs in Matthew forty-four times ; in Mark, five times ; in Luke, twenty times ; in John, one hundred and twenty-one times. In no other Gospel, therefore, when God is spoken of, does the name of *Father*, *the Father*, *my Father*, recur so often, in its special and exclusive relation to Jesus. It is a direct consequence of this relation of God as a Father, that John's is the Gospel of the giving *grace* of God. "As all things in this Gospel are viewed and represented in their highest causes, in their deepest foundations; in like manner do we find in it the word and the idea of God's *gift* and *giving*, occurring with the same frequency. The first cause in all things is the *gift of God.* What the Father *hath given* to the Son, what anew the Son *gives* or *hath given* to men, to those who believe in him, is again and again pressed on the attention."

So John's is in an important sense the Gospel for *all the world.* It has been shown that Luke's is the Gospel for the Greek, the representative of universal humanity in its unrenewed condition. So it appears that John's is in a peculiar sense the Gospel for renewed humanity. Matthew uses the word *world* nine times; Mark, three times; Luke, three times; John, seventy-nine times. John sometimes employs the word to express mankind collectively as distinguished from or opposed to God their Creator, as in the words to Nicodemus, "God so loved the *world*" (John iii. 16); sometimes the majority of the race as opposed to Israel or to believers, as in the Samaritan's exclamation, "We know that this is indeed the Christ, the Saviour of the *world*" (John iv. 42); sometimes an indefinite multitude or extension, as in the exclamation of the Pharisees, "Behold the *world* is gone after him" (John xii. 19). The use of the word in the first two senses is so frequent as to demonstrate the universal reach and application of the last Gospel.

In like manner the fourth Gospel, judged by its vocabulary is the Gospel of spiritual *truth*, *light*, and *life*. Matthew uses *truth* once; Mark, three times; Luke, three times; John, twenty-five times. The first three Evangelists use the word *true* only once, while John uses it twenty-one times. Men are freed from spiritual bondage and sanctified through the truth. Christ before

Pilate declared himself to be a King, establishing a kingdom not of this world, — a kingdom of truth (xiv. 6). Matthew uses the word *light* seven times; Mark, once; Luke, six times; John, twenty-two times. Matthew uses *life* seven times; Mark, four times; Luke, six times; John, thirty-six times. Matthew uses *everlasting life* three times; Mark, twice; Luke, three times; John, seventeen times. It has often been remarked that with John these expressions bear a peculiarly mystical and spiritual character. He links the life and the light with each other and identifies Christ with the truth, the light, and the life.

Peculiar Words. The spiritual truth and Christian aim of the fourth Gospel appear with equal clearness in words and expressions altogether peculiar to itself. The Evangelist uses to some extent a vocabulary of his own in speaking of Christ and his work.

In the opening sentence of the Gospel, Christ is thrice designated as the *Word* (Logos). No one has shown this Word to us, in his incarnation, in such a multiplicity of aspects as John, — in contact and controversy with men, arguing with sinful men, and enduring their reproaches and scoffs; called a Samaritan and one that hath a devil; the hand of man incessantly lifted up against him to seize him, to stone him, to crucify him.

John alone calls Jesus *the Lamb of God.* He alone represents Jesus himself as declaring, that "as Moses *lifted up* the serpent in the wilderness even so must the Son of man be *lifted up;*" and that "I, if I be *lifted up,* will draw all men unto me."

No other Evangelist uses the expression, *Verily, verily,* even once, but John uses it twenty-five times. As the others make use of the single *verily* only, it has been suggested that the second word is John's own, "the response of his faith to the faithfulness of his Lord, like the instantaneous echo by the rocks of a peal of thunder." The careful observer, however, will note the fact that the double word is uniformly connected with sayings peculiar to John, in short, with his expression of the great life-and-death truths of Christianity. The double verily is therefore better explained as being, what it purports to be, an expression from the lips of Jesus himself, and intended to emphasize those great spiritual truths which do not appear in the same form in the other Gospels. If any one will write out the passages from John that are prefaced by it, he will see that they sum up all the glorious and solemn verities of the Gospel in its relation to life here and hereafter, so that, if John's Gospel is *the heart of Christ*, the double verilies are *the heart of the heart of Christ.*

II. *Other Peculiarities.*

In addition to these indications of the Christian aim of John's Gospel, drawn from its conceptions and doctrines, there are still others of a different character which at the same time mark its late origin and fit it for the Christian Church.

First of these may be noticed the manner in which the Gospel deals with the Jewish Scriptures.

Unlike the Gospels according to Mark and Luke, that according to John constantly refers to the Old Testament Scriptures. In this respect it is like that according to Matthew. It is therefore certain that John wrote for those who were familiarly acquainted with the Scriptures. This was true of the Christian Church throughout the world at the close of the first century, while it certainly was not true of the Romans and Greeks at the time when Mark and Luke wrote for them.

That John did not write for Jews alone is proved by the fact that he is careful to describe places in Judæa

(iv. 5; v. 2; xviii. 1); to explain the manners and customs familiar to all Jews (ii. 6, 13; iv. 9; v. 1; vi. 9; x. 22; xi. 33, 44, 55; xix. 31, 39–42); and to interpret Hebrew words (i. 38, 42; ix. 7; xix. 13, 17; xx. 16). He must therefore have written for persons unacquainted with the country, customs, and language of Palestine.

That he did not write merely for those who understood the Greek language only, or best, appears from the fact that, while the other Evangelists appeal for the most part to the Septuagint or Greek version of the Old Testament, John appeals sometimes to it (i. 23; ii. 17; vi. 45; x. 34; xii. 14, 15; xv. 35; xix. 24, 36); but sometimes turns to the Hebrew original, as if to the final standard of appeal (xii. 40; viii. 18; xix. 37). He writes not only for those who are acquainted with the Septuagint, but for all the world of Christians.

It is likewise in conformity with this view and confirmatory of it, that John so often refers his readers to the prophecies of the Scriptures. It has already been seen that he makes a score or more of such references; that these usually take for granted that the persons addressed are acquainted with the Scriptures; and that, while in the first half of his Gospel the references are chiefly confined to fact and law, in the second half they are confined to the prophecies fulfilled in Christ's unfolding of the Christian life and familiar to all Christians. Da Costa has well remarked that these passages are "for the greater part entirely new, and, so to speak, fresh in St. John, never having been cited anywhere before in the New Testament. The form or manner of the quotation, too, is somehow differently modified, and has a depth and subtlety not to be found in the other Gospels; as when, at the purification of the Temple, after recording the words of our Lord: '*Take these things hence; make not my Father's house an house of merchandise*' (ii. 16);

we find this followed by the quotation of one of the prophetical sayings in the book of Psalms: '*And his disciples remembered that it was written, The zeal of thine house hath eaten me up*' (Ps. v. 17)." This peculiarity in the manner of quotation is also illustrated in the discourse with the Jews in the synagogue at Capernaum (vi. 44, 45); in the call on the last day of the feast of Tabernacles (vii. 37, 38); in Christ's reproof of the Jews for their unbelief and hardness of heart (xii. 36–41); when the traitor is pointed out at the supper (xiii. 18); in what fell from Christ's lips at the paschal feast (xv. 25); among the last words on the cross (xix. 28); and when the legs of the malefactors were broken (xix. 36). It will readily be seen that these passages also illustrate with equal force the eminently spiritual view which John takes of the various facts in the life of Christ to which they refer. Of such references to prophecy it may be said that none of them are made, as are those in Matthew, for the purpose of demonstrating for the Jew the Messiahship of Jesus, but rather all of them for the purpose of bringing out the profound spiritual truths involved and of supreme interest to the soul of the believer.

The student of the Gospels will readily observe for himself the same features in John's references to what was prophetical in *our Lord's own words*, as when he compares his approaching crucifixion and resurrection to a destroying and building up again of the temple of God (ii. 22), and in the record of Pilate's sentence (xviii. 31, 32); and again in the record of the *unconscious prophecies of enemies*, as when Caiaphas urges the Sanhedrim to take measures against Jesus (xi. 49–51), and when Pilate places the title, in the three representative languages, over the cross (xix. 19–22).

A second of these peculiar indications of John's later

date and Christian aim is found in the manner in which he deals with the Jewish people.

Matthew uses the appellation *Jews*, five times; Mark, seven times; Luke, five times; John, seventy-one times. This furnishes evidence that the fourth Gospel was written subsequently to the others, at a period when the Christian body, whether Hebrew or Gentile, had crystallized into the Church, and detached themselves entirely from the apostate and hostile Jews, whom they regarded as a separate body, and who were then known over the world as *Jews*. "Throughout this Gospel," as Wordsworth has said, "*the Jews*, represented by their leaders, the priests and Pharisees, are contemplated *ab extra*, and are spoken of in the third person as a separate body, such as they *had become* after the fall of Jerusalem, when those who adhered to Judaism were distinguished by bitter hostility to the Church."[1]

Moreover, the intimate connection of Judaism and Christianity rendered it necessary that the Evangelist for the Christian Church should explain the great and everywhere patent fact of the apostasy of the Jewish race, which fact might else have furnished a powerful *à priori* argument against Christianity itself. Hence it is that in the fourth Gospel the conflict of light and life with darkness and death takes shape in the conflict of Jesus with the carnally minded Jews. The central and closing portions of the Gospel are filled with the record of the strife. The effort to bring Jesus to a judicial trial is followed by attempts to mob and stone him, and these again by the plottings of the great Jewish Council which result in his apprehension and crucifixion. John's sketch of the conflict between the blind, hypocritical, and malignant Jewish formalists, and the sincere, spiritual, and divine Christ, was needed to strip the apostate Jews of

[1] Wordsworth, *St. John's Gospel*, Introduction.

the power they would otherwise have possessed, and which they would most certainly have exercised, to corrupt and destroy the Church of Christ.

Still another, and third, of these peculiar indications of John's Christian aim is found in the complete unfolding of the Jewish practical religion exhibited in this Gospel.

The old religion was the precursor of the new, and contained its germ. The proper development of the old was intended to lead to the new. In other words, the Jewish religion was the world-religion in its typical and undeveloped form, while the Christian religion was the same world-religion in its spiritual and developed form. "The law was given by Moses, but grace and truth came by Jesus Christ." As the old Jewish religious life reached its perfection in connection with the religious institutions and festivals, it was both natural and necessary that the new Christian life should first be developed in connection with these.

Da Costa has brought out the marked prominence of the religious festivals in the fourth Gospel, with great clearness. "While the other three Gospels speak of but one of these, the Passover, and principally, if not solely, of *that* Passover at which Jesus was crucified; our fourth Gospel mentions many such festive occasions, and several different paschal feasts." [1]

Vastly more significant and important, however, is the fact that John makes these religious festivals the central points in the presentation of the truths of the Gospel for the Christian soul. The entire unfolding of spiritual truth by Christ is thus connected with the central places and movements of the Jewish religious life, which held

[1] For the Passovers mentioned, see John ii. 23; v. 1; vi. 4; xii. 1. John also mentions the feast of Tabernacles (vii. 2), and the feast of the Dedication (x. 22).

embodied the highest truth of the old dispensation. He is the Lamb of God, himself the sacrifice, the fulfillment of all the sacrifices, the Passover. His lifting up is therefore naturally and necessarily identified with the Jewish Passover. The Jewish and Christian stages of the world-religion were thus shown to be but parts of the one plan of God, so that the latter could only appear among men as it was unfolded from the former.

A fourth, last, and most conclusive of these indications of the Christian aim of John is to be found in the prominence which his Gospel gives to the relations of Christ, through his sacrifice, to the Christian life.

Jesus is the Lamb of God, the sin bearer of the world (i. 29, 36), who gives his own flesh and blood for the life of the world. Matthew and Mark speak *once* each of the time of Christ's sacrifice as *the hour:* "Behold the hour is at hand and the son of man is betrayed into the hands of sinners" (Matt. xxvi. 45); "It is enough, *the hour* is come" (Mark xiv. 41). But in John's Gospel the hour of the cross is regarded as the central hour in the whole ministry of Christ, to which everything moves forward and in which everything centres. This is seen in his declining on various occasions to make a public manifestation of his Messiahship, because his hour is not yet come (John ii. 4; vii. 30; viii. 20). It is the central hour of the world's history. At the last Passover his hour is heralded by the coming of certain Greeks, as representatives of the world, who desire to see him (xii. 23). It is the central hour in God's plan of all things, and on this ground Jesus, in the opening of the intercessory prayer, bases his plea for his glorification (xvii. 1).

In the *I ams* which fell from the lips of Jesus himself, as given by John, is summed up the fullest possible exhibition of his person and work, and of that perfect satisfaction for the spiritual wants of all men which is to be found only in him.

To the woman of Samaria he said, "*I* that speak unto thee *am*" the Messiah (iv. 26); to the disciples in the storm on the sea, "it is I (literally *I am*); be not afraid" (vi. 20). To the Jews he declares, "*I am* the bread of life" (vi. 36, 48); "*I am* the bread which came down from heaven" (vi. 41, 51). In presenting his relation to the Father, he says, "*I am* from him and he hath sent me." "*I am* the light of the world" (viii. 12; ix. 5). "Verily, verily, I say unto you, Before Abraham was, *I am*" (viii. 58).

Still more tenderly does he present himself to his own. "*I am* the door of the sheep" (x. 7, 9). "*I am* the good shepherd: the good shepherd giveth his life for the sheep" (x. 11, 14). "*I am* the resurrection and the life" (xi. 25, 26). "Ye call me Master and Lord; and ye say well; for *I am*" (xiii. 13). "*I am* the way, and the truth, and the life" (xiv. 6). "*I am* the true vine, and my Father is the husbandman" (xv. 1). "*I am* the vine, ye are the branches" (xv. 5). "Jesus saith unto them, *I am* he. And Judas also which betrayed him, stood with them. As soon, then, as he had said unto them, *I am* he, they went backward, and fell to the ground" (xviii. 5, 6). "Thou sayest that *I am* a King" (xviii. 37).

So completely does Jesus, according to John's Gospel, present himself as the *centre* of all things, — of self-existence, of eternity, of immutability, of omnipotence, of all the resources that are found in God; the *source* of all things, — of light, of life, of comfort, of strength, of blessedness, of immortality, of all the treasures that the Christian soul can desire.

SUMMARY.

In the light of the survey which has been taken of John's Gospel, its Christian aim and adaptation cannot reasonably be doubted.

It has been shown to be a historical fact that John, the beloved disciple, a man eminently fitted for the work both by his character and experience, wrote this Gospel at the end of the first century for the Christian Church, a spiritual organization made up of men saved out of all the great races of the apostolic age through the instrumentality of the earlier preaching of the Gospel and by faith in Christ. This is the firm historical basis for the true theory of the fourth Gospel.

It has also been shown that the Gospel itself bears throughout the evidence of its Christian origin and aim. Its plan is but the unfolding of the central idea of the Incarnate Word as the light and life of the world. Its omissions and additions of material were made to suit it to the Christian soul and its needs. All its incidental changes, its doctrinal system, and its special peculiarities, unite in demonstrating its Christian adaptation. In short, the Christian idea shapes and moulds everything in it from the organic idea down through the rhetorical forms to the very vocabulary itself.

It may therefore be justly claimed, that the historical and critical views combine to establish the theory that John was originally the Gospel for the Christian, and to make it plain that this theory furnishes the true key to the Gospel.

CONCLUSION.

THE GOSPEL FOR ALL THE WORLD.

THE answer proposed to the question, Why four Gospels? is patent from the preceding studies of the Evangelists. It entered into the purpose of God from the beginning, to give the divine religion of the Christian revelation to all mankind. The great commission sent the Apostles to preach the Gospel to every creature. In its fulfillment it required just so many and just such Gospels to meet the wants of the world of the apostolic age in commending Jesus to all men as the Saviour from sin. It is hoped that the view presented may commend itself to the Christian reason, as not only simple and satisfactory, not only based upon the sound principles of philosophy and the undoubted facts of history; but as also, and more than all, helpful to the better understanding of these precious portions of the Scriptures and of the incarnate Word revealed therein, and to a quickened progress in that divine life of faith which ever contemplates as a chief aim the conquest of the world for the crucified and risen Christ.

In conclusion, it may be profitable to direct the attention to the two main facts of the Gospels, — the first, the element common to all the four, and the second, the element peculiar to each, — as suited and doubtless intended to give the productions of the Evangelists a perpetual freshness and fitness for the race of man.

I. *The Gospel for Man.*

There is a central mass of fact and truth around which Matthew, Mark, Luke, and John alike group their other material. This is the essential, fundamental element which must make the productions of the Evangelists *Gospels*, *good news*, to man the sinner wherever and whenever they come to his hearing. These chief facts and truths may be summed up in four particulars.

The first is found in the incarnation of the Son of God. The four Evangelists set it forth in such a way as to make it patent to every candid reader. With Matthew, Jesus is Emmanuel, God with us, in fulfillment of prophecy; with Mark, he is the Son of God in human form exercising his almighty power; with Luke, he is the descendant of Adam and the child of the virgin, yet the Son of the Highest; with John, he is the eternal Word made flesh.

The second is found in the life of the Son of God on earth in human form and subject to human conditions and laws. This makes up the central portion of each of the Gospels. With Matthew, it is the life of Messiah; with Mark, of the almighty worker and victor; with Luke, of the divine and universal man; with John, of the incarnate Word.

The third of these common particulars is found in the death upon the cross. As this is the all-essential fact, all the Gospels devote large space to it, delineating also the events centring in it. In short, here is the ground which all the Evangelists traverse most fully and carefully. They all give the triumphal entry into the Holy City, which was the public claim of Jesus to be the Messiah, the Saviour of the world; the Passover supper, which was his act of putting himself voluntarily in the place of the Paschal Lamb, as the one whose sacrifice alone could deliver from the destruction of sin; the agony and betrayal in Gethsemane, which marked his voluntary submission to drink the cup of his Father for the salvation of the lost; the trial and condemnation, which were at once the public vindication of the innocence of the Redeemer, and his public rejection by the ancient Jewish and Gentile world; the death by crucifixion, which was his actual sacrifice for the sins of the world; and his burial, which signalized his subjection to death for a season. All these are the constituent parts of the great fact of the cross, or of Christ's sacrifice for the sins of mankind.

The fourth and last of these common features is found in the rising of Jesus from the dead on the third day, in his subsequent intercourse with his disciples, in his giving to the Apostles their great commission to preach the Gospel to all the world, and in his ascension to heaven, at once establishing his claim to be the Saviour of mankind and organizing and beginning his saving work.

All these — the incarnation, the life, the death, the resurrection — are the essential facts and truths of the Gospel, those which at the first made it *good news* to men. Without any one of them all it would cease to be good news; for, without the incarnation, the Son of God would have no part in our human nature; without the life on earth, he could neither be our righteousness nor our example; without the death he could not be our sacrifice for sin; and without the resurrection and ascension his claims would be proved baseless and the world would be left to perish without a Saviour. The Son of God became incarnate, lived, died, rose from the dead, for the redemption of the lost, — this cannot grow old but must be glad tidings for man, the sinner, till the end of time.

II. *The Gospel for all Men.*

There is an element of fact and truth peculiar to each of the Evangelists. It was by means of this, as has been seen, that the essential and fundamental Gospel truth was brought by Matthew, Mark, Luke, and John, favorably before the minds of the Jew, Roman, Greek, and Christian, and Jesus of Nazareth commended to them all as the Saviour of the World. It is this fourfold difference that completes the rounded, perfect fitness of the four Gospels to constitute the perpetual Evangel for the world of the ages subsequent to the apostolic.

Not only is it ever true that man is a sinner and needs the good news of Christ's incarnation, life, death, and resurrection; but it remains equally true that the world of mankind is always divided into the same great classes and always exhibits the same generic phases of thought. In all ages the Jewish, Roman, and Greek natures reappear among men, and, in fact, make up the world of natural men; while the Christian nature and wants likewise remain essentially identical. From age to age the four Gospels appeal to the classes who, in temperament, mental constitution, training, and modes of thought, are like those for whom of old, in obedience to the inspiring breath of God, they were prepared. Thus it is that these brief but all-important productions have had power to captivate men by a perpetual fitness and a perennial freshness.

For the man with nature inclined to bow to authority, to appreciate divine religious forms, to exalt the peculiar position of the people of God, and to trace the marvelous plan of God in the preparation for the Messiah and in the progress of his kingdom, the Gospel which Matthew wrote for the Jew must possess a permanent and absorbing interest.

For the man of power, reverencing law, given to action, fitted to be an actor or leader in pushing forward the conquest of the world for Christ, the Gospel which Mark wrote for the Roman must retain its old significance and an ever-potent inspiration as the battle-call of the Almighty Conqueror.

For the man of reason and taste, of philosophic and æsthetic culture, the man longing for the perfect manhood, cherishing a world-wide sympathy with mankind, delighting to contemplate the universal reach of the grace of God the Father to sinners, the Gospel which Luke wrote for the Greek must maintain an increasing reasonableness and an undying influence as the voicing of the infinite Reason of the one Divine Man.

For the man of faith saved by the incarnation and atonement of the Son of God, the man of the new and divine life of obedience and devotion to Christ, the man enlightened, guided, and helped by the Holy Ghost, the Gospel which John wrote for the Christian Church cannot fail to retain an immortal fascination and to furnish a supreme satisfaction as the utterance of God's eternal Word to the believing soul.

It is on this wise that the one Gospel of God in fourfold form, which was exactly fitted to commend Jesus of Nazareth to the ancient world, and which could not then have been put in other shape without a radical change in the races and history of the apostolic age, is still so perfectly adapted to meet the wants of the modern world, that it would require a revolution in the mental structure and experience of man, before any other number of Gospels or any different ones from the four in the New Testament could meet the necessities of ruined and redeemed humanity. God appears, therefore, in his Word no less than in his world, as a God of order. The same perfect, divine plan which science is finding in the latter, a rational and reverential study finds in the former. The Gospels are the perfect thought of God for the restoration of a lost world.

The four Gospels, therefore, in their essential unity and harmony and in their fourfold difference and contrast, illustrate at once and equally well the wonders of the divine love and the comprehensiveness of the divine plan, — a love reaching out after and laying hold of all the great classes of sinners to be found in the race; a plan comprehending and providing for the spiritual wants of all men to the end of time. In contemplating, in the writings of the Evangelists, this sublime plan of the Heavenly Father, who "so loved the world that he gave his only begotten Son, that whosoever believeth in Him should not perish, but have everlasting life," the devout soul must ever bow with a humble, grateful adoration, growing with increasing knowledge, and exclaim, —

To God alone be all the glory.

A NEW TEXT-BOOK ON MORAL SCIENCE.

CHRISTIAN ETHICS; OR, THE TRUE MORAL MANHOOD AND LIFE OF DUTY. A Text-book for Schools and Colleges. By D. S. GREGORY, D.D., Professor of the Mental Sciences and English Literature in the University of Wooster, Ohio.

CONTENTS OF THE WORK.

Part II.

PRACTICAL ETHICS.—DUTIES IN THE LIFE OF DUTY.

Division I—Individual Ethics—Duties Toward Self.

Chapter I—Duty of Self-Conservation.

Section 1. Self-Preservation—Life.
Section 2. Self-Care—Health.
Section 3. Self-Support—Well-Being.

Chapter II—Duty of Self-Culture.

Section 1. Physical Self-Culture.
Section 2. Spiritual Self-Culture.

Chapter III—Duty of Self-Conduct.

Section 1. Self-Control.
Section 2. Self-Direction.

Division II—Social Ethics—Duties Toward Mankind.

Chapter I—General Ethics. Duties Toward Men in General.

Section 1. Duty of Social Conservation.
Section 2. Duty of Social Improvement.
Section 3. Duty of Social Direction.

Chapter II—Economical Ethics. Duties in the Household.

Section 1. Duties of the Marriage Relation.
Section 2. Duties of the Parental Relation.
Section 3. Duties of Master and Servant.

Chapter III—Civil Ethics. Duties in the State.

Section 1. Duties of the State.
Section 2. Duties of the Citizen.

Division III—Theistic Ethics—Duties Toward God.

Chapter I—Supreme Devotion of the Intellect to God.

Section 1. The Binding Force of the Duty.
Section 2. The Range of the Duty.

Chapter II—Supreme Devotion of the Heart to God.

Section 1. The Binding Force of the Duty.
Section 2. The Range of the Duty.

Chapter III—Supreme Devotion of the Will to God.

Section 1. Obedience Toward God.
Section 2. Worship of God.
Section 3. Acceptance of Moral Reconstruction.

FEATURES OF THE WORK.

The work of Dr. Gregory possesses among others the following peculiar features:

1. It is the most complete and comprehensive treatise on this subject that has been brought before the public, containing almost twice the matter of any other work similar in aim and form.

2. A new, logical and systematic form has been given to the whole subject, which makes the science at once easy to master and to retain.

3. It is so constructed as to meet the wants of three classes of pupils. *Practical Ethics* furnishes a complete text-book for the younger and more immature, as in the Public Schools; the book may be studied entire by ordinary Seminary or College classes; or the matter in larger type may be made the basis of a system of lectures for those who desire a Syllabus for guiding the investigations of mature minds.

4. By means of graded type, the relative importance and dependence of the different parts, propositions and discussions, are made to appear at once to the eye of the teacher and of the pupil of average intelligence.

5. The entire treatment is fresh and abreast with the age, dealing with the great ethical questions in living rather than dead form and thereby arousing the natural enthusiasm of the youthful mind.

6. The work aims throughout to present the science of right and noble living from the point of view of the enlightened Christian conscience, so as to keep before the pupil the highest attainable human character and life, and the most powerful motives for attaining them.

The attention of educators is particularly invited to the following points, usually either overlooked or hastily treated:

The elements of personal agency.

The thorough analysis of the moral nature.

The full discussion of the nature of virtue.

The scientific presentation in the philosophy of duty.

The full treatment of the great questions of the will.

The discussion of the problem of moral reconstruction, and the testing of the various schemes proposed.

The new analysis of Practical Ethics.

The principles governing the choice of work in life.

The theory of education and its application, under self-culture.

The treatment, under Self-Conduct, of the great End of Life, of the considerations which should influence in the formation of the plan for life, and of the principles which should govern in the use of the personal powers, the forces of nature, wealth, and time, in carrying out that plan and accomplishing the grandest possible life-work.

The enlarged and unselfish view of duties to mankind.

The fresh discussion of such topics as the duties of the State to the world and to God; of prayer; of the Sabbath, etc.

WHAT LEADING EDUCATORS SAY OF THE WORK.

President M. B. ANDERSON, D.D., LL. D., Rochester University, N. Y.

"The book throughout shows the action of a clear, vigorous, and well-disciplined mind, strongly imbued with the loftiest conceptions of Christian morality. It is admirably fitted for a text-book and is exhaustive in the range of the topics treated."

President JAMES MCCOSH, D.D., LL. D., Princeton College, N. J.

"Dr. Gregory's work is one of the very best of the few good books that we have on Christian Ethics. It is at once philosophic and practical expounding grand principles and applying them to particular precepts.'

President NOAH PORTER, D.D., LL. D., Yale College, New Haven, Conn.

"A valuable addition to the manuals of instruction which we have. It certainly does great credit to the scholarship and ability of the author."

Professor L. H. ATWATER, D.D., LL. D., Professor of Logic, Metaphysics and Political Economy, in the College of New Jersey, Princeton. (From *The Presbyterian Quarterly and Princeton Review.*)

"A work of this kind is to be estimated according to two principal standards: first, as a manual for teaching the science of which it treats, and, next, as an exposition of or contribution to that science itself. . . . Professor Gregory's book very strongly exemplifies both sorts of excellencies. While it takes note of the views of others, and incorporates the marrow of them, it combines with all this a vein of original thinking, which brings the whole out as it has been fused and recast in the alembic of his own mind. It is no mere combination or rehash. It is a construction of his own, which, illuminating with whatever light it can borrow from the great masters, gives many cross and side lights of its own which are new. While it has value so far as an original work, it has still greater value in its plan and method as a text-book."

President MILTON VALENTINE, D.D., Pennsylvania College, (*Lutheran Quarterly Review.*)

"It is a work of very great merit, and will doubtless soon take, as it deserves, a prominent place among the manuals of instruction in academic and collegiate institutions. . . . The work on the whole is so sound and Christian, as well as so clear and well arranged, that we regard it the very best manual now offered for instruction in Moral Science."

DR. H. L. WAYLAND, Editor of the *National Baptist* (late President of Kalamazoo College, and son of Dr. FRANCIS WAYLAND).

"The book is based upon a very rigid, logical, and comprehensive outline. . . . The author takes the highest possible ideal of life and duty, and he discusses his theme with an enthusiasm and directness which are sure to make an impression.

"The book evinces great breadth of scholarship, and a familiarity with all the recent literature upon the subject; and very frequently in evolving his own view, he will place side by side the views of those who differ from him, and in this way he condenses into a paragraph the contents of many volumes; and his criticisms bring the subject down to the present year of grace.

"But the cultus of the book does not surpass its outspokenness. The author sees sin where sin is and does not tamper with it. The warm, earnest, practical, dignified spirit of the volume is in perfect accord with its scientific character.

"The spirit of the book corresponds to Dr. Lyman Beecher's definition of eloquence, viz.: 'Logic set on fire.' Dr. Gregory has set his logic on fire with his pen. We doubt if his voice could better it."

COL. ROBERT D. ALLEN, Superintendent Kentucky Military Institute, and Member of State Board of Education.

"I am persuaded that Gregory's *Christian Ethics* is the only work on the subject, published in America, that is adapted to the class-room. Every man that values knowledge on this subject should study this splendid work with care."

Professor J. P. LACROIX, D. D., Ohio, Wesleyan University, translator of Wuttke's *Christian Ethics.*

"This book presents the *new* ethics. It bears the science *from God.* It gives a clear, positive, *Christian* solution to the great problems of human life.

President THOMAS WARD WHITE, D.D., Greenboro Female College, Alabama.

"I do not hesitate to pronounce it superior to any production of the kind which has come under my observation for years. It is more in accordance with Scripture than Paley, more lucid than Alexander, much more simple than Wayland, freer from professional technicalities than Abercrombie; in short, a *post bellum* production eminently suited for the progressive development of physical and moral womanhood in the South.

"We shall adopt it, at once, in our classes, and would cordially commend it to those engaged in female education."

President THOMAS CHASE, Haverford College, Pennsylvania.

"I am impressed with the great excellence of the work. It is philosophical in its arrangement, sound in its teachings, and happy in its practical applications of the great truths with which it deals."

President C. NUTT, D.D., Indiana State University.

"Such a book has been long needed. It is thorough and up with the times. I shall adopt it as a text-book in this University."

Professor R. BETHUNE WELCH, LL. D., Union University, N. Y.

"It seems to me admirably adapted to its special purpose as a text-book; and, in this respect, cannot fail to meet an urgent need in the department of ethical instruction."

President KENDALL BROOKS, D.D., Kalamazoo College, Michigan.

"It is no discredit to Francis Wayland to say, that forty years after the publication of his Moral Science, which has rendered admirable service for so many years, another is issued better in some respects than his. Dr. Gregory's book seems peculiarly adapted to the class-room."

President N. R. MIDDLETON, College of Charleston, S. C.

"It is a very complete and large-minded analysis of a subject so often discussed in a narrow and sectarian spirit."

President OVAL PIRKEY, Abingdon College, Ill.

"It is the best text-book I have yet found on the subject of which it treats. Condensed, systematic, and plain."

President B. HELING, D.D., Wittenberg College, Ohio.

"The wide range of topics presented, upon what he so fitly terms 'the science of right and noble living,' makes the book a real treasury of truth and knowledge upon its special subject."

President John R. PARK, M.D., University of Deseret, Utah.

"In general plan, in arrangement, and in all that makes a text-book effective in the class-room, I have yet seen nothing equal to it."

President R. L. ABERNETHY, Rutherford College, N. C.

"I am so well pleased with it that I shall adopt it as one of my text-books in this college, next term. The book combines more of mental with the normal of man's nature than any other book I have examined. Its typography and manual execution cannot be easily surpassed."

Professor J. W. SCOTT, D.D., L.L.D., West Virginia University.

"It seems well adapted to the purpose intended. As a text-book, better than any of those in common use."

President L. A. DUNN, Central University, Iowa.

"Decidedly the best of anything I have seen upon this subject."

Professor JAMES HARPER, D.D., United Presbyterian Theological Seminary, Newburg, N. Y.

"I should be glad to know that the work had been adopted as a text-book in all our colleges, and outside of college walls. It is admirably adapted to promote a high moral tone; while it furnishes powerful evidence in behalf of that Christianity toward which, by thoughtful steps from first principles, it conducts the student."

Professor WM. ALEXANDER, D.D., Presbyterian Theological Seminary of the Pacific, Cal.

"The definitions are admirable, clear cut and distinct, and at the same time comprehensive and complete. Another notable feature is, that the author has ventured to depart from the beaten track without departing from the truth. I am delighted with the boldness and directness with which he pushes his principles to their just conclusion."

Professor C. S. REINKE, Moravian Theological Seminary, Bethlehem, Pa.

"I think it an admirable work."

Professor T. S. WYNKOOSS, Theological Seminary, Allahabad, India.

"Tell Dr. Gregory that I take with me to India a package of his Christian Ethics, and shall select the best of my young men and put them through as thorough a course in it as possible."

Principal JOHN W. ARMSTRONG, State Normal School, Fredonia, N. Y.

"The book is uncommonly rich in material. The general impression made by it is, variety and excellence in matter, thoroughness in investigation, and adaptation to the wants of the recitation room."

Principal J. ESTABROOK, State Normal School, Ypsilanti, Michigan.

"I am delighted with it. The arrangement of topics is admirable, and the discussion of them very able."

President C. R. POMEROY, D.D., State Normal School, Emporia, Kansas.

"The classification and arrangement under General Divisions, Chapters, Sections, and Topics, are valuable helps to both teacher and scholar. Add to this the aid afforded by the type, and we have little left to desire in form for a *model text-book.* As to the discussion of the subject matter, Part 2d, upon Practical Ethics, is especially valuable. Its careful study cannot fail to ennoble character, and give a truer conception of the truth and value of the Christian religion.

President J. H. BRUNNER, Hiwassee College, Tennessee.

"On receipt of Gregory's Christian Ethics, I laid the book aside as being no better than what we already had in use; but subsequent events led me to a thorough review of the book. In no other work have I found so many points of excellence. . . .

"We make it a rule to use none but the best books we can find, in the several departments of instruction. This rule will require us to place the Christian Ethics in our course of study for the next year.

"I am at loss for language suitably to express my high appreciation of the work, both as to its intrinsic matter and its typographical excellence as a text-book."

PRICE, $1.50.

Liberal terms to Teachers and School Officers desiring copies for examination or first introduction.

PLEASE ADDRESS THE PUBLISHERS,

ELDREDGE & BROTHER,

17 NORTH SEVENTH STREET,

PHILADELPHIA, PA.

www.ingramcontent.com/pod-product-compliance
Lightning Source LLC
LaVergne TN
LVHW010152110826
845151LV00002B/495
* 9 7 8 1 4 2 5 5 3 7 4 9 4 *